Study Guide to accompany

BECOMING LOGICAL

Study Guide to accompany

Robert Paul Churchill's

B E C O M I N G   L O G I C A L
An Introduction to Logic

Prepared by

Peter Hutcheson

and

Glenn C. Joy
both of Southwest Texas State University

ST. MARTIN'S PRESS   NEW YORK

For information, write:
St. Martin's Press, Inc.
175 Fifth Avenue
New York, NY   10010

ISBN: 0-312-07068-3

Prepared by Peter Hutcheson and Glenn C. Joy for P.S. Associates, Inc.,
Brookline, Massachusetts

DEDICATION

In memory of my father, Peter Wesley Hutcheson, VI,
who introduced me to arithmetic and its logic.

Peter Hutcheson

CONTENTS

PREFACE

This Study Guide covers almost all the topics treated in Robert Paul Churchill's *Becoming Logical*. Because mere repetition of Churchill's words would not help a student who turns to this book for clarification, we have explained the concepts in our own words. We have even defined some terms that are not defined in *Becoming Logical* when we thought it necessary or advisable (for example, the definitions of "asymmetrical relation" and "conclusive disconfirmation"). Because practice helps a person develop and refine logical and analytical skills, we have included many exercises, which range from easy to challenging. Since students will want to measure their progress without constantly asking their professors, we have included solutions to the exercises. Being especially interested in the application of logical and analytical skills to philosophical issues, we have included several philosophical arguments. We have at times considered matters that are not discussed in *Becoming Logical*, because the text naturally led to those topics. Occasionally going beyond the text clarifies the topics even further, as in the reduction of the laws of the probability calculus from five to three, or the discussion of the difference between an explanation and an argument for its correctness.

You should use this book, then, for a different way of putting many of the same points, for occasional clarification of a topic beyond the explanation in the text, for additional exercises, and for a means of checking how well you are learning the material. This is not to mention the sheer pleasure you will experience in working the more challenging exercises!

Professor Kenneth Merrill, a colleague at the University of Oklahoma, generously shared several examples of informal fallacies. Ann-Marie Hutcheson supplied several examples of scientific reasoning. Jerlyn Skrocki, Daphne Green, Rose Ena Karm, Chris Bernal, and Joyce Hull typed the entire manuscript. Many thanks to these friends.

Study Guide to accompany

BECOMING LOGICAL

PART ONE: LOGIC AND ARGUMENT

CHAPTER 1
RECOGNIZING ARGUMENTS

OVERVIEW

Because logic is the study of arguments, this chapter is devoted to techniques for recognizing them. In order to recognize an argument, you need to know its parts, clues for identifying those parts, and which sentences are not constituents of arguments. This chapter introduces the appropriate terms and concepts.

This chapter is a crucial foundation for everything else in the text. A logic course is somewhat like a mathematics course, inasmuch as familiarity with previous material is taken for granted. You have to be able to multiply and subtract if you are to do long division. Similarly, you must be able to recognize arguments and their parts before you can study the rules for evaluating deductive arguments. The terms introduced here will be used throughout the book, but they are explained only in this first chapter.

An argument consists of statements only (see the definition of argument in Section 1-2), so we begin by drawing the distinction between a sentence and a statement.

SECTION REVIEWS
1-1

Sentences and Statements

Section Objective

1. Recognize the differences between sentences and statements.

Key Term Review

1. **Sentence:** a string of words (in a specific language) that conforms to grammatical rules and comprises a complete grammatical unit.
2. **Statement:** what a sentence expresses when it is used to claim something, the expressed claim being either true or false.

Summary

The text discusses four ways in which a sentence differs from a statement. The first two are as follows:

1. Two different sentences can express the same statement.

2. Though a sentence is always part of a particular language, statements are not peculiar to any of the languages in which they are expressed.

Actually, the second point is only an instance of the first. "Snow is white" and "Schnee ist weiss" are two different sentences, but, because they have the same meaning, they express the same statement. The fact that two different sentences (even within the same language) can express the same statement is important, because you will have to recognize sentences with the same meaning in order to evaluate arguments in which those sentences occur.

Learning logic requires paying careful attention to the meanings of sentences. When a sentence is judged different from a sentence with the same meaning, a good argument can mistakenly be assessed as bad (or vice versa). Such mistakes occur when someone looks at words inattentively and fails to understand their meaning.

One can also make a mistake by mechanically rendering the same sentence as the same statement. However, the text points out that

3. The same sentence can, in different contexts, be used to convey different meanings.

and thus

4. The same sentence can, in different contexts, express different statements.

Understanding the distinction between a sentence and a statement can help you avoid careless and mechanical renderings of sentences.

When does a sentence express a statement? How can someone tell when two different sentences express the same statement? The basic questions we ask to resolve these issues are as follows:

1. Is this sentence either true or false? If the answer to this question is "yes," the sentence expresses a statement. If the answer is "no," the sentence does not express a statement.

2. Do these two sentences (which are either true or false), in their context, have the same meaning? If the answer to this question is "yes," the sentences express the same statement. If the answer is "no," the two sentences express different statements.

Please note that the first question must be asked before the second. If the sentence does not express a statement at all, we need not ask whether it expresses the same statement as another.

Practice Exercises

Identify the function of each of the following sentences and justify your answer. In the space to the left, indicate whether the sentence is informative (I), is ceremonial (C), is evaluative (E), expresses feeling (F), directs behavior (D), requests information (Q), or none of the above (N). Please note that some sentences may have more than one function. Explain your answers if it is necessary.

1. _____ What time is it?

2. _____ Please photocopy these notes.

_____

3. _____ At constant temperature, the volume of a gas is inversely proportional to the pressure exerted upon it.

_____

4. _____ Happy Birthday!

_____

5. _____ I shall return your exams Friday.

_____

6. _____ You acted wrongly by stealing that money.

_____

7. _____ No statement is valid in the logical sense.

_____

8. _____ The faculty will wear academic regalia at commencement. (memo
to faculty from the vice president of the university)

_____

9. _____ "Warning: The Surgeon General has determined that cigarette
smoking is dangerous to your health."

_____

10. _____ I'm pleased to meet you.

_____

11. _____ Please remit $15 with the order form.

_____

12. _____ Can you identify the statements in this exercise?

_____

13. _____ That's a pretty dress.

_____

14. _____ At constant pressure, the volume of a gas is directly proportional to the absolute temperature.

_____

15. _____ Green ideas sleep furiously.

_____

16. _____ "Abandon hope, all ye who enter here."--Dante

_____

17. _____ "Working men of all countries, unite!"--Marx

_____

18. _____ God exists.

_____

19. _____ Suppose there are several automobile accidents at a particular curve in the road.

_____

20. _____ Dad's birthday is the sixth of November.

_____

21. _____ There is human life on distant planets.

_____

_____ *1-2*

Premises and Conclusions

Section Objectives

1. Identify arguments and their constituents (premises and conclusions).

2. Distinguish between the logician's definition of the term _argument_ and the ordinary use of that word.

3. Arrange passages containing a single argument into logically proper form.

Key Term Review

1. _Argument_: a set of statements in which at least one statement is put forward as a reason for accepting another statement as true.

2. _Premise_: the statement(s) in an argument that are offered as reasons.

3. _Conclusion_: the statement in an argument that the premise(s) are supposed to establish.

4. _Logically proper form_: an argument with its premises and conclusion explicitly identified, the conclusion stated last, and the asymmetrical relationship between premises and conclusion revealed.

5. <u>Asymmetrical relationship</u>: X is asymmetrically related to Y if and only if X's bearing that relationship to Y means that Y <u>cannot</u> bear that relationship to X. An example of an asymmetrical relationship is "is the mother of." Within a <u>single</u> argument, the relationship "is a reason for" (between premises and conclusion) is asymmetrical.

6. <u>Fallacy or fallacious argument</u>: an argument rendered defective by an error in reasoning.

Summary

Because an argument consists of statements only, we began by making the distinction between a sentence and a statement. A sentence must express a statement in order to be part of an argument.

But not every set of statements is an argument. Someone who formulates an argument is trying to prove something, to give reasons for believing something is true. To formulate an argument, then, is to claim that there is a certain relationship between the constituent statements. That is, to formulate an argument is to claim that at least one of the statements is a reason (a premise) for believing another statement (the conclusion). Not every set of statements involves the relationship between premise and conclusion, so not every set of statements is an argument.

To label a statement a premise or a conclusion is to say something about its role in the passage. To say that a statement is a premise, for example, is to say that it is offered as a reason for another statement, the conclusion. Thus no statement can be either a premise or a conclusion in isolation from at least one other statement.

An argument is a set of statements in which an attempt is made to prove one on the basis of the other(s). An argument thus consists of at least one premise and exactly one conclusion. However, what we ordinarily call an argument involves some sort of disagreement--often an unpleasant one. If the people who disagree with one another do not try to establish the truth of anything, they have <u>not</u> formulated an argument in the logician's sense. Moreover, an argument can be formulated even where there is no disagreement. This is true despite the fact that arguments are most often put forward in the context of disagreement. For example, we argued above for the conclusion that not every set of statements is an argument, although there was no disagreement about the matter.

The relationship between premises(s) and conclusion is asymmetrical. Although the premise is a reason for the conclusion, the conclusion cannot be a reason for the premises (within a single argument). Thus it is impossible to label premises and conclusion without understanding the passage. But how can we tell whether a passage contains an argument? And how are premises and conclusions identified? We ask ourselves the following questions:

1. Is the author trying to prove something in the passage? If the answer to this question is "yes," the passage contains an argument. If the answer is "no," the passage does not contain an argument.

2. Which statement is the author trying to prove? The answer to this question is the conclusion of the argument.

3. Which statement(s) is (are) a reason for the conclusion? The answer to this question yields the premise(s) of the argument.

4. Does the argument, thus interpreted, look funny or ridiculous? Asking this question helps you check for misinterpretations. If the answer to this question is "yes," return to Question 1 and start over; you may very well have misinterpreted the passage.

Bear in mind the definition of the term <u>fallacious argument</u>, because much of logic is devoted to stating ways in which arguments often fail to prove their conclusions. Avoiding fallacies goes hand-in-hand with following the rules for good arguments. Several kinds of fallacies will be discussed in subsequent chapters.

Practice Exercises

Which of the following passages contain an argument? In the space to the left, indicate which passages contain an argument (A) and which contain no argument (NA). Then put those that contain an argument into logically proper form. Indicate why each of the other passages does not contain an argument.

1. _____ I know there is a God because the Bible says so.

_____

_____

_____

2. _____ Either Miss Texas or Miss New Mexico is Miss U.S.A. Miss New Mexico is the first runner-up. Thus, Miss Texas is Miss U.S.A.

_____

_____

3. _____ "For a long time I have hesitated to write a book on woman. The subject is irritating, especially to women; and it is not new." --Simone de Beauvoir, <u>The Second Sex</u>.

_____

_____

4. _____ "Obsessional ideas, as is well known, have an appearance of being without meaning, just as dreams do. The first problem is how to give them a sense and a status in the mental life of the individual, so as to make them comprehensible and even obvious.... The wildest and most eccentric obsessional or compulsive ideas can be cleared up if they are investigated deep enough."--Sigmund Freud, <u>Three Case Histories</u>, p. 45.

_____

_____

6

5. _____ "The reasons for accepting Einstein's law of gravitation rather than Newton's are partly empirical.... Einstein's law of gravitation gives very nearly the same results as Newton's when applied to the calculation of the orbits of the planets and their satellites. If it did not, it could not be true, since the consequences deduced from Newton's law have been found to be almost exactly verified by observation. When, in 1915, Einstein first published his new law, there was only one empirical fact to which he could point to show that his theory was better than Newton's. This was what is called the motion of the perihelion of mercury."--Bertrand Russell, The ABC of Relativity.

_____

_____

_____

_____

_____

6. _____ "Nor does this full assurance [that others' acts are thoroughly predictable, given thorough knowledge] conflict in the smallest degree with what is called our feeling of freedom. We do not feel ourselves the less free, because those to whom we are intimately known are well assured how we shall will to act in a particular case. We often, on the contrary, regard the doubt what our conduct will be, as a mark of ignorance of our character, and sometimes even resent it as an imputation."--John Stuart Mill, A System of Logic.

_____

_____

_____

_____

_____

7. _____ "The stick which looks straight in the air looks angularly bent when in water. There are good reasons for thinking that no such change of shape takes place in the stick. Yet there is something straight in the one case and something bent in the other, and there is no good reason for supposing either is less or more of an existent than the other. The straight-stick appearance and the bent-stick appearance are sense-data."--W. H. F. Barnes, "The Myth of Sense-Data."

_____

_____

7

8. _____ "Sometimes creationists plunge more deeply into dishonesty by taking statements of evolutionists out of context to make them say the opposite of what was intended. For example, when in an article on adaptation, I described the outmoded nineteenth-century belief that the perfection of creation was the best evidence of a creator, this description was taken into creationist literature as evidence of my own rejection of evolution."--R. C. Lewontin, in Scientists Confront Creationism, p. xxiv.

---

9. _____ "The first idea that comes to mind is that responsibility is de-termined by the presence or absence of premeditation--the opposite of 'premeditated' being, presumably, 'unthinking' or 'impulsive.' But this will not do, both because some acts are not premeditated but re-sponsible, and because some are premeditated and not responsible." --John Hospers, "What Means This Freedom?"

---

10. _____ The theory of evolution is not inconsistent with the belief that God created the universe. After all, evolution is a theory of the development of life-forms. It is not a theory of the creation of the universe.

---

11. _____ There is water all over the garage floor because the air condi-tioner is leaking.

---

12. _____ The number 119 is not prime because it is evenly divisible by 7 and 17.

_____

_____

_____

_____

13. _____ "Capacity for the nobler feelings is in most natures a very tender plant, easily killed, not only by hostile influences, but by mere want of sustenance; and in the majority of young persons it speedily dies away if the occupations to which their position in life has devoted them, and the society into which it has thrown them, are not favorable to keeping that higher capacity in exercise."--John Stuart Mill, Utilitarianism.

_____

_____

14. _____ "A contractual democracy is legitimate, to be sure, for it is founded upon the citizens' promise to obey its commands. Indeed, any state is legitimate which is founded upon such a promise. However, all such states achieve their legitimacy only by means of the citizens' forfeit of their autonomy, and hence are not solutions to the fundamental problem of political philosophy."--Robert Paul Wolff, In Defense of Anarchism.

_____

_____

_____

_____

_____

15. _____ "Or, more precisely, it has the publics' attention. Note the placement of the apostrophe, which tells the essential truth of American politics. On an issue like tax reform, the public (definite article, 'the') is a fiction. There are lots of little publics with rival interests."--George Will, 30 May 1985, Austin American-Statesman.

_____

_____

_____

_____

Features of Arguments

Section Objectives

1. Arrange passages containing more than one argument into logically proper form.

2. Distinguish between the component parts of arguments and non-argumentative phrases or sentences within a single passage.

3. Identify premise indicator words and conclusion indicator words, and distinguish their use in arguments from their other uses.

Key Term Review

1. <u>Premise indicator words (or phrases)</u>: words or phrases that frequently alert the reader (or listener) to the fact that a premise is being given.

2. <u>Conclusion indicator words (or phrases)</u>: words or phrases that frequently alert the reader (or listener) to the fact that the conclusion is being given.

3. <u>Extended (or complex) argument</u>: a passage that contains two or more entwined (or interrelated) arguments. Although an extended argument is, strictly speaking, at least two arguments, it is called "an argument" because the arguments are interrelated and ultimately aim at a single conclusion (the final one).

Summary

This section lists several features of arguments, the mastery of which is essential for correct analyses of passages containing arguments. Let us consider most of them briefly.

1. <u>An entire argument can be expressed in a single sentence.</u>

Every argument contains at least two statements: a premise and a conclusion. Because a sentence can express more than one statement, a single sentence can express an entire argument. For example, the preceding sentence is comprised of two statements.

2. <u>The premises and conclusion of an argument can occur in any order.</u>

If a single argument is in logically proper form, its conclusion always appears last. But in ordinary discourse, the conclusion occasionally appears first, or sometimes between the premises. It follows that not all arguments in ordinary discourse are in logically proper form.

The fact that the order in which the statements appear does not determine their role in the argument raises the problem of how to identify premises and conclusions. Here are some clues:

3. <u>Some arguments contain words or phrases that indicate that a statement is a premise (or a conclusion, depending on the word or phrase).</u>

These words and phrases are helpful. However, they are not mechanical guides that can substitute for a careful reading of the passage, because the words (phrases) do not always indicate that a statement is a premise (or conclusion).

Furthermore,

4. Some arguments do not contain indicator words.

Third, premise and conclusion indicator words occasionally occur next to one another, as in this argument: "All philosophers are mathematicians. So, because Bertrand Russell is a philosopher, he is a mathematician." You should therefore rely on the questions for identifying arguments and their parts (set out in Section 1-2) rather than on the indicator words. If we ask what the author is trying to prove in the argument about Russell, the answer is clear: that Russell is a mathematician. The other statements are the premises.

The text points out that the words since and because have non-argumentative uses. The same is true of other words and phrases in the text. The words for and as are premise indicators, for example, only when they are used as conjunctions and not as prepositions or adverbs. But even their being used as conjunctions is no guarantee that they are premise indicators, for they sometimes introduce explanations instead.

Thus far you have dealt with passages containing only one argument. However,

5. Some passages contain two or more arguments that are entwined.

A logical consequence of this is the fact that

6. One and the same sentence can be both a conclusion and a premise (but not relative to the same argument).

Consider an example given in the text:

(1) Matter is activity.
(2) Therefore, a body is where it acts.
(3) Every particle of matter acts all over the universe.
(4) Every body is everywhere.

Line (2) is both a conclusion and a premise. It is a conclusion, since it is derived from line (1). But it is also a premise, because it is a basis for line (4). Line (2) is a conclusion relative to the argument that consists of lines (1) and (2), but it is a premise of the argument consisting of lines (2), (3), and (4). An argument has at least one premise and exactly one conclusion. Strictly speaking, therefore, the foregoing passage consists of two arguments.

To label a statement a premise is to say that it is a reason for the conclusion and that, relative to the argument in question, it is not defended with reasons. A conclusion is a statement that the arguer tries to establish or prove. Since the arguer tries to establish (2) with (1), (2) is a conclusion. But if we ignore (1) and concentrate only on the argument consisting of (2) through (4), we see that, relative to that argument, (2) is a premise.

The final feature of arguments that we shall discuss is the eighth one mentioned in the text.

7. <u>Not everything said in the course of an argument is a premise or a conclusion</u>.

It is tempting, when putting an argument into logically proper form, to try to include every detail. Passages that contain arguments, however, often include extraneous (or extra-logical) material, such as expressions of emotions, literary flourishes, parenthetical comments, illustrations, and explanations. Such extraneous material is not part of the argument. An argument consists of at least one premise and exactly one conclusion. Everything else is extra-logical. Accordingly, when you attempt to put an argument into logically proper form, you need to ask some questions about each sentence:

> Does this sentence express a statement? How many statements?

> Is each statement either a premise or a conclusion? Identify each premise or conclusion as such.

> Are there words within the premises that play no role in the derivation of the conclusion? Are there extra-logical words in the conclusion itself?

When analyzing a passage in order to put the argument into logically proper form, you need to pare it down to the argument only. If you first eliminate all sentences that do not express statements, you will have excluded at least part of the extraneous material. Some statements may be neither premises nor conclusions, and those statements must be deleted as well. Furthermore, sentences that contain a premise or a conclusion may yet include extraneous words that play no role in the derivation of the conclusion and should be deleted. The result is the argument.

Practice Exercises

In the space to the left, indicate which of the following passages contain <u>at least one</u> argument (A) and which contain no argument (NA). If the passage is an extended argument, identify any line that is both a conclusion and a premise by putting the letters 'C' and 'P' next to it. Then put the arguments into logically proper form.

1. _____ Several other brands of diet soft drink couldn't beat diet 7-Up for taste. So, many people believe diet 7-Up has the best taste. So, you should buy diet 7-Up.

_____

_____

_____

2. _____ No one is wiser than Socrates. So, Socrates is the wisest.

_____

_____

_____

12

3. _____ "The terrifying impression of helplessness in childhood aroused the need for protection--for protection through love--which was provided by the father; and the recognition that this helplessness lasts throughout life made it necessary to cling to the existence of a father, but this time a more powerful one. Thus the benevolent rule of a divine providence allays our fear of the dangers of life."--Sigmund Freud, The Future of an Illusion.

_____

_____

_____

4. _____ "To abrogate SALT II limits would send a bad signal to Moscow at a delicate moment in the arms-control process. So, we should continue U.S. compliance with the unratified SALT II treaty."--George Will, 6 June 1985, Austin American-Statesman.

_____

_____

_____

5. _____ "The Soviet Union has been conducting 'Star Wars' research on its own. The U.S. cannot afford to have anything like a Soviet breakthrough for which the U.S. is unprepared. Thus, the U.S. should continue its 'Star Wars' research, despite Soviet objections."--James J. Kilpatrick, 6 June 1985, Austin American-Statesman.

_____

_____

_____

6. _____ "Again, if, as is shown in the Posterior Analytics, the knowledge of the principles of demonstration takes its origin from sense experience, whatever transcends all...sense experience seems to be indemonstrable. That God exists appears to be a proposition of this sort and is therefore indemonstrable."--Thomas Aquinas, Summa Contra Gentiles, p. 84.

_____

_____

_____

7. _____ "Phenomenalism is the view that the existence of a physical object is dependent upon its being perceived; that is, a physical object is a construct made up of percepts that are the immediate objects of perception. It follows directly from this that the physical world is

completely dependent on some perceiver(s) for its existence and that, if all perceivers were to be annihilated, the physical world would, accordingly, cease to exist."--William Halverson, _A Concise Introduction to Philosophy_.

_____

_____

_____

_____

_____

_____

8. _____ It is sometimes said that opponents of abortion inconsistently support the death penalty. They should oppose the death penalty, it is said, because they are against the taking of human life unless some-one else's life is in danger. But there is no such inconsistency, for opponents of abortion oppose the taking of innocent human life. Where-as an embryo or fetus is innocent of wrongdoing, someone who (in their opinion) merited the death penalty would not be.

_____

_____

_____

_____

_____

9. _____ Opponents of abortion have given no good reason for opposing only the taking of innocent _human_ life. Animals are innocent, too, and a person's survival would not be threatened by refraining from eating animals, since he could survive on plants and animal by-products. Until such time as opponents of abortion have given a good reason for singling out human life for special considerations, therefore, they should be vegetarians.

_____

_____

_____

_____

_____

_____

10. _____ Street crimes are more frequently and severely punished than "white-collar" crimes. Law breakers of the economic classes lower than white-collar workers, therefore, are the victims of injustice. The only way to eliminate such injustice is to change the economic system so radically that society becomes classless. So we should take Marx's advice.

_____

_____

_____

_____

_____

_____

_____

_____

Enthymemes: Arguments with Missing Parts
Finer Points of Detecting Arguments

Section Objectives

1. Identify enthymemes and specify the suppressed premise(s) or conclusion in such arguments.

2. Distinguish between explanations and arguments.

3. Distinguish between conditional statements and arguments.

4. Recognize various non-standard arguments.

Key Term Review

1. <u>Enthymeme or enthymatic argument</u>: an argument in which at least one of the constituents (premise or conclusion) is unstated.

2. <u>Suppressed premise (or conclusion)</u>: the premise (or conclusion) that is unstated in an enthymeme.

3. <u>Simple statement (provisional definition)</u>: a statement that does not contain any other component statement.

4. <u>Compound statement (provisional definition)</u>: a statement that contains at least one other component statement.

5. <u>Conditional statement</u>: a compound statement that is usually expressed by a sentence of the form "If X, then Y" (where X and Y are statement variables).

6. <u>Antecedent</u>: the part of a conditional statement that follows the word <u>if</u> (represented above as X).

7. <u>Consequent</u>: the part of a conditional statement that follows the word <u>then</u> (represented above as Y).

8. <u>Explanation</u>: an attempt to understand something taken as fact.

9. <u>Practical argument</u>: an argument with a non-standard conclusion.

<u>Summary</u>

Every argument that is in logically proper form explicitly identifies all its premises and conclusion. Enthymemes, however, leave at least one of the argument's constituents unstated. Consequently, no enthymeme is in logically proper form. So, in order to put enthymemes into logically proper form, you have to be able to identify the suppressed premise(s) or conclusion.

You may not be able to identify unstated constituents unerringly at first; the study of rules of correct reasoning is usually necessary before a person can always identify the unstated parts confidently. But because the simplest rules of correct reasoning are fairly intuitive, the unstated parts should be intuitively clear in many cases. It is useful and enlightening to develop skill at identifying suppressed parts of arguments, since someone who has that skill can more readily spot errors in her or his reasoning and that of others. Occasionally people use enthymemes because they want you to supply a questionable (or false) premise that is needed to support the conclusion. Advertisers often use enthymemes to prompt people to believe they are making up their own minds about the product's quality.

Nevertheless, it is important to be cautious and charitable in interpreting enthymemes. As the text says, a premise (or conclusion) may be supplied if it can truly be said to be implicit in the assumptions of the arguer or the audience--if it is part of the general fund of common knowledge, if the arguer can reasonably believe the audience possess the information in question, or if the "missing link" is logically required for the conclusion.

8. <u>A series of statements can be asserted in such a way that the truth of one depends on the truth of another without the statements being an argument</u>.

There are passages (or sets of statements) that may appear to be arguments at first but that, in fact, are not. Students frequently mistake them for arguments. Accordingly, you are advised to study this section carefully.

An argument is a set of statements in which an attempt is made to prove one (the conclusion) on the basis of the other(s), the premise or premises. Thus, if there is no attempt to prove anything in the set of statements, it is not an argument. Consider these two examples:

(a) There is water all over the floor because the pipes burst.

(b) Fritz insulted his wife; so she slapped him.

The word <u>because</u> in (a) seems to indicate that "the pipes burst" is a premise, whereas "there is water all over the floor" is the conclusion. But there is no attempt to prove that there is water all over the floor. Anyone who said (a) would be offering an explanation of the fact that there is water all over the floor.

The word so in (b) seems to be a conclusion indicator. But once again, there is no attempt to prove that Fritz' wife slapped him. Someone who said (b) would be explaining why Fritz' wife slapped him. An explanation is an attempt to understand something taken as fact, rather than an attempt to establish that something is a fact.

This may leave you puzzled because you are aware that there can be competing explanations of facts. Suppose someone said

(c) There is water all over the floor because someone left the bathtub water running.

Suppose (c) is a competitor with (a). It is easy to imagine someone considering arguments for which explanation is correct, such as:

(d) If the pipes had burst, I probably would have found the breaks when I looked underneath the floor. But I found none. So (c) is probably the correct explanation.

Now (d) is an argument. It is an attempt to prove something--namely, that explanation (c) is correct. However, we need to distinguish (d) from (a), (b), and (c), because there is no attempt to prove anything in (a), (b), and (c). To offer an explanation is not the same thing as arguing for its correctness. An explanation is a statement that can occur in an argument, but it is not itself an argument.

Conditional statements also are sometimes mistaken for arguments. Consider this conditional statement:

(e) If Smith makes an A in logic and a B in all her other courses, then her grade point average will be above 3.0.

It may appear that the consequent of (e) is the conclusion. If it were, however, the (e) would be an attempt to prove that Smith's G.P.A. will be above 3.0. But there is no attempt to prove that in (e). In order to establish that, it would have to be shown that Smith made an A in logic and a B in all her other courses. But (e) does not categorically state the antecedent of the consequent. Rather, it states that if the antecedent were true, then the consequent would be true. Since (e) does not constitute an attempt to prove anything, (e) is not an argument, but a conditional statement.

Item 9 introduces a paradox.

9. The conclusions of some arguments are not statements but directives: commands, imperatives, prescriptions.

However, the text defines an argument as a set of statements in which one or more statements are put forward as reasons for accepting another statement as true. It would seem that the definition of argument would have to be modified in order to accommodate item 9. Item 10, however, offers a way of resolving the paradox.

10. Some arguments can be recognized more easily if you paraphrase the premise(s) and/or the conclusion.

Consider the argument in the text: "You need three credits of science; astronomy would fit into your schedule; the professor is a fantastic lecturer; and the work load isn't heavy. Therefore, sign up for astronomy." The sentence "Sign up for astronomy" expresses no statement. However, it can be paraphrased as "You should sign up for astronomy," which can be construed as a statement. If the conclusions of genuine "practical arguments" can be similarly recast, there is no need to change the definition of <u>argument</u>.

In subsequent chapters we shall be concerned not merely with identifying arguments but with evaluating them as well. Logic, the study of argument, includes the study of the principles for distinguishing between good and bad arguments.

Practice Exercises

I. The following passages are enthymemes. Write out each argument in logically proper form, supplying the suppressed premises (identify them by adding SP) and suppressed conclusions (identify them by adding SC) needed to complete each argument.

1. Because every compatibalist is a determinist, Professor Klotzmeyer is a determinist.

_____

_____

_____

2. "Whoever makes things in which there is evil, which could have been made without evil, or the making of which could have been omitted, does not choose the best. God has made a world in which there is evil, a world which could have been made without any evil, or the making of which could have been omitted. Whoever does not choose the best is lacking in power, knowledge, or goodness."--G. W. Leibniz, <u>Theodicy</u>.

_____

_____

_____

_____

_____

_____

_____

_____

_____

3. If we know that there are trees, then we know that there is not an invisible demon who prompts us to believe, falsely, that there are trees. There is no way to rule out the possibility of the invisible demon. Thus, we do not know that there are trees.

_____

_____

_____

_____

_____

_____

_____

_____

4. If you know that you are reading a logic text now, then you know for certain that you are awake. But it is possible for you to be dreaming that you are reading a logic text. You cannot specify the differences between dreaming that you are reading a logic text and actually reading it.

_____

_____

_____

_____

_____

_____

_____

_____

_____

5. If you knew a thing's properties by seeing it, then this straight stick would not appear to be bent when immersed in water. Therefore, you do not know a thing's properties by seeing it.

_____

_____

_____

_____

_____

_____

6. All cats are mammals. So, Merlin is a mammal.

_____

_____

7. No argument is true or false. Accordingly, this enthymeme is neither true nor false.

_____

_____

_____

8. Some arguments are valid. But no argument is true.

_____

_____

_____

9. A human being's existence is an issue for him. But a person's existence could not be an issue for him unless he had some understanding of his existence.

_____

_____

_____

_____

10. Every statement is either true or false. But no argument is either true or false.

_____

_____

_____

II. Some of the following passages are explanations (E), whereas others are arguments (A). A few may be neither (N). Identify each passage as one of these by entering the appropriate letter.

1. _____ John shut the door because he wanted to speak to Linda privately.

2. _____ "But still, it is advisable always to bear in mind (a) that the distinctions embodied in our vast and, for the most part, relatively ancient stock of ordinary words are neither few nor always very obvious, and almost never just arbitrary; (b) that in any case, before indulging in any tampering on our own account, we need to find out what

it is that we have to deal with; and (c) tampering with words in what we take to be one little corner of the field is always <u>liable</u> to have unforeseen repercussions in the adjoining territory."--J. L. Austin, <u>Sense and Sensibilia</u>.

3. _____ "For many doctrines, though, there is this protective argument: you (pointing to the follower of the scientific establishment) can't disprove it! And to be sure, many of these theories that lie on or beyond the fringe of believability cannot be definitively shown to be wrong. Indeed many of them are cast in terms that are so cloudy that it is hard to know what would count as a refutation of them; for they are not intelligible in the first place. And here the naivete of the believer may blend with his instinct for giant-killing. He thinks that the fact that his belief can't be knocked all the way over is additional ground for embracing it."--Quine and Ullian, <u>The Web of Belief</u>.

4. _____ "Many theories, good and bad, do not admit of absolute proof or disproof.... Sadly, it is not just false science that has wantonly traded on this. A few years ago there were large advertisements in major newspapers in which cigaret manufacturers proudly announced that they were about to have independent researchers prove that there was not, after all, any causal connection between cigaret smoking and lung cancer. Evidence amassed in support of the connection was already overwhelming, and it should have been acknowledged as such. But, grasping at the realization that a causal connection had not been shown to exist with absolute certainty, these advertisers were magnifying the less than reasonable residual doubt into a proclamation of confidence in the opposite claim."--Quine and Ullian, <u>The Web of Belief</u>.

5. _____ The sun appears to rise each morning because the earth rotates.

6. _____ When a ship appears on the horizon, its top is first visible; gradually the lower parts can be seen. This is because the earth's surface is curved, the earth itself being basically spherical.

7. _____ "Freud knew he would be reviled for publishing case histories, in which sexual questions are discussed with utter frankness and the organs and functions of sexual life are called by their proper names." --Sigmund Freud (ed. Philip Rieff), <u>Three Case Histories</u>.

8. _____ That heavenly body does not twinkle like a star because it is the planet Venus, and planets do not twinkle.

9. _____ "You may think yourself bold by spitting in God's face, but know assuredly that god (sic) is sorely vexed and displeased with you; for all ungodly men are a 'stench in God's nostrils.' When the great day of wrath arrives, your mocking will abruptly cease in the presence of God's fury.... Only then will you ever come to know personally His love, kindness, and mercy to those who faithfully follow His will." --Letter in <u>University Star</u>, 30 March 1982.

10. _____ "'Scientific creationism' is a self-contradictory, nonsense phrase because it cannot be falsified. I can envision observations and experiments that would disprove any evolutionary theory I know, but I cannot imagine what potential data could lead creationists to abandon their beliefs. Unbeatable systems are dogma, not science.

Lest I seem harsh or rhetorical, I quote creationism's leading intellectual, Duane Gish, Ph.D., from his recent (1978) book, _Evolution? The Fossils Say No!_ 'By creation we mean the bringing into being by a supernatural Creator of the basic kinds of plants and animals by the process of sudden, or fiat, creation. We do not know how the Creator created, what processes he used, _for he used processes which are not now operating anywhere in the natural universe_ (Gish's italics). This is why we refer to creation as special creation. We cannot discover by scientific investigations anything about the creative processes used by the Creator.' Pray tell, Dr. Gish, in light of your last sentence, what then is 'scientific' creationism?"--Stephen Jay Gould, _Hen's Teeth and Horse's Toes_.

CHAPTER 2

ANALYZING ARGUMENTS

OVERVIEW

Since the nature of an argument has been clarified, we can refine our study of logic by learning to distinguish among various kinds of arguments. The two major kinds of arguments are deductive and inductive, but there are distinctions to be made within those major categories. The goal is to learn to assess arguments. We want to distinguish deductive and inductive arguments that establish their conclusions from those that do not. In order to do that, we must be familiar with the classifications of arguments. This chapter is devoted to that topic.

SECTION REVIEWS _2-1 and 2-2_

Deduction and Induction
Validity, Soundness and Reliable Inductive Inference

Section Objectives

1. Distinguish between deductive and inductive arguments.

2. Distinguish between valid and sound arguments.

3. Distinguish between valid and invalid arguments.

4. Draw some distinctions between stronger and weaker inductive arguments.

Key Term Review

1. Deductive argument: an argument that, from the point of view of its advocate, is sound (see the definition of "sound argument").

2. Inductive argument: an argument in which its advocate claims that the premises provide some (usually) strong, but not absolutely conclusive, reason for believing the conclusion.

3. Valid argument: a deductive argument having a form such that if all the premises were true, the conclusion would have to be true (see the definition of "argument form").

4. Invalid argument: a deductive argument having a form such that it is possible for all the premises to be true although the conclusion is false.

5. Sound argument: a deductive argument that is valid and has all true premises.

6. Strength (of an inductive argument): the probability of the conclusion, given the premises.

7. <u>Form</u> (provisional definition): of an argument or statement, (a) the pattern that remains the same throughout changes in its content; (b) the pattern that results from replacing content with variables.

8. <u>Variable</u> (in logic): a letter that, depending on context, can stand for any statement or part of a statement whatsoever.

9. <u>Reliable inductive argument</u>: an inductive argument that establishes its conclusion to the degree claimed for it.

Summary: Evaluating Deductive Arguments

Both <u>deductive argument</u> and <u>inductive argument</u> are defined in terms of the beliefs or intentions of someone who advocates the argument. The advocate's beliefs show us how the argument is to be evaluated. If the advocate believes that the argument is sound, we use deductive standards of evaluation. But if the argument's advocate believes that the premises provide only some reason for believing the conclusion, we use inductive standards. Ascertaining (figuring out) what someone's belief or intention is can be difficult but isn't always. If the argument's advocate uses words that show that he believes that the premises absolutely guarantee the conclusion, it is appropriate to use deductive standards. When used in the conclusion, words and phrases such as <u>must</u>, <u>cannot</u>, <u>could not</u>, and <u>this guarantees</u> frequently show that the argument is deductive. On the other hand, words and phrases such as <u>probably</u>, <u>it is likely that</u>, and <u>this gives us some reason to believe that</u>, when used in the conclusion, show that the argument is inductive. Unfortunately, these words do not always appear in arguments. So there is no substitute for paying careful attention to just what is being argued.

Although someone's belief about the nature of his argument is "subjective," the standards for evaluating arguments are not. Let us consider deductive standards first of all. A deductive argument is either valid or invalid. There are no degrees of validity or invalidity. Some (but not all) valid arguments are sound. No invalid arguments are sound. A deductive argument is valid or invalid <u>regardless</u> of the advocate's (or anyone else's) beliefs. Validity or invalidity is thus an objective feature of an argument. The terms <u>valid</u> and <u>invalid</u> are technical terms and do not have the same meanings in logic as in ordinary language. Two points are noteworthy:

1. <u>Valid does not mean true.</u>

2. <u>Invalid does not mean false, doubtful, or unknown.</u>

We shall use the terms <u>valid</u> and <u>invalid</u> in the technical senses. <u>Only</u> arguments can be valid or invalid. <u>No</u> statement is either valid or invalid. However, <u>every</u> statement is either true or false. Furthermore, <u>no</u> argument is either true or false. This shows the differences between validity and truth and between invalidity and falsehood.

These statements may seem surprising to you, especially since you are probably accustomed to using the words <u>valid</u> and <u>invalid</u> in the ordinary ways. As in any discipline, you need to learn some technical vocabulary. It will help you to evaluate arguments. We noted above that no argument is either true or false. Yet arguments consist of statements, which are either true or false. Can these two statements be reconciled? Yes. The reason is that what is true of the parts of a whole (the statements) need not be true of the whole (the argument). When we speak of an argument, we are not concerned with the individual statements that comprise it, but with the <u>rela-tionship</u> between the premises and conclusion. This relationship is neither true nor false.

Here are two valid arguments:

1.	All human beings are mammals.	1.	All cats are trees.
2.	All women are human beings.	2.	All dogs are cats.
3.	Therefore, all women are mammals.	3.	Therefore, all dogs are trees.

A valid argument is a deductive argument <u>having a form</u> such that <u>if</u> all the premises <u>were</u> true, the conclusion <u>would</u> have to be true. Even though the premises of the argument at the right are all false, the argument is never-theless valid. Please note that the definition of a valid argument does <u>not</u> state that all the premises <u>are</u> true--only that if they <u>were</u>, the con-clusion would have to be true also. And <u>if</u> all cats were trees and all dogs were cats, all dogs would have to be trees.

The two arguments above are valid for the same reason, for they both have the same <u>form</u>, namely:

1. All m are p.
2. All s are m.
3. Therefore, all s are p.

The first part of the definition states that a valid argument is a deductive argument <u>having a form</u> such that.... <u>The validity of an argument is a func-tion of its form alone</u>. Because both arguments are instances of the same form, they are both valid. This is true regardless of the fact that one argument contains only false statements. It also means that you can sub-stitute any term you please for the variables s, p, and m, and the result will be a valid argument, provided that you substitute consistently.

You have encountered variables in mathematics courses. For example, if $a = b$ and $b = c$, then $a = c$. The difference is that in math the instances of the variables are numbers, whereas in the argument form above the in-stances are class terms. Later you will encounter variables for statements, individuals, and properties.

The foregoing argument form is only one of many valid argument forms. In subsequent chapters you will learn several other valid argument forms.

The invalidity of an argument is also a matter of its form alone. Consider these examples:

1.	All insects are animals.	1.	All horses are animals.
2.	All bees are animals.	2.	All bees are animals.
3.	Therefore, all bees are insects.	3.	Therefore, all bees are horses.

Both of these arguments are invalid. They are invalid for the same reason; that is, they are both instances of the same argument form, namely:

1. All p are m.
2. All s are m.
3. Therefore, all s are p.

You should not be misled by the fact that all the statements in the argument at the left are true. Invalidity is a function of the argument's form alone. When we assess an argument, we are concerned with whether the premises prove the conclusion, rather than with the truth of the conclusion. And the argument at the right proves that the argument at the left is invalid. It is what is known as a refutation by analogy. An invalid argument is one that has a form such that it is possible for the premises to be true although the conclusion is false. Thus, we can prove an argument invalid by constructing an analogous argument with the same form, all true premises, and a false conclusion. When constructing a refutation by analogy, you should choose premises that are clearly true as well as a conclusion that is clearly false, so that the invalidity of the argument you are refuting will be clear to your audience.

A deductive argument is either valid or invalid. But some valid arguments have false conclusions and some invalid arguments have true conclusions, as our examples show. However, the point of an argument is to prove that its conclusion is true. So why are logicians concerned with validity? There are at least two answers to this question. First, no invalid argument proves that its conclusion is true. Even if the conclusion happens to be true, an invalid argument does not establish it. Second, some valid arguments do prove that their conclusions are true, since some valid arguments are sound. A sound argument is valid and has all true premises. Because it is impossible for the premises of a valid argument to be true without the conclusion being true, every sound argument has a true conclusion.

For example, you can substitute any terms you please for s, p, and m in the valid argument form above. If you substitute consistently and the result is all true premises, the conclusion must be true. By identifying valid argument forms, therefore, we create a general framework with which we can formulate deductive arguments that prove their conclusions.

To ask the question "Does this deductive argument prove its conclusion?" is to ask "Is this deductive argument sound?" We analyze that question into two, namely:

1. Is it valid?
2. Are all of its premises true?

If the answer to either of these questions is "no," the deductive argument does not prove its conclusion. Occasionally it is necessary to add a third question:

3. Are all the premises known to be true?

This question arises, of course, when we suspect that the answer to Question 3 is "no." If it were, the answer to Question 2 would be "indeterminate," which leaves open the possibility of a sound argument that is not known to be sound. But if the answer to all three questions is "yes," we know that the argument is sound.

Summary: Evaluating Inductive Arguments

Thus far we have described standards for evaluating deductive arguments. We need a different set of standards for assessing inductive arguments. When someone advocates an inductive argument, he is making a weaker claim for the argument than when he endorses a deductive argument. When someone advocates a deductive argument, he is claiming that the premises guarantee the conclusion. But when someone advances an inductive argument, he is not claiming that the premises guarantee the conclusion. Rather, he is stating (at least tacitly) that the premises make the conclusion (more or less)

26

probable or likely. Thus we need a different set of standards for evaluating inductive arguments.

As with deductive arguments, we shall not spell out the several principles for assessing inductive arguments. We shall merely indicate in a general way how inductive arguments are appraised, just as we discussed validity without setting out several valid argument forms.

Inductive arguments are evaluated in terms of their strength. The strength of an inductive argument is a function of the probability of the conclusion, given the premises. We can put it in the form of a question:

1. If we suppose the premises are true, how probable is the conclusion?

This is the inductive counterpart to the question about the validity of deductive arguments. The question "Is it valid?" can be recast as follows:

> If we suppose the premises are true, must the conclusion also be true?

Supposing, for the sake of evaluation, that the premises are true does not rule out the further question:

2. Are all the premises true?

If the probability of the conclusion (given the premises) is high and the premises are true, the inductive argument establishes its conclusion. Of course, there are varying degrees of strength claimed for the conclusion, depending on the argument. Thus, it is useful to speak of establishing the conclusion to such-and-such a degree. In general, the greater the degree of probability claimed for the conclusion, the greater the evidence for it must be.

Suppose a prosecuting attorney presents the following argument during a trial of Shlomo for the murder of Snurdley:

1. The coroner testified that Snurdley died from a gunshot wound.

2. Ballistics tests show that the gun used is exhibit A.

3. Records show that exhibit A belongs to Shlomo.

The prosecuting attorney naturally aims for the conclusion that Shlomo is guilty as charged. But if the premises above were the attorney's entire argument, it would be wrong to say Shlomo has been proven guilty "beyond a reasonable doubt." The reason is that the conclusion is not sufficiently probable, given those premises, to constitute the high probability of "beyond a reasonable doubt." Suppose that the prosecutor has further evidence:

4. Snurdley's little black book, exhibit B, shows a record of blackmail payments from Shlomo.

5. Klotzmeyer, Snurdley's "collection agent," testified that Snurdley had been blackmailing Shlomo.

The probability of the conclusion is higher with this additional, relevant evidence. Further suppose that:

6. Two of Snurdley's neighbors testified that they saw Shlomo enter Snurdley's apartment just before they heard a disagreement and a gunshot.

The probability is higher still. It is possible to conceive of further evidence that would strengthen (or weaken) the prosecutor's argument.

7. Snurdley's neighbors testified that Smedlap (who was also being blackmailed by Snurdley) entered Snurdley's apartment with Shlomo.

8. Three of Smedlap's neighbors testified that Smedlap had threatened to murder Snurdley.

These premises, if true, would weaken the prosecutor's argument.

In general, then, the higher the probability of the conclusion, given the premises, the stronger the inductive argument. In addition, the premises must be true in order to raise the probability of the <u>truth</u> of the conclusion. Although premises 4, 5, and 6 raise the probability of the prosecutor's conclusion, they raise the probability of the conclusion's <u>truth</u> only if they are true.

If we were to evaluate inductive arguments with deductive standards, every inductive argument would be invalid. Even if an inductive argument is very strong, its premises do not guarantee the conclusion. But it is unhelpful and misleading to apply deductive standards to inductive arguments. If we did, the result would yield no difference between the strongest and the weakest of inductive arguments. Sometimes we are justified in accepting inductively established conclusions even though no inductive argument is valid. Sometimes we are justified in rejecting inductive arguments--but because they are weak, not because they are invalid.

A problem remains. How do we distinguish invalid deductive arguments from inductive arguments? We know that if an argument is valid, it is deductive, regardless of its advocate's beliefs. But we seem to need to know the advocate's intentions for other arguments so that we can tell which standards to apply. Here we need to rely on the context, especially the words used in the conclusion, as mentioned earlier. <u>Occasionally</u>, though not often, it is necessary to evaluate an argument using both deductive and inductive standards. Frequently the context of the argument will give some clue, even when words such as <u>probably</u> and <u>must</u> are absent. But when classifying and interpreting arguments, we need to follow certain principles, such as the principles of charity and fair play (discussed in Section 2-4).

Practice Exercises

I. In the space at the left, identify each of the following arguments as either deductive (D) or inductive (I).

1. _____ John's class schedule shows that his logic class is in session now. He's a conscientious student who always has gone to class unless he's sick. I'm his roommate, and I know he wasn't sick an hour ago. So I'll bet he's in his logic class.

2. _____ Allison's education class is in session now. But she says she regularly cuts that class because it's a waste of time. She says she spends her time more profitably studying biology on the tenth floor of the library. I'd check the library first. If you don't find her there, you should go to the education classroom.

3. _____ If 6,561 were a prime number, it would not be divisible evenly by 3. But it is. So 6,561 is not a prime number.

4. _____ The murderer's blood type is A positive. However, my client's blood type is AB negative. It follows that my client is not the murderer.

5. _____ Suppose that there are two omnipotent (all-powerful) beings: A and B. If A is omnipotent, then A has power over B. But if A has power over B, B is not omnipotent. The same is true if "B" is substituted for "A," and "A" for "B." The same is true for any number greater than two. Therefore, there cannot be more than one omnipotent being.

6. _____ This library book is over a year past due. Since the fine is 25 cents per day and the cost of replacing it is twenty dollars, you will save money if you pay the replacement cost rather than the overdue fine.

7. _____ Religious belief cannot be discussed rationally because people are peculiarly apt to be irrational about that subject. (a paraphrase from Antony Flew, God & Philosophy.)

8. _____ People do things for reasons of which they are unaware. But if such unconscious motives control what a person does, the belief in free will is an illusion. Therefore, there is no free will.

9. _____ It is theoretically possible to build a machine that looks and acts just like a human being (or anything else, such as a cat, that appears to have a mind). If I knew that there were other minds merely by observing something that looks and acts like a human being, then I would know that such a machine has a mind.

10. _____ If I knew that there were other minds merely by observing something that looks and acts like a human being, then I would know that a machine that looks and acts like a human being has a mind. But I know that such a machine does not have a mind. Therefore, it is not the case that I know that there are other minds merely by observing something that looks and acts like a human being (or any other mind-endowed subject).

11. _____ If my knowledge of other minds is not based merely on the observation of something that looks and acts like a mind-endowed subject, then either I can read other minds, or there is some other factor in my knowledge of other minds, or I do not know that there are other minds. I cannot read other minds. Therefore, either there is some other factor in my knowledge of other minds, or else I do not know there are other minds.

12. _____ Three witnesses testified that Becky was in Montreal March the third. The break-in occurred on that date in Los Angeles. So Becky did not participate in the break-in.

13. _____ It is hard to explain how owls could be intelligent and yet bang their heads repeatedly on barn roofs. I'll bet that owls are not intelligent.

14. _____ This coin has landed tails up 15 times in a row. So it's very likely that it will land heads up this time.

15. _____ Klotzmeyer has AIDS. He's no Haitian. So he's either an intravenous drug user or a homosexual.

16. _____ We know that a watch is the product of planning or design on someone's part because its parts work together for a purpose, that of telling the time. We find a similar arrangement of parts in nature. Thus there is a designer of nature.

17. _____ If a person's mind were identical with his brain, it would make sense to say that a thought was to the left of another part of the brain. It would also make sense to speak of the size, weight, and color of a thought, since parts of the brain have all of these properties. But such talk does not make sense. Therefore, a person's mind is not identical with his brain.

18. _____ Plants need water to live. We forgot to ask our neighbors to water our indoor plants while we were on our two-week vacation. Yet the plants are still thriving. So our neighbors probably watered our plants.

19. _____ A male fruit fly inherits its eye color from its female parent. The male parent in our experiment has apricot-colored eyes. So the sons will not have apricot-colored eyes.

20. _____ The male fruit fly inherits its eye color from its female parent. All the male offspring of the female in this vial have white eyes. Therefore, the female parent has white eyes too.

21. _____ All acids turn blue litmus paper red. Placing this piece of blue litmus paper in this solution had no effect on the paper's color. Thus, this solution is not an acid.

II. Follow the same directions for the arguments given in Exercises 1-2, 1-3, 1-4, and 1-5 of Chapter 1.

2-3

Necessary and Empirical, or Contingent, Statements

Section Objectives

1. Distinguish necessary from contingent statements.

2. Distinguish empirical from *a priori* statements.

Key Term Review

1. Necessary statement: (a) a statement that, if true, could not be otherwise or, if false, could not be otherwise; (b) a statement that must be true or that must be false.

2. Contingent statement: (a) a statement that, even if true, could have been false or, if false, could have been true; (b) a statement that is (not "must be") true (or is false), but might have been otherwise.

3. *A priori* statement: (a) a statement that can be known to be true (or false) merely by understanding its meaning (or logical form); (b) a statement that can be known to be true (or false) without evidence supplied by observation.

4. Empirical statement: a statement the knowledge of which requires evidence supplied by observation in addition to understanding its meaning (or logical form).

Summary

Consider the statement "There are 45 desks in the classroom." We can distinguish two things required for knowing whether the statement is true: (1) understanding its meaning, and (2) knowing whether it is true (or false) —that is, having the required evidence. It is because we understand the statement's meaning that we know what further would be required in order for us to know whether it is true. We must go to the classroom and count the desks in order to know whether it is true. Counting the desks is gathering evidence supplied by observation. Thus, the statement "There are 45 desks in the classroom" is an empirical statement.

Now consider the statement "Blue is a color." Here there are not two things required for knowing whether the statement is true, because to understand its meaning is to know that it is true. No observation is required in order to know that it is true. Thus, the statement "Blue is a color" is an *a priori* statement (or is knowable *a priori*).

The statement "There are 45 desks in the classroom" is also a contingent statement. To say that a statement is contingent is to say that its truth (or falsehood) is contingent (dependent) on a certain state of affairs obtaining. The truth of the statement in question is dependent on there being 45 desks in the classroom. But there might have been more or fewer than 45. "There are 45 desks in the classroom," therefore, is a contingent and empirical statement.

"Blue is a color" is also a necessary statement or, more precisely, a necessarily true statement. Although there might have been more or fewer than 45 desks in the classroom, blue could not be anything but a color. The facts could not be otherwise. "Blue is a color," therefore, is a necessary and *a priori* statement. "No bachelor is single" is a necessarily false statement.

It is important not to confuse the statement "Blue is a color" with the different statement that the word blue is an English word for a color. That statement is contingent, because we might have had a different word for that color. But that fact has no bearing on the necessity of the truth that blue, the property named by the word, is a color. Even if we might have had a different word for blue, blue would still be, and must be, a color. If the word were different, we would express the truth differently. But the truth itself would be necessary. The same is true when we consider the possibility that we might have used the word blue to mean something else, or that the word blue has more than one meaning, or that there are no things that are blue. We are designating a certain color with the word, so "Blue is a color" is necessarily true. This is true of other examples as well.

The two examples we have considered thus far are neatly paired: the empirical statement is also contingent, just as the *a priori* statement is also necessary. However, it is important not to confuse either necessary with *a priori* nor contingent with empirical. Note that <u>necessary statement</u> does <u>not</u> mean the same thing as *a priori* <u>statement</u>. Nor does contingent statement mean the same thing as empirical statement. The terms *a priori* and <u>empirical</u> refer to ways in which a statement is <u>known</u>; the terms <u>necessary</u> and <u>contingent</u> do not. Rather, <u>necessary</u> and <u>contingent</u> refer to the status of the stated truth (or falsehood), regardless of anyone's knowledge. Because many statements are neatly paired in the way described above, some philosophers believe that all and only necessary statements are *a priori* and that all and only contingent statements are empirical. A few even define <u>necessary statement</u> and <u>contingent statement</u> in terms of knowledge. However, those beliefs have not been proven. Thus, it is best to recognize the distinctions and to leave open the question of whether all and only necessary statements are known *a priori*.[1]

There are a couple of other mistakes that can be made. Consider the statement "Cordates have hearts." Because this statement may send you to the dictionary to find out the meaning of <u>cordate</u>, you may mistakenly believe that the statement is empirical, inasmuch as it involves a procedure similar to counting the desks. However, the statement is *a priori*. *A priori* means that the statement can be known simply by understanding its meaning. This means that, <u>if</u> you understand its meaning, you know on that basis alone that it is true (or false). But if "Cordates have hearts" sent you to the dictionary, you did not understand its meaning in the first place.

Some empirical statements are so obviously true that their empirical character may be overlooked. Take "You are sitting at a desk now" as an example. Suppose you are sitting at a desk and thus know immediately that the statement is true. Your knowledge involves no procedure such as counting desks. The statement is nevertheless empirical; you have to observe the desk in order to know that the statement is true, even though no elaborate procedure is involved.

Some necessary statements are true (or false) because of their logical form (as opposed to their meaning). Such necessary statements are called logical truths (or logical falsehoods). "All rotifers are rotifers" is an example of a logical truth, whereas "Some marsupials are not marsupials" is a logical falsehood. This is because they are instances of the statement forms "All *p*'s are *p*'s" and "Some *p*'s are not *p*'s," respectively.

There are some statements that cannot be classified with assurance as necessary, contingent, *a priori*, or empirical. Nevertheless, many can. For those that cannot, it is useful to ask how they could be understood to fall in one (or more) of these categories. This can yield a deeper understanding of the statement's meaning.

---

[1]Saul Kripke argues for the distinction between <u>a prioricity</u> and necessity (and between empirical and contingent) in "Identity and Necessity." It appears in Stephen P. Schwartz, ed., <u>Naming, Necessity, and Natural Kinds</u> (Ithaca, N.Y.: Cornell University Press, 1977), pp. 84–85. Kripke also argues that some necessary statements (namely, identity statements) are empirical. I have not included that thesis in the text.

Practice Exercises

I. Identify each of the following statements as either necessary (N) or contingent (C). Identify the necessary statements as either necessarily true (NT) or necessarily false (NF). Lastly, indicate whether the statement is *a priori* (AP) or empirical (E).

1. _____ Mark Twain is identical with Samual Clemens.

2. _____ "Mark Twain" is a name Samuel Clemens used.

3. _____ All ravens are black.

4. _____ It is risky to generalize about the color of a species.

5. _____ The sun will rise tomorrow.

6. _____ If yesterday was Monday, today is Tuesday.

7. _____ Canada is north of South America.

8. _____ Every necessary statement is contingent.

9. _____ If this ball is blue all over, then its other side is not red.

10. _____ Streets are not parallel with avenues.

11. _____ Most English people enjoy tea.

12. _____ The winner of a U.S. presidential election receives the majority of popular votes.

13. _____ The word it's means "it is."

14. _____ The morning star is identical with the evening star.

15. _____ If Smith is an auditor for the I.R.S., then she has a bachelor's degree in accounting.

16. _____ All sodium salts burn yellow.

17. _____ Every triangle with a 90 degree angle is isosceles.

18. _____ Leibniz and Newton independently discovered calculus.

19. _____ Historical persons existed at one time.

20. _____ If there is no bank error and my bank balance is lower than it was on the same date last month, then I spent more than I deposited this month.

21. _____ Einstein's theory accounts for the perihelion of Mercury.

22. _____ Libraries contain books.

23. _____ An ophthalmologist is an eye doctor.

24. _____ Everything is caused, and there is a first cause.

25. _____ There is a first cause, but everything that begins to exist is caused.

26. _____ Fictitious entities do not exist.

27. _____ If someone knows that something is the case, then he is justified in believing it.

28. _____ If someone believes that something is the case, then he may or may not be justified in believing it.

29. _____ Charles remembers having seen a first-class performance of Richard III at Dartmouth College.

30. _____ There are no ghosts.

31. _____ All ravens are ravens.

32. _____ The square root of two went to the football game.

33. _____ No invalid argument proves that its conclusion is true.

34. _____ Shakespeare is the author of King Lear.

35. _____ Every sound argument proves that its conclusion is true.

II. Explain your answers to each of the following questions in Part I: 1, 6, 10, 12, 14, 19, 22, 24, 25, 26, 27, 30, 32, 33, and 35. If any example is ambiguous, show why it can be interpreted in more than one way.

1. _____

_____

6. _____

_____

10. _____

_____

12. _____

_____

14. _____

_____

19. _____

_____

22. _____

_____

24. _____

_____

25. _____

_____

26. _____

_____

27. _____

_____

30. _____

_____

32. _____

_____

33. _____

_____

35. _____

_____

2-4

Argumentation and Ethics

Section Objectives

1. Identify instances of the "straw man" fallacy.

2. Identify the principles of responsible expertise, fair play, charity, and tolerance.

Key Term Review

1. Fallacy of "straw man": presenting a weaker version of an adversary's

position or argument, refuting the weaker version, and inferring that one's opponent's position or argument has been refuted.

2. Principle of responsible expertise: the obligation (of a person conversant with logic) to try to raise the level of debate and to expose faulty reasoning.

3. Principle of fair play: the obligation to avoid using sophistry and other "underhanded" techniques in a debate.

4. Principle of charity: the obligation to interpret written or spoken arguments in the best possible way.

5. Principle of tolerance: the obligation to do one's best to recognize situations wherein argumentative analysis does not apply.

Summary

Logic and morality are two different things. Logic, like mathematics, is a science of non-moral facts. Logic itself does not consist of any moral judgments. Rather, it consists of such non-moral truths as "Every argument with a logical truth as its conclusion is valid." However, as we are people who can abuse our knowledge of this non-moral science, we will do well to consider the four "principles" defined above.

The distinction between proving something and persuading someone of it has a lot to do with the morality of debate and argumentation. Unfortunately, someone can establish something without persuading others of it. Sometimes prejudice or failure to understand the argument explains this phenomenon. Worse still, someone can persuade others of something without a single good argument. Sometimes the inability to formulate any good argument for the belief explains the fact that people resort to sophistry in order to persuade others of a belief. Much advertising and political debate are attempts to persuade people without making a good case for the belief.

There is a practical goal of the study of logic: to be persuaded by all and only good arguments. This is no easy task. We are assailed with sophistical rhetoric frequently, and we do not always have the time (or interest) to consider such sophistry from a logical point of view. Your careful study of logic can help you identify sophistry more frequently and quickly. And it can help you formulate good arguments.

To be persuaded by all and only good arguments is, in large measure, to be free. It is to be free from prejudice, free from being a victimized pawn of those who would enslave you with artful, but logically empty, persuasion. Thus, the practical goal of the study of logic is worthwhile.

This is not a matter of merely academic interest. Hitler did not use good arguments in his successful attempt to persuade many of Germany's citizens that Jews were the cause of Germany's problems. Joseph McCarthy did not use good arguments when he successfully persuaded many that several people were Communists. More recently, U.S. citizens were given a weak argument for the conclusion that taxes could be lowered significantly and military spending raised dramatically without increasing the federal deficit. Reason can make an important difference.

One such logical shortcut is the "straw man" fallacy. As an error in reasoning, it consists of the erroneous inference that because a weaker, caricatured version of one's adversary's view has been refuted, the adversary's actual belief has been proven false. This is standard practice in politics. Of course, one must be at least somewhat familiar with the opponent's position in order to identify the argument as a "straw man" fallacy. The fact that people are uninformed or unwilling to inform themselves is a primary reason why politicians get away with such misrepresentations.

The goal of being persuaded by all and only good arguments is difficult to achieve. Part of the difficulty is the fact that you sometimes encounter poor arguments <u>for</u> your own beliefs. You may feel uncomfortable criticizing a poor argument for something you believe. However, you should bear in mind that criticizing a poor argument is <u>not</u> the same thing as rejecting the argument's conclusion. For example, I pointed out in this chapter that an argument leading to the conclusion "All bees are insects" was invalid. But my criticism of that argument does not commit me to rejecting that truth. In general, then, there is a world of difference between these two statements:

This argument does not prove that its conclusion is true.

and

This conclusion of this argument is not true.

However, this distinction is not a pretext for being smug with one's own beliefs. A rational person must be prepared to abandon a belief that is indefensible. But here we must distinguish between indefensibility and a particular person's inability to make a case for a belief. Someone may be unable to defend a belief that is, in fact, defensible. Part of the practical goal of the study of logic is to examine the case for your own beliefs and to replace bad arguments with good ones.

Practice Exercises

Analyze the following passages. Explain how each of them involves fallacious reasoning.

1. Julian Bond: "We must reject this stupid idea of patriotism that has made us first in war, last in peace and last in the hearts of our countrymen."

    Political opponent, referring to Bond's statement: "Julian Bond says that partiotism is stupid."

    _____

    _____

    _____

    _____

    _____

2. Senator Ted: "I believe this legislation, which regulates ownership of 'Saturday night special' handguns, will make life safer for the American people."

Senator Snort: "Senator Ted believes that handgun legislation will make walking outside at night completely safe. But that's no solution to the problem."

_____

_____

_____

_____

_____

_____

_____

_____

_____

3. Senator Snuff (commenting on the same statement to a National Rifle Association convention): "Senator Ted wants to prevent you from using your rifle to hunt wild game. But that's a ludicrous position. So I'll fight against gun control legislation."

_____

_____

_____

_____

_____

4. Senator Snort: "There is no way we can defend the Panama Canal against terrorist attacks. There is good reason to believe that there will be no attacks if we ratify the Panama Canal Treaty. Besides, ratifying the treaty will improve relations between the U.S. and Panama. Basically, our choice is either to ratify the treaty, in which case our ships can move through the area safely, or to try to defend the area against terrorist attacks, which means that no one will be safe in the area."

Senator Swine (speaking to the members of the True Conservative Caucus): "Senator Snort wants to give away the Panama Canal!"

_____

_____

5. From a letter to the editor of a newspaper in Pensacola, Florida: "What little objectivity there is in your editorial about the underground newspaper is shrouded, even eclipsed, by the use of emotionally charged words. Those words are used to sway the audience where the evidence is insufficient."

Headline over the letter, placed by the editor: "Objectivity Attacked."

OVERVIEW

The practical goal of the study of logic is to be persuaded by all and only
good arguments. Some persuasive uses of language can impede the pursuit of
that goal. People sometimes use language in order to avoid having to produce evidence for questionable or false claims. We need to study such uses
of language. We also need to investigate ways in which people can use language in order to prompt themselves and others to make fallacious or misleading inferences. By doing so, we will be better equipped to distinguish
good from bad (but persuasive) arguments.

SECTION REVIEWS   *3-1 and 3-2*

Language and Thought
Levels of Meaning

Section Objective

1. Identify the various functions that linguistic expressions have.

Key Term Review

1. Referential theory of meaning: the thesis that the meaning of a word
    is the object, or entity, the word designates.

2. Ideational theory of meaning: the thesis that the meaning of a word is
    the idea, or mental image, with which the word is associated when
    spoken, read, or heard.

3. Behavioral theory of meaning: the thesis that the meaning of a word is
    the kinds of activities that prompt someone to speak or write the word
    and the range of the hearer's usual responses.

4. "Use theory" of meaning: the thesis that the meaning of a word consists
    in how it is used.

5. Performative utterance: an expression that, when spoken in the appro-
    priate circumstances, accomplishes the action it reports. (That is,
    saying it in the appropriate circumstances is doing it, as in "I
    promise.")

Summary

Section 3-1, "Language and Thought," is an introductory section designed to
prompt you to think about the relationship of language to thought. To what

extent is a person't thought shaped by the language(s) he speaks? To what
extent do we shape language to suit our (linguistically independent)
thoughts? The text reviews the evidence and conclusions of some investiga-
tors.

Section 3-2, on the other hand, briefly defines four different theories of
meaning. The "use theory" provides the most promising guidelines for exam-
ining the meanings and functions of linguistic expressions. It directs us
to examine language within the context of human behavior and the purposes
and intentions of speakers. We can clarify linguistic expressions by exam-
ining how they are used.

Because our goal is to appraise arguments objectively, we need to isolate
the informative function of sentences in an argument from their other functions. Only the informative function is logically relevant to the derivation of the conclusion. Some of the other functions may be psychologically
relevant to a person's inference, but they are extra-logical.

We can begin by recognizing that one and the same sentence can have a number
of functions. You have already encountered the informative, directive,
emotive, evaluative, and ceremonial uses. Language can also be used per-
formatively when such verbs as <u>advise</u>, <u>suggest</u>, <u>accept</u>, <u>apologize</u>, <u>baptize</u>,
<u>bid</u>, <u>concede</u>, <u>congratulate</u>, <u>greet</u>, <u>promise</u>, <u>pronounce</u>, <u>thank</u>, and <u>warn</u> are
used.

Consider the following sentence:

> Warning: The Surgeon General has determined that cigarette smoking is
> dangerous to your health.

This sentence has several functions. First, the reader is <u>informed</u> of the
Surgeon General's findings. Second, the sentence is a warning and is thus
<u>performative</u>. The Surgeon General (presumably) has warned the reader with
the sentence on each cigarette package. Third, the sentence is politely
<u>directive</u>. Although no direct order is given, the intent of the warning is
to prompt smokers to quit (or to discourage potential smokers from starting).
Its very politeness is evidence for such an intent; smokers would be less
likely to respond to a direct order. Fourth, the sentence is (at least
mildly) <u>emotive</u>. Although the word <u>dangerous</u> is not highly charged with
emotion, it replaced the milder word <u>hazardous</u>. Thus, the warning is intended to stir some emotional response regarding the Surgeon General's
findings.

The informative content of such a sentence could occur in an argument, such
as the following:

1. The Surgeon General has determined that cigarette smoking is danger-
    ous to one's health.
2. Cigarette packages would not have such a warning on them unless
    there were good reason to believe that cigarette smoking is danger-
    ous.
3. So, cigarette smoking is dangerous.
4. So, if you want to avoid that danger, you should quit smoking.

Consider a different example. Suppose someone asks, "Have you stopped
smoking?" On the face of it, this is a request for information. Suppose
the question is being asked by a non-smoking friend who is trying to en-
courage the smoker to quit but who knows that the smoker has not. In that

event, the sentence would be a polite directive, an encouragement to quit smoking. The sentence can also be informative about the speaker's continued concern about the smoker. Note that the question presupposes that the person to whom it is addressed <u>has</u> smoked. This presupposition would not occur to us ordinarily, because it seems that we would not ask such a question unless we knew that the person smoked.

Sometimes, however, people ask loaded questions. Someone can introduce questionable, false, or misleading presuppositions in the very formulation of a question. Suppose an interviewer asks someone, "Do you prefer communism to apartheid?" The simple response of "yes" can create misleading impressions. Suppose the person being interviewed is not an advocate of communism but disapproves of apartheid so strongly that he believes he can register that disapproval effectively by answering "yes." But the interviewer might take the response as advocacy of communism, especially if the interviewer were predisposed to that belief. The interviewer might then dismiss whatever the interviewee has to say. The problem is that the very question proposes certain terms to the interviewee, as though the only alternative to apartheid were communism. The situation calls for <u>dividing the question</u>. This amounts to identifying the presupposition of the question and refusing to answer the question directly because it is loaded. The response might then be "I do not think of the apartheid issue in those terms," or "I prefer majority rule, with constitutional protection for minorities, to both white minority rule and communism."

Not all presuppositions of questions are false, misleading, or questionable. However, a questioner can put words into the mouth (make a statement) of someone being questioned by asking a loaded question. This is why good lawyers are adept at identifying loaded questions. And some clever ones are skillful at posing them! Complex questions are discussed in Section 12-2 of the text.

It should be noted that we must usually consider context in order to ascertain how an expression is being used. I imagined various contexts in order to specify the possible uses of the three examples considered. When analyzing a sentence, it is useful to ask yourself the following questions:

1. What is the most obvious use of the sentence?

2. What are the less obvious uses (if any)?

3. Under what circumstances would the sentence have other uses? What would those other uses be in those circumstances? (The variations here should be limited to possible ordinary uses.)

4. If the sentence is in question form, is it merely rhetorical? Or is it a genuine request for information?

5. Does the question include presuppositions? What are those presuppositions?

6. Are any of the presuppositions (relative to a certain context) questionable, false, or misleading? Why?

Practice Exercises

I. Consider items 4, 5, 8, 10, 16, 17, and 19 in the first exercise in Chapter 1. Each of these sentences can, under appropriate circumstances, have more than one of the following functions: informative (I), directive

(D), emotive or expressive (F), evaluative (E), ceremonial (C), requests informative (Q), or performative (P). On a separate sheet of paper, specify different contexts that would permit the alternative interpretations you select. Use the questions posed above and the examples discussed as guidelines.

II. Follow the same set of directions. Use the space provided for the letters, but specify the circumstances under which those interpretations obtain on a separate sheet of paper.

1. _____ Have you stopped beating your wife?

2. _____ Why did you lie about your age?

3. _____ I missed the test because my grandmother died.

4. _____ A student will be permitted to take a make-up test only if he has a good and documented reason.

5. _____ If find you so attractive.

6. _____ Renoir is one of my favorite painters.

7. _____ Renoir is one of the world's greatest painters.

8. _____ I find her so attractive.

9. _____ I love you.

III. For each of the following terms, present at least one definition in addition to the literal meaning of the word. Use the space provided.

1. Pig _____

_____

2. Cat's meow _____

_____

3. Joint _____

_____

4. Clown _____

_____

5. Stuffy _____

_____

Section Objectives

1. Identify words, phrases, and techniques that <u>can</u> be used to mask the weakness of a statement or argument.

2. Identify some cases of misuse of those words, phrases, and techniques.

Key Term Review

1. <u>Literal meaning</u>: the informative content of an expression.

2. <u>Emotive meaning</u>: the attitude, judgment, or point of view suggested or elicited by the use of an expression.

3. <u>Euphemism</u>: an expression with pleasing or neutral connotations, which is substituted for one with disagreeable connotations (where both expressions have the same literal meaning).

4. <u>Slanting</u>: a speaker or writer's use of euphemisms or words with disagreeable connotations to create an impression about a subject that is not warranted by the evidence.

5. <u>Assuring</u>: (a) reference to shared beliefs with such expressions as "it goes without saying," "everyone agrees that," "as we all know," "it needs no comment," "in fact," "undoubtedly," "of course," and "obviously;" (b) indicating that proof can be produced on demand by using such expressions as "according to an informed source," "recent studies have shown," and "the experts agree that."

6. <u>Slanting use of assuring</u>: doing (a) in order to bypass the need to defend a controversial, questionable, or indefensible claim; doing (b) when no evidence or only insufficient evidence can be produced.

7. <u>Hedging</u>: limiting the scope of a claim to the extent that it is unlikely to be challenged.

8. <u>Slanting use of hedging</u>: Hedging in order to insinuate things that, for lack of evidence, are not explicitly stated.

9. <u>Fallacious use of hedging</u>: inferring that a statement is established from a guarded, or "hedged," form of that statement.

10. <u>Innuendo</u>: an indirect intimation about a person or thing (usually produced by irony, understatement, or overstatement).

11. <u>Discounting</u>: the use of certain conjunctions (such as <u>but</u>, <u>although</u>, <u>however</u>, <u>nevertheless</u>, <u>still</u>, <u>yet</u>, and <u>nonetheless</u>) to bind together diverging but not necessarily contradictory expressions.

12. <u>Slanting use of discounting</u>: the use of those conjunctions to create an impression not warranted by the evidence.

13. <u>Hypostatization</u>: treating an abstraction as though it had existence.

14. <u>Reification</u>: a kind of hypostatization in which an abstraction is thought to exist because the words that designate the abstraction are ordinary nouns.

15. <u>Personification</u>: referring to an abstraction in terms that apply to human beings; attributing human intentions and activities to an abstraction.

16. Con-artistry: a host of techniques used to control information and in-fluence attitudes, such as (a) the selection of certain facts and the omission of others; (b) the distortion of information by arranging facts to suggest relationships that do not exist; (c) name-calling; (d) the oversimplification of complex issues; (e) lifting statements out of context; (f) distraction by the use of a red herring, inappropriate humor, or completely irrelevant considerations.

17. Doublespeak: the selection or invention of emotively neutral—often technical sounding—terms to dull the force of what is being said and thus make acceptable what otherwise might be unacceptable.

18. Fallacy of false dilemma: an argument in which someone tries to win agreement with a conclusion by reducing the alternatives to fewer than there are (usually to just two).

19. Fallacy of suppressed evidence: an argument in which someone tries to obtain agreement with a conclusion by withholding evidence that is damaging to it.

Summary

This section covers many techniques of persuasion. A few are easy to iden-tify; most are not. That is why they are used effectively time and again. Since the practical goal of the study of logic is to evaluate arguments im-partially, you need to be aware of these techniques and just how difficult it can be to identify instances of their use. We hope your study of this chapter will make you more wary of these techniques, better able to identify instances of their use, and less likely to accuse someone indiscriminately of using them in an irrational way.

When appraising an argument, we need to isolate the informative content of what is being said. Only the literal meaning is relevant to the derivation of the conclusion. The emotive meaning of the words used can impede us in our effort to assess an argument or statement impartially. Suppose a city council is considering whether to grant a permit to a business that plans to show sexually explicit films. Suppose citizens are presenting arguments for and against. One and the same set of films might be described as "smut," "sexploitation," or "adult films." Yet these words differ in their emotive content. We are invited to adopt very different attitudes, depend-ing on which word is used. Thus, we are invited to draw very different—in this case, competing—conclusions on the basis of the same facts. In order to appraise an argument or statement dispassionately, it is often useful to replace emotionally charged words or phrases with neutral ones (just as long as such a "translation" does not result in distortion or "doublespeak").

Words have a lot of uses, and it is certainly not wrong to use emotionally charged words. The point, rather, is that such words can be used to take an unwarranted logical shortcut. They can be used to sway you to accept a conclusion that is not justified by the evidence. And if you want clear comprehension of the argument itself, you will try to resist slanting by re-casting it in neutral language.

Although we have referred to slanting as though someone else were responsi-ble for it, you, too, are capable of slanting. It is perhaps most difficult to recognize slanting in your own case.

We have said that emotionally charged words <u>can</u> be used to create an impression that is not justified by the evidence. This means that we are left with the problem of ascertaining <u>when</u> the use of those words is slanting. The first step is to recast the statements into neutral language. We are then in a position to see whether the premises justify the conclusion--and thus whether the emotionally charged words amount to slanting.

Assuring has legitimate uses. That is why there is a distinction between assuring and its slanting use, described in the review of key terms. Suppose you are talking with some fellow students about which courses to take and someone proposes enrolling in Professor Kingsfield's course. Suppose you have heard many students with differing abilities all say so and back up their claim by listing the course requirements. In that case it would be legitimate to say, "Kingsfield is obviously a tough professor, so you should enroll in his class only if you're willing to work hard."

But reputations can be deserved or undeserved. Suppose, on the other hand, that you do not know the students who have "passed the word along." Suppose that none of them backed up the claim by listing the course requirements. Alternatively, suppose many had not even had a course with Kingsfield or, if they did, regularly cut class and did not obtain notes from other students. To "pass the word along" by saying "Kingsfield is obviously a tough professor, etc." under those circumstances would be a slanting use of assuring.

This constitutes a difficulty both for the person who is spreading the rumor and for the person to whom it is told. Presumably, the student spreading the rumor knows that he does not know the students from whom he heard it and knows that they did not corroborate their claim. In that case, he would be spreading a rumor for which <u>he</u> did not have sufficient evidence. Not knowing the students from whom he heard it, however, may leave him unsure whether they could have produced the evidence. He may be uncertain whether <u>there</u> <u>is</u> sufficient evidence for the statement, regardless of whether <u>he</u> has that evidence. The person who hears the rumor has similar difficulties but can inquire into the nature of the evidence. Thus, the discussion of the slanting use of assuring has not so much to do with truth (whether there is sufficient evidence) as with whether the speaker or writer <u>has</u> sufficient evidence. The objectionable nature of the slanting use of assuring is a function on the fact that we do not <u>know,</u> in such a case, that there is sufficient evidence unless we know that the speaker or writer has it. Identifying cases of slanted assuring helps us to distinguish what we know from what we do not know.

If you have independent, sufficient evidence, then you are in a position to confirm or deny the rumor. But this is the exception, rather than the rule, because each of us has first-hand knowledge of only a limited number of things. That is one reason why identifying cases of slanted assuring is difficult. Acquiring first-hand knowledge is hard work.

Hedging also has legitimate uses. Sometimes people introduce a guarded statement because they do not believe that it is true in a less-qualified form (or perhaps know that it isn't true in that form). Consider the preceding sentence as an example. I wrote "sometimes," rather than "most of the time," because I do not have sufficient reason to believe that the statement would be true if I wrote "most of the time."

However, hedging can be used in order to slant or make a fallacious inference. The slanting use of hedging can be an innuendo, as in "Perhaps he
stole the money." The slanting use of hedging is frequently for the purpose
of avoiding responsibility for a less-guarded statement that the speaker
would like to insinuate without defending.

Hedging can also form a part of a fallacious argument. For example, two
proselytizing Christians once claimed that the Bible contains no two statements that contradict one another. They added that historical evidence did
not contradict any statement in the Bible. But then they proceeded to speak
as though they had proven that every statement in the Bible is true. This
is a case of a fallacious inference based on hedging. "Does not contradict"
is a logician's phrase, the technical sound of which can cover up the fact
that the statements are hedged. "Does not contradict" means "is not impossible" or "is possible." The argument, then, is:

1. It is possible for all the statements in the Bible to be true (disregarding external evidence).
2. It is possible for us to accept historical evidence and all the
   statements in the Bible (taking external evidence into account here).
3. Therefore, all the statements in the Bible are true.

The problem is that there is a huge gulf between _possibly_ being true and
actually being true. What is lacking in the argument is any direct evidence
for those statements. Even if there is not conclusive evidence _against_
their truth, that fact does not establish their truth. The same could be
said of some works of fiction. Historical evidence may not contradict any
of a novel's statements. This is not to suggest that the Bible is fiction.
It is only to specify the shortcomings of the argument in question.

Discounting is part of everyday language, although the conjunctions can be
used to slant. That last sentence is itself an example of a legitimate use
of discounting. We are interested in how discounting can be used to slant,
so by using the word _although_, I stressed the slanting use over its unobjectionable use. Consider the example in the text:

Chalmers is an honest politican, but he is reticent and secretive.

Chalmers is reticent and secretive, but he is an honest politician.

These statements present the same facts, although the first sounds critical
and the second does not. These statements could be used for different purposes. The first (but not the second) would be used to argue against
Chalmers. Discounting is a relatively subtle turn of speech. It requires
careful attention to what someone says or writes to identify possible slanting uses of it. In order to ascertain whether there is a slanting use of
discounting, ask the question "What justifies stressing X over Y?" If the
response is not a good one, we have a slanting use of discounting.

Hypostatization, reification, and personification often occur in passages
that are so difficult to read that you may be tempted to think that they
are profound and beyond your comprehension. But a close reading of them
sometimes shows that the passages are anything but profound. Society is an
abstraction that is frequently hypostatized, as when we speak of a prisoner
"paying his debt to society." Society is even personified, as in "society's
interests." Hypostatization and personification can be harmless. On the
other hand, they can form a part of bad arguments, as when someone dis-
guises his self-interest as society's interest or speaks as though society
had interests that were distinct from those of the individuals who comprise
it.

Con-artistry covers many techniques of persuasion of which the student of logic should be aware. Although the word con-artistry evokes the image of someone trying to con you, occasionally the "con-artist" is duped also. Frequently, however, the image is appropriate.

Selecting certain facts and omitting others is standard practice in advertising and politics. The omitted facts are damaging to the arguer's conclusion. That is why the practice is objectionable from the logical standpoint. When facts that are damaging to one's conclusion are omitted, but the conclusion is nevertheless inferred, we have an instance of the fallacy of suppressed evidence.

Consider a commercial for diet 7-Up in which we are told that a recent poll showed that other diet soft drinks "couldn't beat" diet 7-Up for taste. But the fact that other soft drinks "couldn't beat" diet 7-Up only means that the others were not judged to be better. That is perfectly consistent with all of them being equally good. The spokesman does not say that diet 7-Up was judged to have a better taste, yet a series of boxers (representing the competitors' soft drinks) are defeated by diet 7-Up's boxer. Although the action takes place off camera, we are clearly supposed to infer that diet 7-Up defeated the others. Now if the poll had shown that diet 7-Up was better than its competitors, the ad would have said so. We are thus invited to commit the fallacy of suppressed evidence.

Political examples are even easier to find. If a politician is campaigning for re-election, we all know that he (or she) will emphasize the accomplishments and ignore the blunders. Politicians bank on our faulty memories or prejudices, which will lead us to forget the blunders, be blind to them, or downplay their significance.

Lifting statements out of context is a con-artist's ploy that requires either research or background knowledge to identify. That is, you must either read or have read the source from which someone quotes in order to spot a case of quoting out of context. That is why this tactic can be used to persuade even though the argument is poor. One of the exercises in Chapter 1 quotes a passage in which R. C. Lewontin identifies an instance of quoting out of context. Having written the article from which a creationist quoted, he was in a position to know that he had been quoted out of context to create the misleading impression that he endorses a position that he does not endorse. Quoting out of context can be interpreted as a particular version of the fallacy of suppressed evidence, because the person who quotes out of context does not reveal the context of the quotation, which is damaging to the conclusion.

The oversimplification of a complex issue very often is a prelude to the fallacy of false dilemma. That fallacy consists of reducing the number of alternatives to fewer than there are, rejecting all but one alternative, and inferring that the remaining alternative must be accepted. Usually the fallacy consists of reducing the number of alternatives to just two. A slogan from the 1960s, "America: Love it or leave it," is an example of this, because there is at least one alternative other than unqualified endorsement of then-current governmental policies (loving it) and leaving the country. Another example is the loaded question discussed in the previous section; there are many alternatives to apartheid and communism. The fallacy of suppressed evidence is discussed in Section 12-3 of the text.

Humor has its place, even in debate. But humor or something irrelevant can be introduced in order to distract attention from the point under consideration. The effectiveness of talking about irrelevant or tangential matters (red herrings) may be due to the fact that it takes a little time to spot a red herring as such. Besides, it can be rude to interrupt a speaker and call the irrelevancy a red herring. By the time the speaker is finished with the irrelevant considerations, the audience may have forgotten the main point. Thereby some speakers can introduce questionable claims or weak arguments without being challenged.

The practical goal of logic is to be persuaded by all and only good arguments. Pursuit of this ideal requires careful attention to nuances of the signficance and content of what is said or written. It requires research, background knowledge, healthy skepticism, and a willingness to deal with the complexity of issues. Rationality requires self-discipline.

Practice Exercises

The following passages could (or do) contain one or more of the "pitfalls of language" discussed in this section. A few of them contain all the information you need to specify just how the reasoning has gone awry. If so, discuss how the passage involves a pitfall of language. Many of the passages do not contain all the information you need to say with assurance that they involve a pitfall of language. If so, specify the conditions that would make the passage an instance of one or more pitfalls of language. Be specific. That is, do not merely write "if the evidence were insufficient, the passage would be an instance of such-and-such a pitfall." Rather, specify what would make the evidence inadequate. Use the analyses of examples in this section as a guide for formulating your responses. Write you answers on a separate sheet of paper.

1. South African President Botha rejected the one-man, one-vote concept, saying, "I am not prepared to lead white South Africans and other minority groups on a road to abdication and suicide. Destroy white South Africa and our influence, and this country will drift into faction, strife, chaos and poverty."--Quoted by Arthur Hoppe in Austin American Statesman, 23 August 1985, p. A-15.

2. "Opponents of Kassebaum's ceiling (of 20% of the U.S.'s budget, rather than the current 25%) feared that it smacked of a new American isolationism and would undermine our influence in the agency that is the major forum for world opinion. But these worries are exaggerated, based on the discredited notion that uncontrolled spending is the equivalent of respect."--Marianne Means, in Austin American-Statesman, 23 August 1985, p. A-14.

3. "Try your oil against Mazola Corn Oil in a taste test of your own. Just fry some chicken and then take a bite. You'll like ours better. Why are we so confident? Because Mazola beat the other leading oils in taste tests. That's why. We'll even send you $2.00 in Mazola coupons, if you agree that Mazola is the best way to fry. Just send us a proof-of-purchase from a 24-oz. or larger bottle, along with a Mazola certificate from you supermarket. And the $2.00 savings is all yours. If you're one of the very few that doesn't agree, we'll mail you $1.00 in cash. No questions asked."--From an advertisement for Mazola in Austin American-Statesman.

4. Earl Butz (the former Secretary of Agriculture) defended ex-President Ford's plan to allow no family of four that earns over $5000 per year to receive food stamps by saying that one should get food stamps out of the hands of those families who make $12,000 to $15,000 per year and get them to those families that are "really in need." (Butz put forward this argument in 1974 or 1975, when $12,000-$15,000 per year was a middle-class income.)

5. Phanthene Brampton, movie critic of the Mudville Bugle, made the following assessment in a review: "Revenge of the Reptilians is without a doubt a masterpiece of the gut-turning, mindless tripe that has become sickeningly commonplace among graduates of the school of inanely adolescent filmmaking!" (An advertisement for the movie reported critic Brampton as having said: "Revenge of the Reptilians is without doubt a masterpiece of filmmaking!")

6. I bought a cheaper shortening, and my fried foods tasted greasy. I discovered that the cheaper brand had part animal fat, which made my food taste greasy. But Crisco is an all-vegetable shortening. Crisco's worth the difference because you can taste the difference.

7. A 1950 political advertisement for Richard Nixon: "The real import of the contest between Mr. Nixon and Helen Gahagen Douglas is whether America shall continue to tolerate Communist conspiracies within our own borders and Government, persist in condoning bureaucratic profligacy and appeasing totalitarian aggression, or whether America shall victoriously resist these deadly dangers."--Quoted by Howard Kahane in Logic and Contemporary Rhetoric, p. 52.

8. Let's stop the slaughter, the murdering of babies. Support a constitutional amendment to end abortion.

9. A woman has a right to do with her body as she pleases. Support the Supreme Court's decision and resist the reactionary forces who are trying to legislate morality.

10. Congresswoman Smith voted against voluntary school prayer. Her opponent supports the right of students to pray. That's a good reason to vote for Smith's opponent.

OVERVIEW

Because recognizing and evaluating arguments are so dependent on the natural languages used to express premises and conclusions, this chapter concentrates on clarifying meaning, avoiding ambiguity, and recognizing the emotive content of language.

SECTION REVIEWS   *4-1*

The Hazards of Ambiguity

Section Objective

1. Learn to recognize three sources of confusion: amphiboly, accent, and equivocation.

Key Term Review

1. Amphiboly: an amphiboly or amphibolous sentence is a sentence that is ambiguous because of poor sentence construction.

2. Accent: as used here, accent refers to an unclear sentence that results from confusion about what word or phrase is accented or emphasized.

3. Equivocation: the use of the same word or phrase in more than one sense in an argument.

Summary

Amphibolous sentences and sentences that are unclear because of difficulties in understanding what is or should be emphasized or accented are not fallacies. But if such sentences appear in arguments, they may cause confusion about what actually is being claimed. Equivocation often occurs in arguments, and when the shift in meaning from one occurrence to another is slight, it may be difficult to detect. If the structure of an argument appears to be correct but the argument still seems "fishy," it is wise to do a careful examination of the ideas or concepts expressed by the statements to see whether there is an equivocation.

Practice Exercises

Although it is sometimes rather difficult, try to determine whether the confusion in the following examples is the result of amphiboly (AM), accent (AC), or equivocation (EQ). Explain the ambiguity.

1. _____ For sale. 3-2-2 brick house. By owner. See to believe.

2. _____ Charlotte has been received into the holy catholic church. Catholics are not Protestants. So, Charlotte is not a Protestant.

3. _____ Newspaper headline: "After two nights of looting and rioting, the mayor imposes curfew."

4. _____ Some would suggest that abortion be legal until the fetus is "viable." Most people define viable as "capable of independent existence." No one is totally capable of independent existence, so this cannot be a good solution to the problem.

5. _____ From a newspaper story: "Covered with nothing but Saran Wrap, the attractive housewife carried her prize-winning pie to the judges' stand.

6. _____ Landlord: I'm going to raise your rent.
Tenant: Boy, that's a relief because I can't raise it.

7. _____ A gorilla is more like a man than a chimpanzee.

8. _____ Of all the beings in the universe only man is rational. No woman is a man. So, no women are rational.

9. _____ People object to racism and sexism on the grounds of discrimination. But what is objectionable about discrimination? We discriminate all the time--in the cars we buy, the foods we eat, the books we read, the friends we choose. So there is nothing wrong with discrimination against people on the basis of color or sex.

10. _____ I just don't understand the thinking of people who oppose legalized gambling. Gambling is an unavoidable part of life. We gamble when we cross the street, take a job, drive our cars, or get married. To legalize gambling would be only to face up to the facts.

11. _____ Everyone has a right to his or her opinion. Therefore, everyone's opinion is right.

12. _____ I cannot praise his work too highly.

13. _____ Terence is a fast turtle. Terence is an animal. It follows that Terence is a fast animal.

14. _____ He likes his job more than his wife.

15. _____ It had been an exciting confrontation. But now the crowd was gone. Only Sheriff Bart was left. He stood there, wiping his forehead on the courthouse steps.

16. _____ She says she didn't see the reason I deserve a raise.

17. _____ When she's planning to see the boss, I always try to get her to mention my name, in vain.

18. _____ This is a fine place to work.

19. _____ Newspaper: "This is a perfect example of an ill-conceived, poorly executed film."
    Reader: "Hey Bill, let's go see this movie the paper calls 'a perfect film.'"

20. _____ If our senses do not deceive us, scientific theory is true. But if scientific theory is true, our senses deceive us. So if our senses do not deceive us, our senses deceive us.

4-2

Exploiting Vagueness

Section Objective

1. Describe the hazards of vague words and concepts.

Key Term Review

Slippery-slope fallacy: also sometimes called the argument of the beard or the bald-man argument. The fallacy of assuming that if things lie on a continuum, they cannot be distinguished from each other, or the mistake of believing that once a move on the continuum is made, one cannot stop until he "slips down the slope" to the end.

Summary

Nearly all words and concepts are vague to some extent. Hence it behooves us to be aware of the difficulty in communication that derives from this vagueness.

Practice Exercises

Examine each of the following to determine why it involves slippery-slope reasoning. Write a brief response to each.

1. If we let students become members of the Admissions Committee, they will soon want to be voting members of departments, and then they will want to have a student co-dean. Before you know it, they will be hiring and firing the faculty. Obviously, then, we shouldn't allow them on the Admissions Committee.

   _____   _____

   _____

   _____

2. If the Regents grant official recognition to the Gay Alliance, then the way would be clear for the organization and for recognition of similar

groups founded solely on the basis of sexual preferences. Within a few
years the campus would be overflowing with sex-oriented clubs. The
thing would probably snowball and, within a short time, these groups
would become national or even international sex organizations. Just
think of it!

---

3. The mayor of a small Wyoming town proposed an ordinance making it illegal for tavern patrons to carry guns into the tavern. The National
Rifle Assocation opposed the ordinance using the following line of argument: This proposed ordinance, which seems reasonable enough (after
all, who wants to get shot by a drunk?), is in reality pernicious.
It is just the foot in the door that the liberal, anti-gun crowd wants.
If they succeed in banning guns from taverns, they will try to ban the
transporting of guns in pickups or cars. They will not stop until they
have made it illegal to own a gun. We must nip this insidious plot in
the bud.

---

4. The argument against legalizing marijuana is really simple and straight-
forward. Once we legalize marijuana, sure as shootin' legalized co-
caine, amphetamines, and heroin can't be far behind.

---

5. Argument against abolishing the foreign-language requirement for majors
in the College of Arts and Sciences: If we abolish the foreign-
language requirement, why not the English requirement, the history requirement, the government requirement? Pretty soon, nothing would be
required.

---

6. Consumer groups that lobby for increased product safety are deluding
themselves. Automobiles are a case in point. No car, however carefully and ingeniously designed, can protect its occupants if it is
driven into a bridge support at 90 miles per hour. Likewise, practically any toy can cause injury if a child uses it to beat another

over the head. It is just not possible to eliminate every conceivable risk associated with consumer products.

_____

_____

_____

7. Some people are contending nowadays that animals have rights. It is argued, for example, that chickens have the right not to be kept in tiny cages that prevent them from moving about; and the same goes for cows being fattened for slaughter. But if we say that chickens and cows have rights, it won't be long before we are forced to say the same about fish and insects. And then come plants and bacteria. Pretty soon we will be afraid to eat or to use antibiotics for fear of violating some entity's rights.

_____

_____

_____

8. No matter how nobly motivated and well-intentioned, attempts to outlaw pornography threaten basic civil rights and should be abandoned at once. If pornography--even so-called hard-core pornography--is out-lawed, censorship of newspapers and news magazines in only a short step away. After that, there will be censorship of textbooks, politi-cal speeches, and the content of lectures by university professors. Complete mind-control by the central government will be the inevitable result.

_____

_____

_____

9. Vegetarians would have us quit eating meat, on the grounds that killing animals for food is both cruel and unnecessary. But look where that sort of reasoning leads us. Fish are living creatures too, so we should stop eating fish. And we can't stop there: plants are also living things. If we followed the vegetarians' advice, we would soon be starving.

_____

_____

_____

10. As communism has taken one country at a time, so the Japanese are tak-ing over one industry at a time: automobiles, motorcycles, television, electronics, lawn mowers, machine tools--you name it. It's the same way with the communists. We sit idly by and say: "Oh, well, there goes Afghanistan."

_____

_____

_____

11. If the "don't knows" get away with banning trapping, it won't be long
     before someone starts a crusade to save the fish and worms and hell-
     grammites from the mean old fisherman. (Adapted from a circular oppos-
     ing a constitutional amendment banning the use of leghold traps in
     Ohio)

_____

_____

_____

12. First they put ratings on movies; then come records. Soon there'll be
     ratings for magazines, newspapers, and book classics. Then, maybe,
     ratings for hair style, make-up, and clothing.

_____

_____

_____

_____
4-3

Types of Dispute and Disagreement

Section Objectives

1. Recognize different types of dispute and disagreement.

2. Become aware that resolving a controversy or disagreement may require
    techniques appropriate to the type of dispute or disagreement involved.

Key Term Review

1. Factual dispute: a disagreement about the correctness of one or more
    claims.

2. Disagreement in attitude: a difference in how the persons involved
    feel about some situation.

3. Verbal dispute: a disagreement that would appear to be a factual dis-
    pute but is actually the result of different meanings being attached to
    words or concepts.

Summary

Failure to realize that the nature and type of disagreements vary may result in needless frustration when trying to cope with them.

56

Factual disagreements involve questions about who stole the book, whether the player crossed the plane of the goal line, or whether it is likely to rain soon. This is quite different from disagreements about whether John showed <u>admirable</u> ingenuity in obtaining by stealing a book he could not afford or whether we should rejoice about the prospect of rain. And these are different from a third type of disagreement about meanings. We might discover that a long argument about weather forecasting was really only a disagreement about what each of us meant by "soon." These three types of disagreement are, respectively, factual disputes, disagreements in attitude, and verbal disputes.

Practice Exercises

I. Assume that two people disagree about whether some given argument is valid. Discuss how you would classify the type of disagreement involved.

_____

_____

II. In each of the following, determine the type or types of disagreement involved.

1. Green: "Abortion is murder."   _____
   White: "No, it's not!"

2. Blue: "He touched the base."   _____
   Gray: "No, he stepped on it."

3. Black: "Billy Ghote-Gruph is
          sure disagreeable in
          class."   _____
   Brown: "No, he's just raising
          interesting questions."

4. Gray: "What a snowstorm! All   _____
          wind."
   Black: "I thought it was a
          blizzard."

4-4

Defining Terms

Section Objectives

1. Distinguish between the various ways in which terms and concepts are defined.

2. Discover the most appropriate techniques for clarifying the meaning of terms.

Key Term Review

1. <u>Ostensive definition</u>: definition by giving examples nonverbally, through gesturing or pointing.

2. <u>Denotative definition</u>: definition by giving examples verbally.

3. <u>Extension of a term</u>: the range of objects to which a general or class term applies. These are the objects denoted by the term.

4. <u>Intension of a term</u>: the attributes or properties shared by the objects denoted by a term. This is also the <u>connotation</u> of the term.

5. <u>Definition</u> (in logic): a transformation rule for replacing some words or phrases in a sentence with equivalent words.

6. <u>Analytical or connotative definition</u>: definition by listing the properties or attributes shared by all the individuals to which the word applies.

7. <u>Definiendum</u>: the expression being defined.

8. <u>Definiens</u>: the expression said to be equivalent to the word being defined.

9. <u>Lexical definition or dictionary definition</u>: the account of how the word is currently used in the language.

10. <u>Definition by genus and species</u>: definition by giving a class to which the denoted objects belong and additionally stating what other properties are shared by this subclass.

11. <u>Definition by limiting conditions</u>: definition by listing the situations or conditions that must be fulfilled in order for the term to be used properly.

Summary

We can clarify meaning by defining the terms or concepts mentioned. This may be done in a number of ways. Pointing to the type of objects is ostensive definition. Naming the objects included in the class is denotative definition. Words with no extension (the class is empty or the word does not refer to objects) must be defined by means of analytical or connotative definition. In general, the methods of analytical definition--definition by genus and species and definition by limiting conditions--are most helpful in clarifying the informative meaning of terms.

Practice Exercises

I. In a game like "charades" try do "define" each of the following words and phrases by pointing:

1. chair	4. arm	7. idea	10. lie
2. male	5. brown	8. noise	11. smile
3. wall	6. index finger	9. to bring	12. happiness

II. Have someone try to guess what word you are "defining" by denoting three or four examples of each of the following words and phrases:

1.	poet	5.	U.S.-made automobile	9.	chair
2.	male human	6.	dictator	10.	idea
3.	actor	7.	sister		
4.	movie actor	8.	arm		

III. Define each of the following words and phrases by genus and species:

1.	chair	5.	noise	9.	automobile
2.	poet	6.	wall	10.	college
3.	actor	7.	brown	11.	university
4.	sister	8.	index finger		

Definitions for Special Purposes

Section Objectives

1. Learn to recognize three types of definitions that are used in special and restricted situations where much precision is required.

Key Term Review

1. <u>Precising definitions</u>: definitions for use in special and restricted situations. The three primary kinds are technical, operational, and stipulative definitions.

2. <u>Technical definition</u>: precising definition that imposes quite precise boundaries on a concept that is often used in a less precise way in ordinary circumstances.

3. <u>Operational definition</u>: a definition in which the meaning of a word is explained by stating a set of techniques or operations for determining how the word is to be applied.

4. <u>Stipulative definition</u>: a definition that is the result of a person of group making and announcing a decision to use a word in a certain way.

Summary

Precising definitions of various sorts are often used, as their name implies, to make a concept as precise as possible. Organizations, disciplines, the law, and science all frequently need precise definitions.

Practice Exercises

Suppose that you are chairman of the Definitions Committee for the Good Logic and Good Times club on your campus. Write a proposed list of technical definitions for each of the following words and phrases:

1. club member　　　　　　　　　3. upperclassman

2. member in good standing　　　4. qualified presidential candidate

Persuasive and Revelatory Definitions

Section Objective

1. Learn two additional ways in which terms or concepts are approached.

Key Term Review

1. Persuasive definition: "definition" or discussion of a concept or term from a particular point of view with the intent of convincing others that that point of view is correct.

2. Revelatory definition: "definition" or discussion of a concept or term that reveals or makes vivid some overlooked but important aspect of the concept.

Summary

Persuasive definitions and revelatory definitions are generally techniques used to influence or change the listener's or reader's attitude or point of view about some subject.

Practice Exercises

Try to write persuasive definitions from a particular point of view for each of the following:

1. Republican　　　　　　　5. divorced woman

2. Liberal　　　　　　　　　6. Dean's List student

3. lobbyist　　　　　　　　　7. student on football scholarship

4. divorced man

PART TWO: DEDUCTIVE REASONING

CHAPTER 5
CATEGORICAL STATEMENTS

OVERVIEW

Some arguments are composed entirely of statements that are about the relationship between classes or sets of objects. In the next chapter, two methods of evaluating such arguments, known as categorical syllogisms, will be explained. The ability to deal with such arguments depends in some measure on a thorough understanding of the categorical statements themselves. This chapter will give you this understanding.

SECTION REVIEWS

5-1

Quantity, Quality, and Categorical Form

Section Objectives

1. Learn the various types of categorical statements and how they are classified.

2. Change nonstandard categorical statements into standard form, retaining as much of the original meaning as possible.

Key Term Review

1. <u>Class</u>: a group, set, or collection of objects that have some characteristic or characteristics in common.

2. <u>Categorical statement</u>: a statement that makes a claim that one class is included (in whole or in part) in or is excluded (in whole or in part) from another class.

3. <u>Subject class</u>: the class that is claimed to be included in or excluded from the other class.

4. <u>Predicate class</u>: the class that the subject class is included in or excluded from.

5. <u>Copula</u>: the verb <u>are</u>, which links the subject and predicate classes in a sentence that makes a categorical statement. In an O statement (see Section 5-1) <u>are not</u> is the copula.

6. <u>Quantifier</u>: the word in the sentence that indicates how many of the subject class are included in or excluded from the predicate class. In the standard categorical form, the quantifier is <u>all</u>, <u>no</u>, or <u>some</u>.

7. <u>Categorical form of a statement</u>: the way the subject and predicate classes are related to each other. There are four types or forms of categorical statements (see Section 5-1).

8. Quantity: the property of a statement that refers to whether all or some of the subject class is involved in the assertion.

9. Universal quantity: the statement makes an assertion about the entire subject class.

10. Particular quantity: the statement makes a claim about some members (at least one) of the subject class.

11. Quality: the property of a statement that refers to whether the subject class is included in or excluded from the predicate class.

12. Affirmative quality: the statement claims the subject class is included, either totally or partially, in the predicate class.

13. Negative quality: the statement claims the subject class is excluded, either totally or partially, from the predicate class.

14. Universal affirmative or A: a statement in which the entire subject class is said to be included in the predicate class, such as "All Danes are redheads."

15. Universal negative or E: a statement in which the entire subject class is said to be excluded from the predicate class, such as "No Danes are redheads."

16. Particular affirmative or I: a statement in which some members of the subject class are said to be included in the predicate class, such as "Some Danes are redheads."

17. Particular negative or O: a statement in which some members of the predicate class are said to be excluded from the predicate class, such as "Some Danes are not redheads."

18. Standard form: a categorical statement expressed by a sentence that begins with all, no, or some; is followed by a description of the subject class; is then followed by the copula are (or are not in an O form); and concludes with a description of the predicate class.

19. Subject term: the word or words that describe the subject class.

20. Predicate term: the word or words that describe the predicate class.

21. Singular statement: a statement whose subject is a single person, thing, place, or time.

Summary

The four standard form categorical statements are:

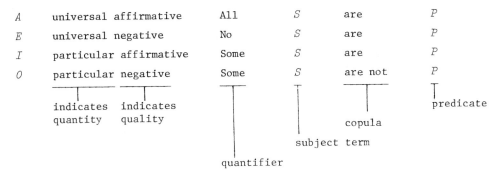

A	universal affirmative	All	S	are	P
E	universal negative	No	S	are	P
I	particular affirmative	Some	S	are	P
O	particular negative	Some	S	are not	P

indicates quantity   indicates quality   quantifier   subject term   copula   predicate

To translate a nonstandard sentence into the standard categorical form, it might be best first to decide what the subject class is and then to ask yourself whether the assertion involves the entire class. You will then know whether the statement is universal or particular. Then decide whether the subject is claimed to be included in the predicate. If it is, you can use an affirmative proposition. If not, use a negative. At this point you will know which of the four standard forms you will be using.

Suppose the sentence "Most Freshmen aren't diligent" must be dealt with. Since part of the class of Freshmen are being excluded from those who are diligent, it should be appropriate to use an O form: "Some S are not P." Keep in mind that, for purposes of logic, some means at least one and that it does not rule out the possibility that the entire subject class may be included in the predicate class.

All that remains is to be sure that the S and P are replaced by class descriptions. For the statement to be in standard form, the subject and the predicate must each be able to stand also as a description of a group or class. The predicate, for example, must not be an adjective or adjectival phrase with some part of the description "understood." Our translation must not be "Some Freshmen are not diligent enough." Instead, it must be "Some Freshmen are not diligent students."

Singular statements must be rewritten so that the subject term describes a class of which the singular item is the only member. The simplest system for doing this is to use a strong notion of identity such that nothing is identical to a thing except that thing itself. Thus, "Socrates is mortal" can be rendered as "All persons identical to Socrates are mortal beings." "Today is Sunday" becomes "All days identical to today are Sundays."

Practice Exercises

Change each of the following statements into a categorical proposition in standard form that is as close in meaning to the original as possible. Underline the subject and predicate terms. Circle the quantifier and the copula.

1. Cats are mammals.

2. Bats are not birds.

3. A few students make all A's.

4. Dogs bark.

5. Most dogs bark.

6. Guppies are ferocious.

7. Every person who passed studied.

8. A few students study too much.

9. Some flutes are not made of wood.

Venn Diagrams and the Distribution of Terms

Section Objective

Learn to diagram each of four types of categorical propositions or statements.

Key Term Review

1. Venn diagram technique: a procedure for representing a categorical statement by means of a certain type of diagram.
2. Universe of discourse: everything that can be named or described.
3. Distributed term: a term in a categorical statement is distributed if the statement in which it appears makes a reference to the entire class that that term represents.

Summary

The subject terms of A and E statements are distributed because the entire subject is being claimed to be either included in or excluded from the predicate. The predicate terms of E and O statements are distributed because the subject is being excluded from the predicate and the relevant members of the subject class are said to be excluded from the entire predicate class.

In other words, the subject terms of universal statements and the predicate terms of negative statements are distributed.

Form	Subject term	Predicate term
A	Distributed	Undistributed
E	Distributed	Distributed
I	Undistributed	Undistributed
O	Undistributed	Distributed

Following a system developed by the English logician John Venn (1834-1923), we can draw a picture or diagram of each type of categorical proposition. Certain conventions are introduced. Bounded spaces or areas will be assumed to contain designated entities if an asterisk (*) is placed within the space.

If this circle is labeled "cows," this diagram shows or says, "Cows exist" or There are cows," or "There exists at least one cow."

If a space is shaded, there are no members of that group.

Unicorns

This indicates that "There are no unicorns" or "Unicorns don't exist." An area with no markings says nothing. Whether a class contains some members (at least one) or does not contain members is left as an open question.

Categorical propositions involve either an inclusive or an exclusive relationship between two classes. Therefore a diagram of a single categorical proposition will be done using two circles. Venn diagrams are always drawn using the same overlapping skeleton:

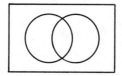

If we overlap two circles labeled S and P we delineate a number of specific spaces or areas.

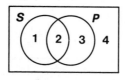

Area 1 is the area in S but not in P.
Area 2 is in both S and P.
Area 3 is in P but not in S.
Area 4 is in neither S nor P.

What does the following diagram say? Take a minute and decide.

Spaniards

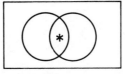

Painters

It says there is at least one entity that is both a Spaniard and a painter. It represents the *I* (particular affirmative) proposition "Some Spaniards are painters."

We have just seen a diagram for "Some Spaniards are painters." How would you represent "Some painters are Spaniards?" Of course the same picture will do. The orientation of the circles does not matter.

Do these diagrams all assert the same thing? Yes, they do. What does the following picture or diagram say?

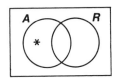

The * indicates that there is something in *A* that is not in *R*, or "Some *A* are not *R*." Or maybe "Some apples are not red objects." Hence this diagram is one that represents an *O* (particular negative) proposition.

1. What does this diagram indicate?

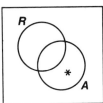

It means "Some *A* are not *R*."

2. What does this diagram say?

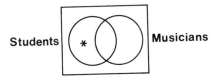

It indicates "Some students are not musicians."

66

3. What does this diagram mean?

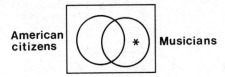

It means "Some musicians are not American citizens."

4. Draw a diagram to indicate "Some disenchanted voters are not persons who are registered to vote in the next election."

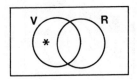

Notice that, for an *O* proposition, a section of the diagram contains an asterisk (*). That section is always this shape:

The section with the x is always part of the circle that represents the subject class of the proposition. Thus, for an *O* proposition, that term will be the one that immediately follows the word <u>some</u>. If you saw the diagram

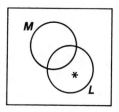

you would know it said "Some *L* are not *M*" because of the * in the *L* portion outside *M*. If you are diagramming an *O* proposition, remember to put the * in the end of the picture that represents the subject class. Thus "Some *V* are not *X*" would look like this:

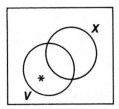

One way to think about an *A* proposition such as "All cats are mammals" is to see that every cat is said to be in (included in) the class of mammals. We label the large circle *M* to represent the set of mammals, and we label the small circle *C* to represent the cats that are included within the group of mammals:

This is not the rear view of a cat!

However, we are required (for reasons that will be clear later) to make a diagram of an *A* proposition via the picture of overlapping circles. So we need to "push" the entire cat circle inside the mammal circle, somewhat like this:

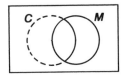

But since we cannot erase the line, we must turn the "cat area" outside "mammals" into a kind of nothingness. We can accomplish this with shading to show that there can be no cats outside the mammal circle.

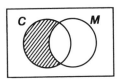

Notice that, for an *A* proposition, a section of the diagram is shaded. That section is always this shape:

The shaded section is always the subject term of the proposition. Thus, for an *A* proposition, it will be immediately after the word <u>all</u>. So if you saw the diagram

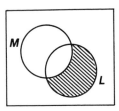

you would know it said "All *L* are *M*" because the *L* portion is shaded. If you are diagramming an *A* proposition, just remember to blacken that portion of the diagram that represents the subject class outside the predicate class. Thus, "All *V* are *X*" would look like this:

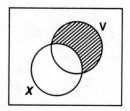

One way to think about an *E* proposition (universal negative) such as "No bats are birds" is to realize that it means the class of bats is totally excluded from, or separated from, the class of birds.

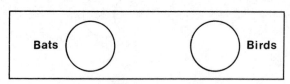

No bats are birds.

To keep two classes apart when using circles that overlap, we can think of the center section as turning to nothingness:

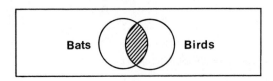

--and the two circles are again separate. In other words, the diagram clearly says or shows that no bats are birds.

Learn the diagram for each of the four types or kinds of propositions.

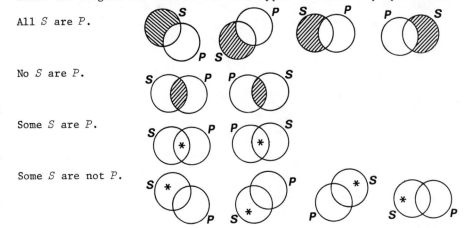

All *S* are *P*.

No *S* are *P*.

Some *S* are *P*.

Some *S* are not *P*.

Practice Exercises

I. Explain what each of the following pictures indicates.

1.

Passenger
pigeons

2.

Loch Ness
monster

3.

Students

4.

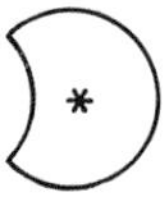

B

5.

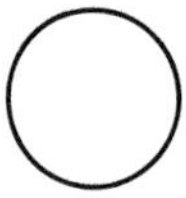

C

6.

D

II. 1. Draw a diagram for "Some chickens are two-legged creatures."

2. Draw a diagram for "Some two-legged creatures are chickens."

3. Draw a diagram to represent "All computers are pieces of electronic equipment."

4. Draw a diagram to represent "All J are K."

5. On these circles, indicate "All orangutans are trumpet players."

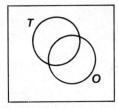

6. What does this diagram represent?

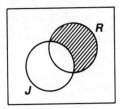

7. What does this diagram indicate?

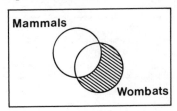

8. Examine the shape of the area that is shaded in the last two diagrams and remember it.

5-3

The Traditional Square of Opposition

Section Objective

Learn the relationships between statements with the same subject and predicate terms but with different categorical forms.

Key Term Review

1. Contradictories: statements that are related such that each always has the opposite truth of the other. *A* and *O* propositions are contradictories, and so are *E* and *I* propositions.

2. Contraries: statements that are related such that they cannot be true, although they could both be false. *A* and *E* statements are contraries.

3. Subcontraries: statements that are related such that they cannot both be false, although they could both be true. *I* and *O* propositions are subcontraries.

4. Subimplication: the process by which the truth of a universal statement

allows inference of the truth of the particular statement with the same quality.

5. <u>Superimplication</u>: the process by which the falsity of a particular proposition allows inference of the falsity of the universal statement with the same quality.

<u>Summary</u>

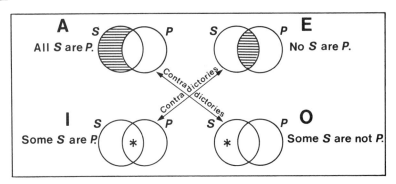

The members of each pair of statements lying diagonally across from each other are contradictories. The *A* and *O* statements contradict each other because the area that is shaded in one has an asterisk in the other. The same is true of the *E* and *I* statements. The area that one says is empty, the other says has at least one member. Hence contradictories must have opposite truth values.

A and *E* statements are contraries. This means that they cannot both be true (assuming that there are some members of the subject class), although they might both be false. They could not both be true because the area that the *E* statement says is empty is the area that would have to contain the *S*s to make the *A* statement true.

I and *O* statements are subcontraries. This means they cannot both be false (as long as there are any *S*s), although clearly they could both be true statements.

The truth of a universal statement (*A* or *E*) allows inference of the particular proposition with the same terms and the same quality. This is the process of subimplication. Of course the falsity of a universal does not allow inference of the falsity of the corresponding particular. However, the falsity of a particular proposition does allow inference of the falsity of the universal with the same terms and the same quality. This is known as superimplication. Of course the truth of the particular does not necessitate the truth of the corresponding universal. The correctness of subimplication and superimplication also requires the assumption that there are members of the subject class.

If we do not postulate that the subject class has members, then the only relationship that would remain is that between contradictories. You are reminded that the diagrams introduced in Section 5-2 are based on the hypothetical viewpoint and hence do not claim membership in any classes when the *A* and *E* statements are involved.

Practice Exercises

Use the square of opposition.

1. If "Some cities are overpopulated places," what is the truth value of:

   a. No cities are overpopulated places. _____

   b. All cities are overpopulated places. _____

   c. Some cities are not overpopulated places. _____

2. If it is false that all dogs that Jeff owns are clean-smelling animals, what is the truth value of:

   a. Some dogs that Jeff owns are not clean-smelling. _____

   b. No dogs that Jeff owns are clean-smelling. _____

   c. Some dogs that Jeff owns are sweet smelling. _____

3. If it is true that no Volvos are cars made in the U.S., what is the truth value of:

   a. Some Volvos are cars made in the U.S. _____

   b. All Volvos are cars made in the U.S. _____

   c. Some Volvos are not cars made in the U.S. _____

5-4

Immediate Inference

Section Objective

1. Learn three types of operations on categorical statements (conversion, obversion, and contraposition and the conditions under which they yield logically equivalent statements.

Key Term Review

1. Logical equivalence: one statement is logically equivalent to another if and only if they necessarily have the same truth value.

2. Immediate inference: an inference from the truth or falsity of a single statement to the truth or falsity of another statement.

3. Conversion: the process of interchanging the subject and predicate terms in a statement.

4. Class complement: the complement of a class is a term referring to all the objects that don't belong to the original class.

5. Obversion: the process of changing the quality of both the statement and the predicate term.

6. <u>Contraposition</u>: the process of replacing a statement's subject term with the complement of the predicate and replacing the predicate term with the complement of the subject.

<u>Summary: Conversion</u>

To convert, do nothing except make the subject and predicate change places. Any proposition can be converted, but the original proposition and its converse are equivalent only when you are working with E propositions and with I propositions.

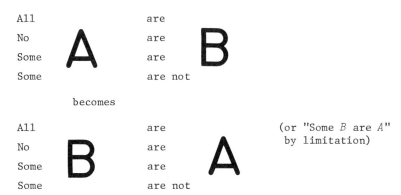

All	are	
No	are	
Some	are	
Some	are not	

becomes

All	are	(or "Some B are A"
No	are	by limitation)
Some	are	
Some	are not	

"All elementary students are persons that are not concerned with foreign policy" becomes "All persons that are not concerned with foreign policy are elementary students."

"No bats are mammals" becomes "No mammals are bats."

"Some citizens are not senators" becomes "Some senators are not citizens."

It might be noted that, even though only conversions of E and I statements yield equivalent statements, traditionally conversion "by limitation" was an allowed procedure for A statements. This meant to reduce the converse from universal to particular. Hence, "All cats are mammals" becomes "Some mammals are cats." If we assume the existential viewpoint (classes have members) and if the original statement is true, then its converse by limitation is true. That is the <u>only</u> valid inference that can be made using coversion by limitation.

<u>Summary: Obversion</u>

To obvert requires two steps because the form of the proposition changes <u>and</u> the predicate changes. Any proposition can be obverted, and the result will always be a pair of equivalent statements.

1. Change in form:

An A proposition always becomes an E proposition, and an E proposition always becomes an A proposition.

An I proposition always becomes an O proposition, and an O proposition always becomes an I proposition.

2. Change in predicate: The predicate is always replaced by its complements. For example,

"Smokers" replaced by "nonsmokers"

"A" replaced by "non-A"

"non-A" replaced by "non-non-A" or "A"

"things that are square" replaced by "things that are not square"

"objects of value" replaced by "valueless objects"

Consider the E proposition   "No bats are birds."

  Step 1: becomes A All _____ are _____.

  Step 2: predicate
         changes   All bats are non-birds.

Consider the I proposition   "Some students are smokers."

  Step 1: becomes O Some _____ are not _____.

  Step 2: predicate
         changes   Some students are not nonsmokers.

Summary: Contraposition

First determine the complement of the subject and that complement of the predicate; then have these complements change places. (This could also be done by taking a proposition and obverting, taking that and converting, and taking that and obverting again.)

Any proposition can be contraposed, but only when working with A propositions or O propositions will you have equivalent pairs.

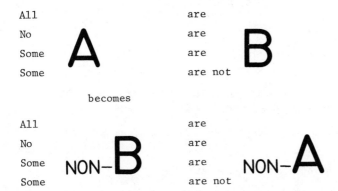

All		are	
No	**A**	are	**B**
Some		are	
Some		are not	

becomes

All		are	
No	**NON-B**	are	**NON-A**
Some		are	
Some		are not	

"Some students are nonsmokers" becomes "Some smokers are nonstudents."

"All cats are mammals" becomes "All non-mammals are non-cats."

Traditionally, contraposition by limitation of the E statement was allowed. This meant to reduce the "true" contrapositive from universal to particular. But, as with conversion by limitation, the only inference that could be made is that, if the original E statement is true (and if we assume the existential viewpoint), its contrapositive by limitation is true.

I. In column 2, state the obverse of each item. Then, in column 3, give
    the obverse of each item in column 2.

Column 1	Column 2	Column 3
1. All A are B.	1.	1.
2. No C are D.	2.	2.
3. Some E are F.	3.	3.
4. Some G are not H.	4.	4.
5. All non-I are J.	5.	5.
6. No non-K are L.	6.	6.
7. Some non-M are N.	7.	7.
8. Some non-O are P.	8.	8.
9. All Q are non-R.	9.	9.
10. No S are non-T.	10.	10.
11. Some V are non-T.	11.	11.
12. Some W are non-X.	12.	12.
13. All non-Y are non-Z.	13.	13.
14. No non-A are non-B.	14.	14.
15. Some non-C are non-D.	15.	15.
16. Some non-E are non-F.	16.	16.

II. Convert each of the following and indicate whether the members of the
     pair are equivalent. (Do not convert by limitation.)

1. No house plants are objects usable for building materials.

2. All healthy persons are non-smokers.

3. Some students are non-smokers.

4. Some machines are mechanisms designed for washing machines.

5. Some non-*A* are *B*.

6. No *C* are non-*D*.

7. All non-*E* are non-*F*.

8. Some *G* are not non-*H*.

III. State the contrapositive of each of the following and indicate whether the members of the pair of propositions are equivalent. (Do not contrapose by limitation.)

1. All healthy persons are non-smokers.

2. Some students are not smokers.

3. Some *M* are non-*O*.

4. Some *A* are *B*.

5. No cowboys are persons who spend their lives indoors.

6. Some basketball players are persons over seven feet tall.

7. Some contrapositions are extremely difficult problems.

5-5

Practical Applications

Section Objective

1. Translate a wide variety of categorical assertions into categorical statements of standard form.

Key Term Review

Exclusive statements: statements that involve none, but, none except, only, or alone, such as "None but citizens may vote.

Summary

Statements in the form "Not all *S* are *P*" and "All *S* are not *P*" are sometimes troublesome. They are negative but the quantity of the statement is unclear.

Unless you have knowledge of context that would allow a different translation, they should be thought of as particular. In other words, they should
usually be translated as O propositions. Another way to think of them is
that they look like A statements with an additional <u>not</u> in them. They can
then be thought of as contradicting the A statement, and the contradictory
of an A is an O statement. Hence, "All TV shows are not second-rate productions" means "Some TV shows are not second-rate productions." Similarly,
"All that glitters is not gold" means "Some things that glitter are not
gold."

Whereas "A few S are P" means "Some S are P," "Few S are P" means to assert
that most S are not P. "Few S are P" should be translated as "Some S are
not P" (Its complete meaning can best be rendered by using both an I statement and an O statement.)

A large number of unlikely candidates for translation can be translated
rather easily if we note that they are about times, or places, or cases
(and so forth) and then use the appropriate word (times, places, cases) in
formulating both the subject and predicate terms. So "Where there's a will,
there's a way" can become "All places/cases/times there is a will are
places/cases/times there is a way." "It's always messy after rock concerts"
becomes "All times after rock concerts are times there is a mess."

Exclusive statements are most often mistranslated by replacing the <u>only</u>,
<u>none but</u>, or <u>none except</u> with the word <u>all</u> and leaving everything else
alone. However, "Only elephants have trunks" does not assert that all elephants have them (even though that may be true), but it asserts that any
animal with a trunk is an elephant: "All creatures with trunks are elephants." "None but citizens may vote" means "All persons who can vote are
citizens." Note that the order of the classes changes when we make these
translations.

<u>Practice Exercises</u>

Translate each of the following into a standard-form categorical <u>statement</u>
that is as close as possible in meaning to the original.

1. Only citizens can vote.

2. None can vote but citizens.

3. Only good players are inducted into the Hall of Fame.

4. Reagan is President.

5. This assignment is not easy.

6. This assignment is important.

78

7. All's well that ends well.

8. Bats are not birds.

9. All that glitters is not gold.

10. He who doesn't study, fails.

11. Some are hungry.

12. Some dogs bark all night.

13. Most cats are friendly.

14. Bats are mammals.

15. Socrates is mortal.

16. Only brave persons are war heroes.

17. He who lives by the sword shall perish by the sword.

18. Most students are able to understand this material.

19. Today is not Sunday.

20. Good furniture isn't cheap.

21. The basement is damp.

22. John is pusillanimous.

23. It's raining.

24. There is a lot trash here.

25. Never does Betty study before an exam.

26. One will make higher grades if one studies.

27. This plant is not rare.

28. All marriages do not end in divorce.

29. Only a fool would engage in that activity.

30. No friend is better than a dishonest friend.

31. He who sows injustice will reap calamity.

CHAPTER 6

CATEGORICAL SYLLOGISMS

OVERVIEW

Many deductive arguments can be analyzed as categorical syllogisms. Once these categorical syllogisms are written in standard form, the Venn diagramming technique introduced in Chapter 5 can be used to develop a complete method for checking them for validity. In addition, a second method of checking validity is introduced.

SECTION REVIEWS

Section Objectives

1. Learn to put a categorical syllogism into standard form.

2. Learn to recognize the mood and figure of categorical syllogisms--that is, their structure or form.

Key Term Review

1. Categorical syllogism: a deductive argument comprised of three categorical statements and containing exactly three terms, each of which appears in two statements.

2. Major term: the predicate term of the conclusion of a categorical syllogism.

3. Major premise: the premise of a categorical syllogism in which the major term appears.

4. Minor term: the subject term of the conclusion of a categorical syllogism.

5. Minor premise: the premise of a categorical syllogism in which the minor term appears.

6. Middle term: the term in a categorical syllogism that appears in both premises (and not in the conclusion).

7. Standard-form categorical syllogism: a categorical syllogism that has all of its statements in standard form and has the major premise stated first, the minor premise second, and the conclusion last.

8. Mood: the listing of the forms of the statements in a categorical syllogism (using the A, E, I, or O designation) in the standard order.

9. Figure: the arrangement of all the terms within a categorical syllogism.

10. Mood and figure: together, mood and figure constitute a complete description of the structure of a categorical syllogism.

Summary

Evaluation of a categorical syllogism is facilitated by turning it into a standard-form categorical syllogism. This involves being sure each statement is itself a standard-form categorical statement and placing each statement in the argument in a certain order. The predicate term of the conclusion is the major term, and the premise with that same term in it is the major premise. It is stated first. The subject of the conclusion is the minor term, and the premise with that same term in it is the minor premise. It is stated second. The conclusion, of course, is last. Listing these statements by their form (using A, E, I, and O) constitutes the mood of a syllogism. The mood of the following standard form argument is EIE:

No students are lazy persons.
Some bankers are lazy persons.
_____

No bankers are students.

A complete knowledge of the structure of a syllogism requires that, in addition to mood, we also take into account the arrangement of terms in the argument. The following four arguments are all AAA, but each has a different arrangement of terms. In fact, only the first of these is valid.

All M are P.	All P are M.	All M are P.	All P are M.
All S are M.	All S are M.	All M are S.	All M are S.
All S are P.	All S are P.	All S are P.	All S are P.

These four arrangements illustrate the four figures:

-- M -- P	-- P -- M	-- M -- P	-- P -- M
-- S -- M	-- S -- M	-- M -- S	-- M -- S
-- S -- P	-- S -- P	-- S -- P	-- S -- P

At first glance it appears that it would be hard to remember all four of these, but if you concentrate just on the middle term (the Ms), you can figure everything else out from that:

M --	-- M	M --	-- M
-- M	-- M	M --	M --
-- --	-- --	-- --	-- --

Because the predicate of the conclusion (P) must appear in the first premise, it is easy to put it in the remaining place. The subject of the conclusion (S) goes in the second premise.

There are four different figures and each statement may be one of four possibilities (A, E, I, or O), so there are a total of 256 different structures possible (4 x 4 x 4 x 4 = 256).

Practice Exercises

I. State the mood and figure of each of the following syllogisms:

_____ 1. No M are P.
Some S are M.
Some S are not P.

_____ 2. All M are P.
All S are M.
All S are P.

_____ 3. All M are P.
All M are S.
All S are P.

_____ 4. Some P are M.
All S are M.
Some S are P.

_____ 5. No G are A.
All A are M.
Some M are not G.

_____ 6. All C are P.
Some M are not P.
Some M are not C.

_____ 7. All R are F.
Some R are I.
Some I are F.

_____ 8. No T are H.
Some C are not T.
Some C are not H.

_____ 9. Some S are not D.
All S are R.
Some R are not D.

_____ 10. All L are T.
No W are L.
No W are T.

_____ 11. All T are B.
Some R are B.
Some R are T.

_____ 12. Some D are S.
Some C are not S.
Some C are not D.

II. State whether each of the following is syllogisms in standard form (SF) or not (NSF).

_____ 1. All S are M.
No M are non-P.
Some D are not R.

_____ 2. All S are R.
Some S are not D.
Some D are not R.

_____ 3. All A are C.
All C are B.
All A are B.

_____ 4. All wombats are marsupials.
Every marsupial is a mammal.
All wombats are mammals.

_____ 5. No students are lazy.
Some bankers are lazy.
No bankers are students.

III. Put each of the following syllogisms into standard form and give its mood and figure.

1. Some A are F, so some I are F, since all A are I.

2. Some B are N; hence, since all S are N, some S are B.

3. Some *C* are not *O*, for some *C* are not *P*, and some *P* are not *O*.

4. Some *M* are not *P*, but all *C* are *P*, which entails some *M* being not *C*.

5. Some winners are not young, because some zealots are not young, and all zealots are winners.

IV. Construct a syllogism for each of the following moods and figures. You may leave the terms as *S*, *P*, and *M* if you wish.

1. *AAA*-1   2. *AAA*-4

3. *EIO*-2   4. *EAO*-3

5. *IAO*-4

The Venn-Diagram Test for Validity

Section Objective

1. Learn to test a categorical syllogism for validity or invalidity by means of a Venn diagram that represents the entire argument.

Summary

Here's an argument: No *P* are *M*.
                    Some *M* are *S*.
                    Some *S* are not *P*.

Although each assertion requires two circles to diagram, there are only three __different__ terms in the entire argument. Therefore, we can deal with the whole argument by starting with this:

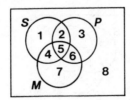

Area 1 represents possible Ss that are known not to be members of P or M. Areas 3 and 7 also indicate locations that are in only one class and are known not to be in the other two classes.

Area 2 can be seen to be a part of both S and P and not a part of M. Likewise, areas 4 and 6 are within two circles and definitely outside the remaining circle.

Area 5 is within all three circles.

Area 8 is outside all three circles.

Think about what it means for an argument to be valid. It means simply that the conclusion follows necessarily from the premises. With that in mind, we should find it easy to understand the Venn-diagram procedure for checking to see whether a syllogism is valid.

Our procedure will be to place a representation of both premises on the three-circle skeleton. We never place or draw anything else on that diagram. When that is properly done, we will have an accurate picture of the premises of the argument. We can then look at that diagram and ask ourselves whether the conclusion follows necessarily from those premises. If we know that it does, we will know that the argument is valid. If is does not follow necessarily, it is invalid.

Let us begin to learn to draw the premises of an argument on a three-circle diagram.

If we are confronted by an argument such as

No P are M.
Some M are S.
Some S are not P.

and by circles such as

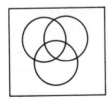

the first question that arises is "Which circle represents what?" Let's stipulate how to label circles. The upper circles are to represent the conclusion. The term on the left of the conclusion (the subject or minor term) will be represented by the upper left circle. The term on the right of the conclusion (the major or predicate term) will be represented by the upper right circle. The middle term will be represented by the lower middle circle. Hence, the circles we are considering would be labeled this way:

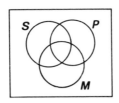

Now let's learn to place each type of statement on the three-circle skeleton.
Let us consider "No S are M." An E proposition always shades the "football"-
shaped area where the two circles that represent the terms in the proposition overlap.

Suppose the skeleton is labeled as follows:

Because the S and M circles are lopsided like this

it is clear that exactly the same area is shaded on a three-circle diagram.

Now consider "No M are P."

To diagram with three circles, either first draw (for yourself) a two-circle
diagram with the circles in the same orientation as in the three-circle diagram, or you can draw this in your mind (if you <u>can</u> draw this in your mind).

The same sorts of considerations apply when dealing with an *A* proposition.
Take "All *S* are *M*."

And take "All *M* are *P*."

Notice the shape of the shaded area. Exactly the same shape is shaded in both the two-circle diagram and the three-circle diagram. Remember that the circle for the subject term (minus the football section it shares with the predicate) is shaded.

Practice Exercises A

Do the following exercises before reading the rest of this section.

I. Label the circles for each of the following arguments.

1. All galloonists are opportunists.
    Some bassoonists are galloonists.
    Therefore, some bassoonists are
        opportunists.

2. No *Y* are *B*.
    Some *X* are not *B*.
    Some *X* are not *Y*.

3. No food products whose nutritional value
        is worth the cost are junk foods.
    No marshmallows are food products whose
        nutritional value is worth the cost.
    All marshmallows are junk foods.

II. Follow the instructions for each of the following items.

1. What two propositions are represented by this diagram?

2. What two propositions are represented by this diagram?

3. Diagram "No W are E."

4. Diagram "No E are T."

5. Draw a diagram for "All F are A."

6. Draw a diagram for "All Y are Z."

7. Diagram "All L are S."

8. Indicate "All wombats are mammals."

9. Diagram "All G are F."

III. What propositions are represented by the following diagrams?

1.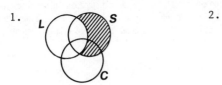

2.

3.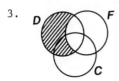

4.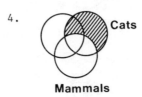

Summary

Different considerations apply to diagramming I and O propositions. Consider "Some S are M."

The entity or entities represented by the asterisk (*) are inside the SM "football," but we don't know exactly where in there they are. Nor are we told anything about their relationship to any other class. Why are these two diagrams <u>wrong</u> ways of saying "Some S are M"?

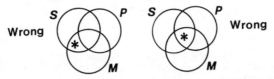

The one on the left is wrong because the * is located outside the P circle. Therefore, what is indicated is "Some S are M and they are not P." The diagram on the right is wrong because it indicates "Some S are M and also P." Since the proposition we are trying to diagram ("Some S are M") says nothing about P, we must be careful to say nothing about P.

We need a new convention for this situation. We need a way to indicate our lack of knowledge about circle P. Here is how we do it:

Note that this explanation of diagramming uses an * on the border of a circle
rather than a bar in the relevant section. This says that there are some
entities but we do not know whether they are members of class P. They are
on the fence, indeterminate. Let's think again about diagramming "Some S
are M."

From our knowledge of two-circle diagrams, we know that the * must be inside
the SM "football."

But in the three-circle diagram the P boundary runs through the "football."
So the * goes on the P boundary where it is inside the SM football.

Note that the * is (and always must be) inside (completely inside) the
appropriate football for any I proposition. Examine the following diagram
for "Some M are P."

Considerations involved in working with O propositions are similar to those
involved in working with I propositions. Consider "Some W are not Y." The
following is tempting but wrong. Why?

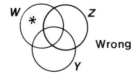

It is wrong because it makes a statement about Z (the * is not in Z) that
we are not allowed to make because we know nothing about Z. Examine the
correct diagram.

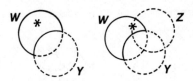

The * goes in the W end of the two-circle diagram. It must remain there on the three-circle diagram, but because the Z boundary runs through the area, it must go on that line. Examine the following diagram for "Some C are not R."

There is only one other thing. Consider the premises in this argument.

> Some R are F.
> All R are I.
> Some I are F.

This diagram would be inadequate:

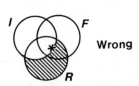

Concentrate on the RF "football":

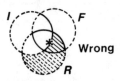

The * was placed in the center of it (on the I line) to indicate that its exact location (with respect to I) was unknown. But now the universal premise has indicated (with shading) that part of the RF football is empty. Taking the two premises together, we would know where the * belongs. Because the area outside I is empty, the * would necessarily be inside I. Our diagram must clearly indicate this, so it must be drawn as follows:

Never put (or leave) an * halfway in a shaded area. Let it fall off the fence into the area that is unshaded.

Consider this argument:

> All C are P.
> Some N are not P.
> Some N are not C.

The *O* proposition would normally be diagrammed in this fashion:

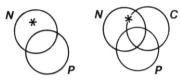

But the universal premise tells us that part of the section in question is empty.

Again, the * moves off the fence and the completed diagram appears this way:

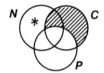

Examine another:

No *O* are *G*.
Some *G* are *J*.
———————
Some *J* are not *O*.

Practice Exercises B

Do the following exercises before reading the rest of this section.

I. Which of the following diagrams are correct for "Some *B* are *C*"? Circle the number of those that are correct.

1.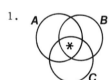

2.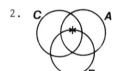

3.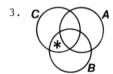

4.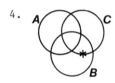

5.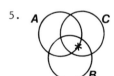

6.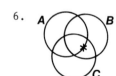

7.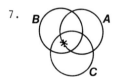

92

II. Diagram "Some X are Y" on the following skeletons.

1.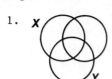

2.

3.

III. Which of the following diagrams are correct for "Some J are not K"? Circle the number of those that are correct.

1.

2.

3.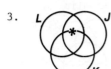

4.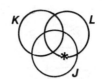

5.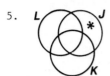

6.

7.

8.

IV. Diagram "Some bats are not wooden objects" on the following skeletons.

1.

2.

3.

Summary (continued)

An argument is valid is the conclusion follows necessarily from the premises. We can therefore put the premises (only) on a diagram and then look at it to see whether the conclusion would have to be the case. Consider:

```
No M are P.
All S are M.
No S are P.
```

Now, DON'T EVER put the conclusion on the diagram. Just look at it to see whether what the conclusion says is illustrated in the diagram. The conclusion "No S are P" asserts that the SP "football" is empty:

The SP area is the only area we now care about. Because that area is shaded on the three-circle picture, the argument is valid. Notice how the two premises work together.

Diagram these two arguments and decide whether they are valid.

```
All R are S.          No D are F.
All T are R.          No E are F.
All T are S.          No D are E.
```

1.  ```
    All R are S.
    All T are R.
    All T are S.
    ```

2.  ```
    No D are F.
    No E are F.
    No D are E.
    ```

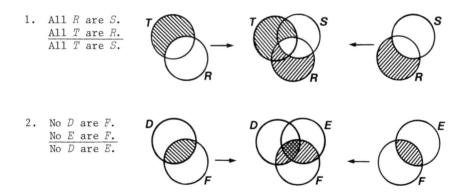

If your diagrams do not look correct, notice that exactly the same area is shaded on two-circle diagrams as on the three-circle diagrams.

Note that the conclusion of syllogism 1 states "All T are S":

Because the area shaded on this two-circle diagram is also shaded on the three-circle diagram, it is valid.

The conclusion of syllogism 2 states: "No D are E":

Not all of this shaded area is shaded on the three-circle diagram, so it is invalid.

A conclusion that is universal (A or E) will not follow necessarily unless it is seen that the entire area in question is shaded. However, a particular conclusion (I or O) requires only an asterisk (*) somewhere in the area in question. Diagram this:

All B are C.
Some A are C.
Some A are B.

The conclusion says the AB "football" has at least one member.

If you did the diagram correctly, it looks like this:

Concentrating on the AB "football," we see that the * is not completely in the "football," so the argument is invalid.

Examine the following invalid argument carefully.

Some M are not O.
All O are L.
Some L are M.

The two invalid arguments that we have just seen had I conclusions. If the circles have been labeled according to our labeling convention, the conclusion will be represented by the top two circles. For the argument to be valid, the * would have to be completely inside the top "football" section. The two invalid arguments first seen had the * on the perimeter of the "football," which means we do not know for sure whether there are members inside the area.

If the conclusion of an argument is an O proposition (and the circles are labeled correctly), the claim is that this section

has members. Again, for the argument to be valid, the * could not be on the perimeter of this section but must be inside it.

Let us examine two more invalid arguments.

Some L are not K.
Some J are L.
Some J are not K.

Some O are P.
Some M are not P.
Some M are not O.

If you label the diagrams properly, it will be easy to check for validity. The conclusion will be an A, an E, an I, or an O assertion.

If the conclusion is an A proposition, you need only check to see whether there is shading like this:

which corresponds to

If sections 1 and 4 are shaded, the argument is valid regardless of what else may or may not be on the diagram.

VALID   INVALID   INVALID

96

If the conclusion is an *E* proposition (and you labeled properly), the conclusion asserts this:

So the area to check is made up of sections 2 and 5.

Premise   VALID
Premise
No *S* are *P*.

                   INVALID

                   INVALID

If the conclusion is an *I* assertion, it asserts this:

The area to check is made up of sections 2 and 5.

If there is an * anywhere in those sections, as long as it is entirely inside, the argument is valid.

Premise   VALID
Premise
Some *S* are *P*.

97

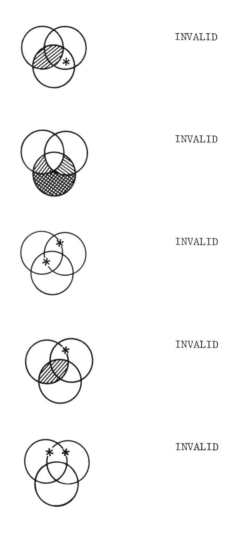

INVALID

INVALID

INVALID

INVALID

INVALID

If the conclusion is an _O_ statement, the area to check is the combination of 1 and 4.

If there is an * anywhere in those sections, as long as it is entirely inside, the argument is valid.

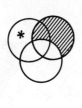

Premise	VALID
Premise	
Some *S* are not *P*.	

VALID

INVALID

INVALID

INVALID

Practice Exercises C

I. Assume each of the following is a correct diagram of the premises of an argument. Examine each diagram to determine whether the indicated conclusion follows necessarily. State whether it is valid or invalid.

1.

Some *S* are not *P*.

2.

No *S* are *P*.

3.

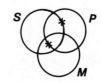

Some *S* are *P*.

4.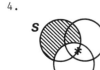

All *S* are *P*.

5.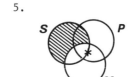

Some *S* are not *P*.

6.

All *S* are *P*.

7.

No *S* are *P*.

8.

Some *S* are *P*.

9.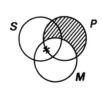

Some *S* are not *P*.

10.

All *S* are *P*.

11.

Some *S* are not *P*.

12.

Some *S* are *P*.

II. Diagram the following arguments and state whether they are valid or not.

1. Some *A* are not *B*.
   All *A* are *C*.
   No *C* are *B*.

2. Some *M* are not *S*.
   Some *C* are *M*.
   Some *C* are not *S*.

3. All *F* are *G*.
   All *H* are *F*.
   All *H* are *G*.

4. No *C* are *B*.
   All *A* are *B*.
   No *A* are *C*.

5. Some P are not G.
   No I are G.
   _____
   Some P are I.

6. Some I are not H.
   No I are G.
   _____
   Some G are not H.

7. Some R are F.
   All R are I.
   _____
   Some I are F.

8. All C are P.
   Some N are not C.
   _____
   Some N are not P.

9. No O are G.
   Some G are J.
   _____
   Some J are not O.

10. Some F are not E.
    Some D are F.
    _____
    Some D are not E.

11. Some C are not B.
    All C are A.
    _____
    Some A are not B.

12. All L are K.
    All J are L.
    _____
    All J are K.

13. Some Y are Z.
    No Z are W.
    _____
    Some W are Y.

14. All *N* are *O*.
    No *O* are *M*.
    No *M* are *N*.

15. Some *R* are not *Q*.
    Some *R* are not *P*.
    Some *P* are not *Q*.

16. No *U* are *T*.
    Some *U* are *S*.
    Some *S* are not *T*.

17. All communists are believers in socialized medicine.
    All persons identical to Professor Jones are believers in social-
    ized medicine.
    Therefore, all persons identical to Professor Jones are communists.

18. All creatures with eight legs are creatures that can fly.
    All cats are creatures with eight legs.
    All cats are creatures that can fly.

19. All artists are human beings.
    Some artists are compassionate beings.
    All compassionate beings are human beings.

20. All *V* are *X*.
    All *W* are *X*.
    All *V* are *W*.

21. Some *B* are not *C*.
    Some *C* are *A*.
    Some *A* are *B*.

Rules of the Syllogism

Section Objective

1. Learn a second method of proof of validity or invalidity of categorical
   syllogisms that involves conformity to a set of rules.

1. **Fallacy of undistributed middle**: an invalid syllogism that breaks the first rule listed below.

2. **Fallacy of illicit distribution**: an invalid syllogism that breaks the second rule listed below.

3. **Fallacy of faulty exclusion**: an invalid syllogism that breaks the third rule listed below.

4. **Fallacy of unwarranted existential assertion**: an invalid syllogism that breaks the fourth rule listed below.

Summary

A second method of checking for validity of a categorical syllogism involves a system of rules. A valid syllogism conforms to all the rules, whereas an invalid syllogism violates one or more of them.

A short set of rules, at least one of which is violated by every invalid syllogism, is as follows:

1. The middle term must be distributed at least once.
2. Every term that happens to be distributed in the conclusion must be distributed in the premise in which it occurs.
3. There must either be no negative statements or exactly two, one of which must be the conclusion.
4. (From the hypothetical viewpoint) If both premises are universal, the conclusion must be universal also.

To apply these rules you may need to refresh your memory about the following items.

1. **Negative statement**: E or O form.
2. **Universal statement**: A or E form.
3. **Distributed terms**: subject term of universal statements (A and E) and predicate term of negative statements (E and O).

Practice Exercises

I. Which rule (1 or 2) is broken in each of the following syllogisms?

    1. All T are B.   2. Some Z are not V.
       Some R are B.   All Z are R.
       Some R are T.   No R are V.

    3. All P are O.   4. Some D are not P.
       All O are M.   Some C are D.
       All M are P.   Some C are not P.

II. Which rule is broken in each of the following syllogisms?

    1. No T are I.   2. Some A are not P.
       Some C are not I.   All W are P.
       Some C are not T.   All W are A.

_____ 3. Some E are not D.
Some D are not B.
Some B are E.

III. Which rules are broken in each of the following syllogisms?

_____ 1. Some D are P.
Some C are not D.
Some C are not P.

_____ 2. Some F are not R.
All C are R.
All C are F.

_____ 3. All E are N.
All I are N.
All I are E.

_____ 4. All S are R.
Some S are not D.
Some D are not R.

_____ 5. All M are S.
All M are F.
Some F are S.

_____ 6. No W are H.
Some J are not W.
Some J are H.

6-4

Practical Applications

Section Objectives

1. Translate some syllogisms that have more than three terms into equivalent syllogisms with only three terms.

2. Recognize that some arguments that appear to have three terms actually have more.

3. Learn to deal with enthymemes.

4. Learn to deal with sorites.

Key Term Review

1. Fallacy of four terms: the fallacy of using a class description in two different ways within a single argument. Also known as the fallacy of equivocation.

2. Enthymeme: an argument with either a premise or the conclusion not explicitly stated.

3. Sorites: an argument containing more than three statements that can be interpreted as a chain of categorical syllogisms.

Summary

Most syllogisms with more than three terms are invalid. However, some such syllogisms, when the "extra" terms are complements of other terms in the syllogism, are valid.

To check for validity by the four rules or by Venn diagram, we must first translate the argument into an argument with only three terms. The operations of conversion, obversion, and contraposition are useful in this regard. An argument with up to six terms may be translated into a manageable argument so long as the extra terms are complements of other terms in the argument.

If an argument had the six terms A, B, C, non-A, non-B, and non-C, the translated argument could have the terms A, B, and C, but it might also equally well be translated to a syllogism containing, say, B, non-A, and non-C. The most important thing to remember is that each of the propositions in the translation must be equivalent to the proposition in the original. Therefore, conversion should be performed only on E and I statements, and contraposition only on A and O statements. Of course, any proposition may be obverted.

The resulting syllogism can be checked for validity by the five rules or by Venn diagram. If the translated argument is valid, the original argument is also valid; if the translated argument is invalid, the original is also invalid.

Consider the following argument:

    (A)   No M are P.
            <u>Some S are not non-M.</u>
            Some non-P are not non-S.

There is not much that can be done with this argument as it stands. Its mood and figure cannot be given, because mood and figure describe standard-form syllogisms. A six-term syllogism could not be diagrammed on three circles, and the rules also apply only to standard-form syllogisms. So translation is required.

The clearest translation (the easiest to understand) would probably be in terms of S, P, and M. If that is attempted, only the second premise and the conclusion need be changed. In the second premise, the "non-M" is in the predicate; obversion always replaces the predicate of a proposition with its complement; therefore, obversion yields "Some S are M." The conclusion has both non-P and non-S in it; contraposition will replace the non-P with S, and the non-S with P; <u>because this is an O proposition</u>, it is acceptable to contrapose to "Some S are not P." The resulting standard-form argument is:

    (A-1)   No M are P.
              <u>Some S are M.</u>
              Some S are not P.

This is easily proved to be valid.

It would be equally correct to have obverted all three statements to yield:

    (A-2)   All M are non-P.
              <u>Some S are M.</u>
              Some non-P are S.

This is not quite in standard form, but it needs only to have the premises reversed. Again, it is easily proven valid. (Of course, the circles in the Venn diagram would be labeled non-P, S, and M.)

Let's consider another argument:

    (B)   Some M are non-P.
            <u>Some S are not non-M.</u>
            Some non-P are not non-S.

Here there are five terms. One member of the pair M and non-M must be removed. One member of the pair S and non-S must also be eliminated. Because one member of each pair is in a predicate location, the easiest approach would be to obvert those two propositions. Then, if we reverse the order of the premises, we have:

(B-1) Some S are M.
       Some M are non-P.
       Some non-P are S.

This is an equivalent translation of the original and it is invalid, so the original argument is known to be invalid.

It would have been equally acceptable to have done the translation in other ways. Because one member of both pairs of complementary terms is in the second premise, and because it is a proposition that contraposes to an equivalent statement, it would have yielded "Some M are not non-S." And putting the premises in proper order, we obtain:

(B-2) Some M are not non-S.
       Some M are non-P.
       Some non-P are not non-S.

Of course, we know that this is also invalid.

What does argument B look like if it is translated into one with the terms S, P, and M? You might want to try to accomplish this before looking at (B-3) below.

(B-3) Some M are not P.   (by obversion)
       Some S are M.   (by obversion)
       Some S are not P.   (by contraposition)

So far we have not made any use of conversion. But consider the following syllogism:

(C) All Z are Y.
     No non-Z are X.
     All X are Y.

It has four terms, and either Z or non-Z must be eliminated. If either one was in a predicate location, all we would need to do would be to obvert. But because conversion moves the subject into the predicate location, and because the second proposition will convert to an equivalent statement, we can achieve the desired results in two steps:

(C-1) All Z are Y.
       All X are Z.   (by conversion and obversion)
       All X are Y.

When a word or phrase is used equivocally, often a bad argument is disguised as a good one. An argument that has four (or more) terms disguised as three is said to commit the fallacy of equivocation or to be an instance of the fallacy of four terms.

In ordinary discourse, it is very common not to state every part of an argument explicitly. (Enthymemes are arguments with either a premise or conclusion not explicitly stated.) This is because persons share a large body of knowledge and it is unnecessary to state the obvious in an argument. Often the conclusion is unstated because it is the obvious inference from the premises. If someone said, "John won't get into Yale because he cannot score well on entrance exams," it is easy to see what is not stated. It is the premise that persons who don't score well on entrance exams cannot get into Yale. In fairness to the arguer we should realize that he is arguing this way:

No persons who perform poorly on entrance exams are persons who will be admitted to Yale.
All persons identical to John are persons who perform poorly on entrance exams.
No persons identical to John are persons who will be admitted to Yale.

This is a valid argument.

On the other hand, we might want to break the news gently to John, so we let him figure out the unstated conclusion: No one who performs poorly on entrance exams will get into Yale and you always perform poorly on them." This is the same valid argument as above.

If you are unable to question the author of the argument about implicit statements, you must use your best judgment in adding reasonable statements.

Sorites are chains of syllogisms that appear like single arguments with more than two premises. They are enthymematic in nature because intermediate conclusions are missing and must be supplied in order to check the sorites for validity. Of course, each syllogism in the chain of syllogisms must be valid for the sorites to be valid.

Practice Exercises

I. Use obversion to change the following arguments (which have more than three terms) into equivalent standard-form arguments. Check each argument by the four rules.

1. No *F* are *E*.
   Some *F* are not non-*D*.
   Some *D* are not *E*.

2. Some *H* are non-*I*.
   Some *I* are *G*.
   Some *G* are not non-*H*.

3. Some *L* are non-*K*.
   No *J* are non-*L*.
   No *J* are *K*.

II. Use conversion and/or obversion to change the following arguments to ones that are equivalent but have only three terms. Check each argument by the four rules.

1. No *N* are *O*.
   Some *M* are not *O*.
   Some non-*N* are *M*.

2. No non-*I* are *G*.
   All *I* are *H*.
   All *G* are *H*.

III. Use contraposition and/or obversion and/or conversion to reduce each of the following arguments to one that has three terms. Check each argument by the four rules.

1. Some *S* are not *H*.
   All *D* are *S*.
   No non-*D* are *H*.

2. No non-*B* are *C*.
   All non-*C* are non-*A*.
   All *A* are *B*.

3. All *A* are *C*, for no *A* are non-*M*, and no *M* are non-*C*.

IV. Evaluate each of the following enthymemes by translating the statement to standard-form propositions and supplying the missing parts.

1. Because every compatibalist is a determinist, Professor Klotzmeyer is a determinist.

2. Whoever makes things in which there is evil that could have been made without any evil, or the making of which could have been omitted, does not choose the best. God has made a world in which there is evil, a world that could have been made without any evil or the making of which could have been omitted. Whoever does not choose the best is lacking in power, knowledge, or goodness.

3. All cats are mammals, so L.C. is a mammal.

4. Any philosopher knows Kant's ethics. So Dr. Y. S. Acre can tell you something about the Categorical Imperative.

CHAPTER 7

TRUTH FUNCTIONS

OVERVIEW

The English language, like any natural language, is a wonderful concoction.
It allows us to question, command, exclaim, assert, and reason. It is a
rich language full of subtleties, nuances, and colloquialisms. It is not,
however, the ideal vehicle for the expression and analysis of arguments.
Consequently, logicians have worked toward development of artificial languages that are especially designed to avoid ambiguity of expression and to
facilitate ease of analysis.

SECTION REVIEWS

7-1

Truth-Functional Compounds

Section Objective

1. Learn the meaning and function of the five logical operators.

Key Term Review

1. <u>Simple statement</u>: a statement that does not have any simple statements
    as component parts.

2. <u>Compound statement</u>: a statement that has one or more simple statements
    as components.

3. <u>Truth function or truth-functional compound</u>: a compound statement
    whose truth value (whether it is true or false) is precisely determin-
    able if we know that truth value of its simple components and under-
    stand the meaning of the logical operators.

4. <u>Logical operator</u>: a symbol that, when combined correctly with a state-
    ment or statements results in a different (compound) statement. The
    five logical operators are the tilde or curl (~), the ampersand (&),
    the wedge (V), the horseshoe (⊃), and the triple bar (≡).

5. <u>Tilde</u> or <u>curl</u>: the symbol for negation or denial (~).

6. <u>Ampersand</u>: the symbol for conjunction (&). Each component in a con-
    junction is a conjunct.

7. <u>Wedge</u>: the symbol for inclusive disjunction (V). Each component in
    a disjunction is a disjunct.

8. <u>Horseshoe</u>: the symbol for forming a conditional (⊃). The component
    on the left side of the horseshoe is the antecedent. The component on
    the right side of the horseshoe is the consequent.

9. <u>Triple bar</u>: the symbol for the biconditional (≡).

10. <u>Dominant operator</u>: the logical operator that applies to the entire (largest) compound in cases where there are compound statements within a larger compound statement.

11. <u>Variable</u>: any of the lower-case letters from the middle of the alphabet (such as p, q, r, and s), which act as mere place holders to indicate where statements (either simple or compound) may appear.

12. <u>Statement form</u>: a sequence of symbols and variables such that replacing the variables with statements results in a compound statement.

13. <u>Substitution instance</u>: any statement that results from replacing the variable or variables in a statement form is a substitution instance of that form.

Summary

Simple statements can become compound statements through the use of a logical operator. All the operators we will use result in truth-functional compounds. This means that, if the truth value (whether true or false) of the simple statements is known, then the truth value of the compound statement is precisely determinable.

<u>Negation</u>: "I am not a crook."--R. M. Nixon

To negate or deny some statement is to use one of the most common logical operators. The new statement that is formed is considered a compound statement, and it will always have a truth value that is opposite that of the original statement. The most common symbol for this operator is called the <u>tilde</u> or <u>curl</u> and it looks like this: ~ . The tilde is always placed in front of (on the left side of) that which is being negated.

If M represents a statement, then $\sim M$ represents the negation of that statement. If C represents the statement "I am a crook," $\sim C$ represents "I am not a crook." If a compound is being denied, the curl is placed before the parentheses, brackets, or braces that contain the compound: ~(compound).

<u>Conjunction</u>: "Charlie's neat and Charlie's sweet."--Anonymous

Another extremely common operator is conjunction. It is used to join two propositions and to assert them both. The symbol we will use for conjunction is called the <u>ampersand</u> and looks like this: &. The ampersand is always placed between the two statements that are being asserted together. Each component of the conjunction is called a conjunct. A conjunction is true if and only if both conjuncts are true.

<u>Disjunction</u>: "To be or not to be."--Shakespeare

"Either...or..." expressions in English are ambiguous. To say "He lives in San Antonio or he lives in Houston" probably means he lives in one and only one of those towns. To say "I'll either read or watch T.V. tonight" probably means at least one of these will be done but would not be considered false if both are done. The first example is known as an exclusive disjunction. However, unless we have strong evidence that exactly one (and not both) of the alternatives is claimed to be true, we will interpret all "either...or..." statements as <u>inclusive disjunctions</u>. A <u>wedge</u> is used to

symbolize the inclusive disjunction: V. The wedge is placed between the
alternatives or disjuncts that may be simple or compound. A disjunction is
true under every condition except one. It is false when both disjuncts are
false.

Conditional: "If you've got the money, honey, I've got the time."
--Lefty Frizzell

The symbol for the conditional is the horseshoe,⊃, and it will be used to
translate "if...then..." statements from English. Because there are a number of slightly different meanings attached to conditional or hypothetical
statements in English, the exact meaning of the horseshoe will reflect a
meaning common to all of them but it cannot be identical to all of them.

The horseshoe stands between two statements. The statement on the left,
known as the antecedent, is the one that would follow the word if in English;
the statement on the right side of the horseshoe is called the consequent.
The only case in which a conditional is false is the case in which the antecedent is true and the consequent is false.

Biconditional: "You will pass if and only if you know the material."
--Ev Ree Teacher

The symbol for the biconditional is the triple bar, ≡, and it translates
the phrase "if and only if." This is the same as a conjunction of an "if..."
statement and an "only if..." statement. The biconditional relation is
sometimes called "material equivalence." The triple bar stands between two
statements. The biconditional is true only under the following conditions:
(1) both statements are true or (2) both statements are false.

Whenever a truth-functional compound has components that are themselves compound, the symbolization must be carefully done. Ordinarily, whenever more
than one symbol appears in a statement, punctuation in the form of parentheses, brackets, or braces must be used to indicate which is the dominant
operator. The dominant operator is the one that applies to the compound as
a whole. Punctuation is often necessary to avoid ambiguity.

The expression

$A \lor B \& C$

is not an acceptable formulation because there is no way to tell whether
the right disjunct is B or the compound $B \& C$. Likewise, the left conjunct
is not clear. If the dominant operator is supposed to be the ampersand, as
in the expression "Either A or B, and C," then the symbolization should be

$(A \lor B) \& C$

On the other hand, if the dominant operator should be the wedge, as in
"Either A or both B and C," the result should be

$A \lor (B \& C)$.

To avoid the use of parentheses in certain cases, we will adopt a convention
about how the curl is read. Consider the following:

$\sim F \& G$

This expression is ambiguous because it is not clear whether the curl is denying the "*F*" or denying the "*F* and *G*" compound. We will henceforth always consider a curl to be applied to the <u>smallest</u> expression that the symbolization allows. Hence "~*F* & *G*" means that just the "*F*" is negated, and the negation of "*F*" is joined to "*G*." If we are required to symbolize the negation of the compound "*F* & *G*," parentheses will allow this: ~(*F* & *G*).

With this convention in mind, we can rewrite the following expressions, eliminating superfluous parentheses.

1.	*D* & (~*E*)	becomes	*D* & ~*E*
2.	(~*X*) & (*A* & *B*)	becomes	~*X* & (*A* & *B*)
3.	(~*X*) ∨ *A*	becomes	~*X* ∨ *A*
4.	[~(*C*)] & (*D* & *E*)	becomes	~*C* & (*D* & *E*)

Do not be tempted to remove all parentheses in numbers 2 and 4. You should note that the expressions "~*X* & *A* & *B*" and "~*C* & *D* & *E*" are technically incorrect. If you examine the first ampersand in the second expression, you will see that it is not clear whether the right side of the conjunction is "*D*" or "*D* & *E*." Similarly, the left side (left conjunct) of the second ampersand might be either "*D*" or "~*C* & *D*." Therefore, one pair of parentheses must remain in the expression.

We will use capital letters to stand for actual individual statements. A different letter will be used to represent different statements, but if the same statement appears more than once in, say, an argument, the same letter must be used each time. (Note that this is quite different from categorical logic, in which capital letters represented class descriptions.)

Lower-case letters (beginning with the letter "*p*") will be statement variables and will indicate the location of any proposition whatever. If they occur within an expression, they are like blanks that can be filled in with any statement.

Examine the following compounds and locate the simple statements in each of them:

1. Whenever I am in trouble, I pray.

2. I will buy the car only if I like the way it handles.

3. It's a nice house; however, it's too expensive.

4. It is not the case that Nixon always avoided uncouth language.

5. I leave if Paul arrives.

If we underline the simple statements, we get

1a. Whenever <u>I am in trouble</u>, <u>I pray</u>.

2a. <u>I will buy the car</u> only if <u>I like the way it handles</u>.

3a. <u>It's a nice house</u>; however, <u>it's too expensive</u>.

4a. It is not the case that <u>Nixon always avoided uncouth language</u>.

5a. <u>I leave</u> if <u>Paul arrives</u>.

Replacing simple statements with capital letters yields

1b. Whenever *T*, *P*.

2b. *B* only if *L*.

3b. *N*; however, *E*.

4b. It is not the case *N*.

5b. *L* if *A*.

Inserting logical operators gives

1c. $T \supset P$

2c. $B \supset L$

3c. $N \& E$

4c. $\sim N$

5c. $A \supset L$

"$T \supset P$," for example, is a substitution instance of the general statement form "$p \supset q$." Every possible conditional is symbolized by "$p \supset q$."

Practice Exercises

I. For each of the following statements, replace any simple statements with capital letters. (Use the underlined letter.)

1. That I understand this material is not true.

_____

2. If John loves Marsha, then he is willing to swim the deepest ocean.

_____

3. I'm staying if the professor arrives.

_____

4. I studied and now I'm doing well in the course.

_____

5. The band played rock and roll.

_____

II. Then, for each of the foregoing statements, replace the simple statements with capital letters and replace the connectives with logical operators so that each answer is an entirely symbolized expression.

1. _____

2. _____

3. _____

4. _____

5. _____

III. Symbolize each of the following, using appropriate logical operations.

1. A and B _____

2. Both A and B _____

3. A, but B _____

4. A, however B _____

5. It's not the case B _____

6. It's not the case both A and B _____

7. Both A and B are not the case _____

8. A or B _____

9. Either A or B _____

10. Neither A nor B _____

11. If A then B _____

12. If A, B _____

13. B, if A _____

14. A is a sufficient condition for B _____

15. All A's are B's _____

16. Only if A, B _____

17. Only A's are B's _____

18. If and only if A, B _____

19. A is a necessary condition for B _____

20. Either A or B, but not both A and B _____

21. If both A and B, then C _____

22. If A, then B and C _____

23. Either A or B, and C _____

24. Either A or both B and C _____

25. A unless B _____

26. *A* if *B* _____

27. *A* only if *B* _____

28. If *B*, then *A* _____

29. *A* and *B* are not both the case _____

30. Neither *A* nor *B* is the case _____

31. It is not the case neither *A* nor *B* _____

32. *A* and *B* are both not the case _____

33. Jones will come if he gets the message, provided that he is still

    interested _____

34. If it is not the case either *A* or *B*, then neither *C* nor *D*

    _____

35. *S* and either *J* or both *A* and *B* _____

IV. What is the truth value of each of the following if *A*, *B*, and *C* are
    considered true and *X*, *Y*, and *Z* are considered false?

1. ~*B* & *X* _____   5. ~*A* V ~*Y* _____

2. ~(*B* & *X*) _____   6. [(*A* ⊃ *B*) ⊃ *C*] ⊃ *Z* _____

3. ~*B* & ~*X* _____   7. *A* ⊃ (*B* ⊃ *Z*) _____

4. ~(*A* V *Y*) _____   8. *X* ⊃ (*Y* ⊃ *Z*) _____

_____

7-2

Truth Tables

Section Objective

1. Learn how truth tables show the truth value of any truth-functional compound statement under all possible truth value conditions.

Key Term Review

1. Truth table: a listing in tabular form of all possible combinations of
   truth values of a given set of simple statements, showing how each combination affects the truth value of a compound statement having those
   as component statements.

2. Base column or guide column: a truth table column showing truth values
   for a simple statement.

Summary

A truth table serves to define a given logical operator. Here is the truth table of the curl or tilde.

		p	$\sim p$
(row 1)	Case 1:	T	F
(row 2)	Case 2:	F	T

A truth table shows all the possible combinations of truth values of statements that replace the variables in the table. In this case the negation symbol is placed in front of a variable. That variable, whether simple or compound, is either true or false. That is why this truth table is only two rows long.

Case 1 covers the true replacements for p; Case 2 covers the false replacements.

Truth tables are "read" across the rows and we can see that, for Case 1 where p is true, $\sim p$ is false. For the second case, in which p is false, $\sim p$, of course, is true.

The truth table for the ampersand looks like this:

		p	q	p & q
(row 1)	Case 1:	T	T	T
(row 2)	Case 2:	F	T	F
(row 3)	Case 3:	T	F	F
(row 4)	Case 4:	F	F	F

Because conjunctions join two statements each of which may be either true or false, there are four possible combinations of truth value. The first possibility is that both statements are true; this is listed as Case 1 on the truth table. Reading on across, it is indicated that the compound p & q is true in that circumstance. The other cases are equally easy to understand.

As we have said, the curl may deny a simple or a compound statement. Likewise, an ampersand may join simples or compounds:

A & $(B$ & $C)$

D & $(\sim E)$

$\sim (F$ & $G)$

The truth table for the wedge is as follows:

		p	q	$p \vee q$
(row 1)	Case 1:	T	T	T
(row 2)	Case 2:	F	T	T
(row 3)	Case 3:	T	F	T
(row 4)	Case 4:	F	F	F

(It is Case 1 that is different from what it would be in an exclusive disjunction.) Note that the only situation that makes the inclusive disjunction false is that in which both disjuncts are false.

The truth table for the conditional looks like this:

p	q	$p \supset q$
T	T	T
F	T	T
T	F	F
F	F	T

This truth table is derived from the fact that the horseshoe is defined to be equivalent to the expression "$\sim(p \ \& \ \sim q)$." A truth table for that expression is constructed in this manner:

p	q	$\sim q$	$p \ \& \ \sim q$	$\sim(p \ \& \ \sim q)$
T	T	F	F	T
F	T	F	F	T
T	F	T	T	F
F	F	T	F	T

Note that the column of truth values for "$\sim(p \ \& \ \sim q)$" is identical to the column on the previous truth table for "$p \supset q$."

A truth table for the biconditional is as follows:

p	q	$p \equiv q$
T	T	T
F	T	F
T	F	F
F	F	T

We can construct a truth table for any expression, no matter how complex, by following a fairly simple procedure.

1) <u>Count</u> the number of simple statements in the expression. That is, count the number of different letters. If the expression contains capital letters they should be changed to variables or lower-case letters.

   a. $p \lor \sim p$ 1 statement

   b. $(p \supset q) \ \& \ (q \supset p)$ 2 statements

   c. $(q \lor r) \supset \sim p$ 3 statements

   d. $(p \supset q) \ \& \ (r \supset s)$ 4 statements

   e. $(p \lor q) \ \& \ [r \supset (s \ \& \ t)]$ 5 statements

2) <u>Determine</u> the number of rows the truth table will have, using the count of variables and the formula 2^n, where "n" is the number of variables. The function of the base columns or guide columns is to list every possible combination of truth values that could occur in the statement form we are dealing with. A statement with one variable, which might be true or might be false, has two rows that indicate these two possibilities.

118

One with two variables has twice as many possibilities: they might both be true, one might be false while the other is true, one might be true while the other is false, or they might both be false. Each additional variable doubles the number of possible truth value combinations.

3) <u>Construct</u> the base columns or guide columns. There are the columns for each variable. We will make them like this:

1 statement (2 rows)

1. T
2. F

2 statements (4 rows)

	p	*q*
1.	T	T
2.	F	T
3.	T	F
4.	F	F

3 statements (8 rows)

p	*q*	*r*
T	T	T
F	T	T
T	F	T
F	F	T
T	T	F
F	T	F
T	F	F
F	F	F

4 statements (16 rows)

p	*q*	*r*	*s*
T	T	T	T
F	T	T	T
T	F	T	T
F	F	T	T
T	T	F	T
F	T	F	T
T	F	F	T
F	F	F	T
T	T	T	F
F	T	T	F
T	F	T	F
F	F	T	F
T	T	F	F
F	T	F	F
T	F	F	F
F	F	F	F

Note that the guide column on the far left in every case alternates T's and F's all the way down. The next column alternates pairs of T's and

F's. Each column alternates twice as many T's and F's as the previous
column. Guide columns for any number of statements can be made this way.

4) Construct a column for the statement in question by referring to the
   base columns. Fill in the column, using your knowledge of the symbols
   and the truth value of the variables for each row. Suppose we want a
   truth table for

$p \supset (p \ \& \ q)$

There are two statements, so there need to be four rows. The base
columns look like this:

p	q		$p \supset (p \ \& \ q)$
T	T		
F	T		
T	F		
F	F		

However, it is rather difficult to determine the column for "$p \supset (p \ \& \ q)$"
because this compound has a component (the consequent) that is itself a
compound. We should first construct an intermediate column for the expression "$p \ \& \ q$."

p	q	$p \ \& \ q$	$p \supset (p \ \& \ q)$
T	T	T	
F	T	F	
T	F	F	
F	F	F	

The column for "$p \ \& \ q$" can be obtained immediately from the "p" column
and the "q" column, because we know a conjunction is true only in the
first row where "p" and "q" are both true. Now we can complete the
table.

	p	q	$p \ \& \ q$	$p \supset (p \ \& \ q)$
(row 1)	T	T	T	T
(row 2)	F	T	F	T
(row 3)	T	F	F	F
(row 4)	F	F	F	T

We determine the last column by realizing that the dominant operator
is the horseshoe and, for each row, checking the truth value of the
antecedent (by looking at the "p" column) and checking the truth value
of the consequent (by looking at the "$p \ \& \ q$" column).

Suppose we are concerned with the statement

$[p \supset (p \ \& \ q)] \equiv (\sim q \supset \sim p)$

Again there are only two statement variables, so we need only four rows.
It is good practice to write our final expression on the far right.

p	q			$[p \supset (p \,\&\, q)]$	$\equiv$	$(\sim q \supset \sim p)$
T	T					
F	T					
T	F					
F	F					

Then we may work to the left, adding intermediate columns for progressively less complex parts, until we get to parts that can be immediately determined from the guide columns.

p	q	$p \,\&\, q$	$p \supset (p \,\&\, q)$	$\sim q$	$\sim p$	$\sim q \supset \sim p$	$[p \supset (p \,\&\, q)] \equiv (\sim q \supset \sim p)$
T	T	T	T	F	F	T	T
F	T	F	T	F	T	T	T
T	F	F	F	T	F	F	T
F	F	F	T	T	T	T	T

Practice Exercises

Construct a truth table for each of the following expressions.

1. $(q \lor r) \supset \sim p$

2. $(p \supset q) \,\&\, (p \supset r)$

3. $(p \mathbin{\&} {\sim}p) \supset q$

4. ${\sim}q \lor r$

5. $[(p \supset q) \mathbin{\&} (q \supset r)] \supset (p \supset r)$

6. $\{[p \supset (q \supset r)] \mathbin{\&} (p \mathbin{\&} q)\} \supset r$

Section Objective

1. Learn to use truth tables to determine whether any two statements are truth-functionally equivalent.

Key Term Review

1. Logically equivalent statement forms: two statement forms that are both true under the same conditions and both false under the same conditions.

2. Truth-functionally equivalent statements: any compound statements that are logically equivalent are truth-functionally equivalent.

3. Transformation rule: a rule allowing a statement of one form to be replaced by a statement of another form, based on the fact that the statements are truth-functionally equivalent.

Summary

When two compounds are true under the same conditions and false under the same conditions, they are truth-functionally equivalent. Because a truth table shows all possible truth value occurrences for expressions, one may be used to detect equivalence or lack thereof.

Students often think the expression "$\sim(p \ \& \ q)$" is equivalent to the expression "$\sim p \ \& \sim q$," but a truth table shows that they are not equivalent.

p	q	$p \ \& \ q$	$\sim p$	$\sim q$	$\sim(p \ \& \ q)$	$\sim p \ \& \sim q$
T	T	T	F	F	F	F
F	T	F	T	F	T	F
T	F	F	F	T	T	F
F	F	F	T	T	T	T

The columns for the two expressions are not absolutely identical, so the two expressions are not truth-functionally equivalent. The conditions in both the second and third rows make "$\sim(p \ \& \ q)$" true but make "$\sim p \ \& \sim q$" false.

On the other hand, "$\sim(p \ \& \ q)$" is equivalent to "$\sim p \lor \sim q$."

p	q	$p \ \& \ q$	$\sim p$	$\sim q$	$\sim(p \ \& \ q)$	$\sim p \lor \sim q$
T	T	T	F	F	F	F
F	T	F	T	F	T	T
T	F	F	F	T	T	T
F	F	F	T	T	T	T

Note that the last two columns are identical.

When two expressions are truth-functionally equivalent and one is allowed to be replaced by the other, we have a transformation rule. The equivalence demonstrated in the above truth table is a traditional transformation rule known as one of De Morgan's laws (after the logician Augustus De Morgan). A replacement by transformation rule may be made on entire statements or on portions of statements. Commutation, for example, allows the entire expression "$X \equiv (Y \equiv Z)$" to be replaced by "$(Y \equiv Z) \equiv X$" or allows only the latter part of the expression to be replaced: "$X \equiv (Z \equiv Y)$." A complete list of allowable transformation rules is given below.

TRANSFORMATION RULES

Absorption (Abs.)	$[p \supset (p \ \& \ q)] \equiv (p \supset q)$
Association (Assoc.)	$[p \lor (q \lor r)] \equiv [(p \lor q) \lor r]$
	$[p \ \& \ (q \ \& \ r)] \equiv [(p \ \& \ q) \ \& \ r]$
Biconditional Exchange (Bicon. Exch.)	$(p \equiv q) \equiv [(p \supset q) \ \& \ (q \supset p)]$
Commutation (Com.)	$(p \lor q) \equiv (q \lor p)$
	$(p \ \& \ q) \equiv (q \ \& \ p)$
	$(p \equiv q) \equiv (q \equiv p)$
Conditional Exchange (Con. Exch.)	$(p \supset q) \equiv (\sim p \lor q)$
	$(p \supset q) \equiv [\sim(p \ \& \ \sim q)]$
Contraposition (Contrapos.)	$(p \supset q) \equiv (\sim q \supset \sim p)$
	$(p \equiv q) \equiv (\sim q \equiv \sim p)$
De Morgan's laws (De M.)	$[\sim(p \lor q)] \equiv (\sim p \ \& \ \sim q)$
	$[\sim(p \ \& \ q)] \equiv (\sim p \lor \sim q)$
Distribution (Dist.)	$[p \ \& \ (q \lor r)] \equiv [(p \ \& \ q) \lor (p \ \& \ r)]$
	$[p \lor (q \ \& \ r)] \equiv [(p \lor q) \ \& \ (p \lor r)]$
Divergence (Div.)	$[\sim(p \equiv q)] \equiv (p \equiv \sim q)$
Double Negation (D.N.)	$P \equiv (\sim\sim p)$
Duplication (Dup.)	$p \equiv (p \ \& \ p)$
	$p \equiv (p \lor p)$
Exportation (Exp.)	$[(p \ \& \ q) \supset r] \equiv [p \supset (q \supset r)]$

Practice Exercises

I. Using the transformation rules, give a truth-functionally equivalent statement in English for each of the following.

1. Neither John nor Mary failed logic.

   _____

   _____

2. Either Bill or Jane passed logic.

   _____

   _____

3. If Stuart graduates then if his parents keep their promise then he'll get a new car.

_____

_____

4. John and Bill passed and Jane passed.

_____

_____

5. If Stuart can pass logic then so can Kim.

_____

_____

6. Pete will graduate and he'll either get a new car or save his money for graduate school.

_____

_____

7. It's not the case that he cannot get into medical school.

_____

_____

II. Replace each of the following with a truth-functionally equivalent compound in accordance with the transformation rule mentioned.

1. $C \supset (A \supset B)$ contraposition _____

2. $C \supset (A \supset B)$ conditional exchange _____

3. $C \supset (A \supset B)$ a different conditional exchange _____

4. $C \supset (A \supset B)$ absorption _____

5. $C \supset (A \supset B)$ exportation _____

6. $\sim(C \& D)$ De Morgan's law _____

7. $\sim(C \& D)$ commutation _____

8. $\sim[(E \& F) \& G]$ De Morgan's law _____

9. $\sim[(E \& F) \& G]$ commutation _____

10. $\sim[(E \& F) \& G]$ a different commutation _____

11. $\sim[(E \& F) \& G]$ association _____

12. $H \mathbin{\&} (I \vee J)$ commutation _____

13. $H \mathbin{\&} (I \vee J)$ a different commutation _____

14. $H \mathbin{\&} (I \vee J)$ distribution _____

15. $(K \supset L) \mathbin{\&} (L \supset K)$ biconditional exchange _____

16. $(K \supset L) \mathbin{\&} (L \supset K)$ conditional exchange _____

17. $(K \supset L) \mathbin{\&} (M \supset N)$ contraposition _____

18. $(K \supset L) \mathbin{\&} (M \supset N)$ double negation _____

19. $(M \supset N) \mathbin{\&} (M \supset N)$ duplication _____

20. $\sim(O \equiv P) \mathbin{\&} (Q \supset R)$ divergence _____

21. $(Q \mathbin{\&} R) \vee (Q \mathbin{\&} T)$ distribution _____

22. $(Q \equiv R) \supset (S \equiv T)$ contraposition _____

23. $(Q \equiv R) \supset S$ absorption _____

Translating from English into Symbolic Logic

Section Objective

1. Learn more skills in translating from English to symbolic expressions.

Summary

The extreme complexity of the English language (or any natural language) means that setting out rules for translation is almost impossible. The best defense against translation mistakes is a thorough knowledge of English and a good understanding of the meanings of the logical operators.

Practice Exercises

I. Which of the following sentences are logically equivalent to "If Clovis loves Mavis, then he will buy her mink"? Use a truth table to help you decide after you symbolize each expression.

   1. If Clovis doesn't love Mavis, then he won't buy her mink.

   2. Clovis won't buy Mavis mink if he doesn't love her.

   3. Clovis will buy Mavis mink unless he doesn't love her.

4. Clovis loves Mavis unless he isn't buying her mink.

5. Clovis isn't buying Mavis mink only if he doesn't love her.

6. Clovis loves Mavis but he isn't buying her mink.

7. Clovis will buy Mavis mink provided he loves her.

8. Clovis loves Mavis only if he'll buy her mink.

9. If Clovis is going to buy Mavis mink, he loves her.

10. If Clovis loves Mavis, he'll buy her mink.

11. Clovis will buy Mavis mink if he loves her.

12. Clovis will buy Mavis mink only if he doesn't love her.

13. In case Clovis doesn't love Mavis, he won't buy her mink.

II. In Exercises 1, 2, and 3 circle the letter of each statement that
asserts the same thing as the given statement.

1. Earl must study his lessons or he will have to stay home from the
picnic.
   a. If Earl doesn't study his lessons, he will have to stay home
   from the picnic.
   b. If Earl studies his lessons, then he must go to the picnic.
   c. If Earl stays home from the picnic, then he must study his
   lessons.
   d. If Earl is not to stay home from the picnic, then he must
   study his lessons.

2. Fred will pass only if he studies hard.
   a. If Fred studies hard, he will pass.
   b. Either Fred studies hard or he will fail.
   c. If Fred does not study hard, he will not pass.
   d. If Fred is to fail, then he must not study hard.

3. If T then U
   a. T only if U
   b. U only if T

          c. *T* if and only if *U*
          d. *U* if and only if *T*

III. Which of the following could be translated as "*p* ⊃ *q*"?

1. *q*, if *p*   2. *p* implies *q*   3. *p* is a sufficient con-
                                                        dition for *q*

4. *p*, only if *q*   5. *q* follows from *p*   6. *q* is a necessary condi-
                                                        tion for *p*

7. *p*, if *q*   8. *q*, only if *p*   9. if *p*, then *q*

IV. Translate each of the following using a ⊃ .   Write your answers out
     fully.

1. Every multiple of 4 is a multiple of 2.

     _____

     _____

2. Warren will sing provided Steve will play the piano.

     _____

3. The game will be canceled in the event of rain.

     _____

4. Two integers whose sum is seven cannot both be even.

     _____

     _____

5. Susie is late when she walks.

     _____

6. He is late only when he sleeps late.

     _____

7. Providing he studies and the exam is easy, he will pass.

     _____

8. Earl must study or he will have to stay home from the picnic.

     _____

9. Fred will pass only if he studies hard.

     _____

10. Texas's beating Oklahoma proves Texas is the better team.

_____

_____

11. In order to pass, you must study.

_____

12. Elementary logic is a prerequisite for symbolic logic.

_____

_____

CHAPTER 8
EVALUATING TRUTH-FUNCTIONAL ARGUMENTS

OVERVIEW

This chapter shows how truth tables can be used to determine whether truth-functional statements are tautologies or contradictions. More important, several techniques are introduced for the evaluation of truth-functional arguments. The use of truth tables is extended to the evaluation of arguments for validity or invalidity. The method of formal deduction and the method of indirect proof are also presented as ways of demonstrating validity. In addition, shorter truth tables are introduced to prove invalidity.

SECTION REVIEWS

Truth Tables and Valid Argument Forms

Section Objective

1. Learn to use truth tables to evelute arguments for validity or invalidity.

Key Term Review

1. <u>Valid argument form</u>: an argument structure such that no argument having that structure could have true premises and a false conclusion. Hence, any argument with that structure is a valid argument.

2. <u>Formal fallacy</u>: an argument (resembling a valid argument) that is invalid because of its form or structure. (A proof can be given that the argument is invalid.)

Summary

A valid deductive argument is such that the conclusion follows necessarily from the premises. This means that, if the premises are true, the conclusion also must be true. Any argument that has a structure such that it allows the possibility of the premises all being true while the conclusion is false is an invalid argument.

Because a truth table covers all possible combinations of truth values for the simple statements, it covers all possible arguments with that structure. If it is possible for an argument to have all true premises and a false conclusion, it will show up on the truth table as one or more invalidating rows. If that is impossible, an invalidating row will not occur in the truth table and this will prove that the argument is valid.

A truth table for any truth-functional argument can be constructed (if one has the time) following a procedure essentially the same as that explained in the previous chapter.

1. Change the argument to its argument form. That is, change capital letters to lower-case letters beginning with "*p*."

A ∨ *M*		*p* ∨ *q*
~*A*	becomes	~*p*
∴*M*		∴*q*

(*C* ∨ *D*) ⊃ *E*		(*p* ∨ *q*) ⊃ *r*
C	becomes	*p*
∴*E*		∴*r*

2. Count the number of simple statements (or variables). That is, count the number of different letters.

p ∨ *q*	
~*p*	has 2 variables
∴*q*	

(*p* ∨ *q*) ⊃ *r*	
p	has 3 variables
∴*r*	

3. Determine the number of rows the truth table will have, using the count of variables and the formula 2^n where n is the number of variables. One variable requires two rows, two variables require four rows, three require eight rows, four require sixteen rows, and so on.

4. Construct base columns for each variable in the manner explained in the last chapter.

5. Construct premise and conclusion columns. A column for every premise and for the conclusion must be made.

    If we are dealing with an argument whose structure is

    p   *q*
    ~*q*
    ∴~*p*

    we would need the following columns:

	p	*q*	*p* ⊃ *q*	~*q*	~*p*
1.	T	T			
2.	F	T			
3.	T	F			
4.	F	F			

    Fill in the columns, using your knowledge of the symbols and the truth value of "*p*" and "*q*" given for each row.

    Your completed truth table should look like this:

p	q	$p \supset q$	$\sim q$	$\sim p$
T	T	T	F	F
F	T	T	F	T
T	F	F	T	F
F	F	T	T	T

6. Read the truth table to determine whether the argument is valid. In the example above, only the fourth row is such that the premises are both true. But the conclusion, $\sim p$, is also true in this row, proving the argument to be valid.

If you must construct a column for a premise or conclusion that is too complex to be determined directly from the guide columns, you may first construct a column or column(s) for the less complex parts of the proposition. If we construct a truth table for this argument,

$p \supset (q \ \& \ r)$
$(q \lor r) \supset \sim p$
$\therefore \sim p$

our completed table will look something like this:

p	q	r	$q \ \& \ r$	$q \lor r$	$\sim p$	$p \supset (q \ \& \ r)$	$(q \lor r) \supset \sim p$	$\sim p$
T	T	T	T	T	F	T	F	F
F	T	T	T	T	T	T	T	T
T	F	T	F	T	F	F	F	F
F	F	T	F	T	T	T	T	T
T	T	F	F	T	F	F	F	F
F	T	F	F	T	T	T	T	T
T	F	F	F	F	F	F	T	F
F	F	F	F	F	T	T	T	T
						premise	premise	premise

This argument is valid because there is not a single row in which premises are true while the conclusion is false.

Every invalid argument for which a truth table is constructed will have at least one invalidating row that exhibits all true premises and a false conclusion. Consider a well-known invalid argument called the fallacy of affirming the consequent:

p	q	$p \supset q$	q	p
T	T	T	T	T
F	T	T	T	F
T	F	F	F	T
F	F	T	F	F
		premise	premise	conclusion

$p \supset q$
q
$\therefore p$

The truth table for this invalid argument appears to the left.

Note that the second row is an invalidating row because it has true premises and a false conclusion. (The last two columns are unnecessary because they are repeats of previous columns. However, it is much easier to "read" a truth table if the conclusion is the last column and the premises are the columns just to the left of it.)

Another invalid argument structure is known as the fallacy of denying the antecedent. It and its truth table follow:

$p \supset q$
$\sim p$
$\therefore \sim q$

p	p	$p \supset q$	$\sim p$	$\sim q$
T	T	T	F	F
F	T	T	T	F
T	F	F	F	T
F	F	T	T	T
	premise	premise	conclusion	

The second row is an invalidating row because it has true premises and a false conclusion.

There are a number of fairly simple valid argument forms that we will make use of soon as rules of inference. Each of the eleven can easily be proven valid by means of a truth table. For example, one that looks quite similar to the fallacy of affirming the consequent is known as *modus ponens*. Let's examine it and its truth table:

$p \supset q$
p
$\therefore q$

p	q	$p \supset q$	p	q
T	T	T	T	T
F	T	T	F	T
T	F	F	T	F
F	F	T	F	F
		premise	premise	conclusion

There is no row in which both premises are true and the conclusion is false.

Here is the entire list of the rules of inference:

Adjunction (Adj.)	p, q; therefore p & q
Biconditional Argument (Bicon. Arg.)	$p \equiv q$, p; therefore q $p \equiv q$, q; therefore p $p \equiv q$, $\sim p$; therefore $\sim q$ $p \equiv q$, $\sim q$; therefore $\sim p$
Chain Argument (Chain)	$p \supset q$, $q \supset r$; therefore $p \supset r$
Conjunctive Argument (Conj. Arg.)	$\sim(p$ & $q)$, p; therefore $\sim q$ $\sim(p$ & $q)$, q; therefore $\sim p$
Conjunctive Simplification (Conj. Simp.)	p & q; therefore p p & q; therefore q
Constructive Dilemma (C.D.)	$p \supset q$, $r \supset s$, $p \lor r$, therefore, $q \lor s$ $p \supset q$, $r \supset q$, $p \lor r$, therefore, q
Destructive Dilemma (D.D.)	$p \supset q$, $r \supset s$, $\sim q \lor \sim s$; therefore, $\sim p \lor \sim r$ $p \supset q$, $p \supset r$, $\sim q \lor \sim r$; therefore, $\sim p$

Disjunctive Addition (Disj. Add.)	p; therefore, $p \lor q$
Disjunctive Argument (Disj. Arg.)	$p \lor q$, $\sim p$; therefore, q
	$p \lor q$, $\sim q$; therefore, p
Modus Ponens (*M.P.*)	$p \supset q$, p; therefore, q
Modus Tollens (*M.T.*)	$p \supset q$, $\sim q$; therefore, $\sim p$

Remember that the variables "p," "q," "r," and so on represent <u>any</u> statement, simple or compound. This means that

X
B
$\therefore X$ & B

is a substitution instance of adjunction, but so is

$X \supset Y$
$A \supset B$
$\therefore (X \supset Y)$ & $(A \supset B)$

The same holds true for other rules as well. Study these:

$(A \lor Y) \supset E$
$A \lor Y$ *modus ponens*
$\therefore E$

$R \lor (S$ & $T)$
$\sim R$ disjunctive argument
$\therefore S$ & T

$(G \supset H)$ & $(I \lor J)$ conjunctive
$\therefore G \supset H$ simplification

$L \supset M$ disjunctive
$\therefore (L \supset M) \lor (L \supset N)$ addition

$J \supset (K \lor L)$
$(K \lor L) \supset (R$ & $S)$ chain argument
$\therefore J \supset (R$ & $S)$

When we are working with the six rules that have two premises, the order of premises is not important. Thus,

$\sim A$
$B \supset A$
$\therefore \sim B$

is just as much an example of *modus tollens* as is

$R \supset (E$ & $\sim F)$
$\sim (E$ & $\sim F)$ or
$\therefore \sim R$

$[J$ & $(\sim K \lor L)] \supset S$
$\sim S$
$\therefore \sim [J$ & $(\sim K \lor L)]$

However, almost everything else about the patterns shown by the rules of inference is important. Neither of the following are examples of disjunctive argument:

$A \lor B$
A
$\therefore B$

$\sim A \lor B$
B
$\therefore A$

On the other hand, <u>all</u> of the following are examples of disjunctive argument:

~B	~B ∨ A	~B ∨ A	B ∨ ~A	(B ⊃ C) ∨ (R & S)
B ∨ A	~(~B)	~~B	~B	~(B ⊃ C)
∴A	∴A	∴A	∴~A	∴R & S

Practice Exercises

I. Which of the following match one of the eleven rules of inference?
    Name the rule or write "none."

1. A ⊃ C
    R ⊃ S
    ∴A ⊃ S

2. A ⊃ B
    A
    ∴B

3. J ⊃ K
    ∴J ⊃ (K & K)

4. A & C
    D
    ∴(A & C) & D

5. R ⊃ J
    C ⊃ R
    ∴C ⊃ J

6. R
    ∴R ∨ R

7. (X ⊃ Y) & (C ⊃ R)
    X ∨ R
    ∴Y ∨ R

8. J & (A ∨ B)
    ∴J

9. R ⊃ ~S
    S
    ∴~R

10. C ⊃ D
    D ⊃ E
    ∴E ⊃ C

11. J ∨ K
    ~J
    ∴~K

12. (L ∨ M) ∨ N
    ~(L ∨ M)
    ∴N

13. F ⊃ G
    G
    ∴F

14. (E ⊃ F) & (G ⊃ F)
    E ∨ G
    ∴F ∨ F

15. A ⊃ X
    ∴A ⊃ (A & X)

16. ~Z ∨ Y
    Z
    ∴Y

17. H ⊃ I
    I
    ∴H

18. R
    ∴R ∨ (S ⊃ T)

19. J ⊃ (K & L)
    ∴J ⊃ [J & (K & L)]

20. (A ∨ B) ⊃ R
    A ∨ B
    ∴R

21. J & K
    ∴K

22. L
    M
    ∴M & L

23. ~L ⊃ M
    ~M
    ∴~~L

24. ~M
    N
    ∴~M & N

25. [R ⊃ (S ∨ T)] & [J ⊃ (C & Z)]
    R ∨ J
    ∴(S ∨ T) ∨ (C & Z)

II. Which of the following match one of the eleven rules? Name the rule
    or write "none."

1. X & Y
    ∴X

2. A ⊃ B
    ∴A ⊃ (A & B)

3. R
    ∴R ∨ S

4. X
    Y
    ∴X & Y

5. C ∨ D
    ∴C

6. X ⊃ Y
    ~X
    ∴~X

7. $C \lor D$
$\sim C$
$\therefore D$

8. $X \supset Y$
$Y \supset Z$
$\therefore X \supset Z$

9. $R \lor S$
$\therefore (R \lor S) \lor T$

10. $B \supset C$
$A \supset B$
$\therefore A \supset C$

11. $(A \supset B) \ \& \ (C \supset D)$
$A \lor D$
$\therefore A \lor C$

12. $(R \lor S) \supset T$
$\therefore (R \lor S) \supset [(R \lor S) \ \& \ T]$

13. $J \supset K$
$K \supset L$
$\therefore L \supset J$

14. J
$(A \supset B) \lor C$
$\therefore (A \supset B) \lor C \ \& \ J$

15. $(\sim B \supset C) \ \& \ (\sim X \supset Y)$
$\sim B \lor \sim X$
$\therefore C \lor Y$

16. $\sim[(R \ \& \ S) \lor (A \lor B)] \supset [(X \lor Y) \ \& \ Z]$
$\sim[(R \ \& \ S) \lor (A \lor B)]$
$\therefore (X \lor Y) \ \& \ Z$

17. $(A \supset B) \ \& \ (E \supset F)$
$A \lor E$
$\therefore B \lor F$

18. $C \lor D$
$\sim E \lor \sim F$
$\therefore (C \lor D) \ \& \ (\sim E \lor \sim F)$

19. $\sim S \supset \sim T$
$\sim \sim T$
$\therefore \sim \sim S$

20. $\sim E \lor \sim F$
$\sim \sim E$
$\therefore \sim F$

21. $C \lor D$
$\sim D$
$\therefore C$

22. $\sim S \supset \sim T$
T
$\therefore S$

23. $[(X \lor Y) \supset Z] \ \& \ [R \supset (S \supset T)]$
$(X \lor Y) \lor R$
$\therefore Z \lor (S \supset T)$

24. $(O \lor P) \lor (Q \ \& \ R)$
$\sim (O \lor P)$
$\therefore Q \ \& \ R$

25. $\sim C \supset \sim D$
$\sim D \supset E$
$\therefore \sim C \supset E$

26. $\sim S \supset \sim T$
T
$\therefore S$

27. $(L \lor M) \supset O$
$(J \ \& \ K) \supset (L \lor M)$
$\therefore (J \ \& \ \sim K) \supset O$

28. $(J \ \& \ \sim K) \supset (L \lor M)$
$\sim L \lor \sim M$
$\therefore \sim (J \ \& \ \sim K)$

III. In each case, tell what third statement follows necessarily from statements 1 and 2. Which of the eleven rules does each match?

A. 1. If today is Saturday then tomorrow is Sunday.
   2. Today is Saturday.

   3. _____

B. 1. If he studies he makes good grades.
   2. But he made a bad grade in basket weaving.

   3. _____

C. 1. If today is Saturday then I am supposed to be at work.
   2. If I am supposed to be at work then I had better hurry.

   3. _____

D. 1. It's either Tuesday or Wednesday.
   2. It's not Tuesday.

   3. _____

E. 1. If this is a logic class, the material will be easy.
   2. The material is hard.

   3. _____

F. 1. If I study I make good grades, and if I don't study I have lots
      of fun.
   2. I'll either study or I won't.

   3. _____

G. 1. If I lie to the hostess she'll feel better, and if I tell the
      truth I'll feel better.
   2. I will either lie or tell the truth.

   3. _____

H. 1. This is either a math class or a logic class.
   2. This is not a math class.

   3. _____

I. 1. If the Cowboys had won in the Super Bowl last year I would have
      won a dollar.
   2. I did not win a dollar.

   3. _____

J. 1. I can either drop or not drop the course.
   2. If I drop the course I will be given an F and if I don't drop
      the course I will get an F.

   3. _____

K. 1. It is Sunday.
   2. It's a beautiful day.

   3. _____

L. 1. If I work hard I will get a promotion.
   2. I am working hard.

   3. _____

IV. Construct truth tables and check each of the following for validity.

1. $p \supset q$
   $\sim p$
   $\therefore \sim q$

2. $p \supset q$
   $q \supset r$
   $\therefore p \supset r$

3. $(p \supset q)$ & $(p \supset r)$
   p
   $\therefore q$ & r

4. p
   $\sim p$
   $\therefore q$

5. p
   $\therefore p$ & q

6. If matter exists, then Berkeley was mistaken. Matter exists if rocks exist. Therefore either Berkeley was not mistaken or rocks exist.

7. If it is raining then if the temperature is below 40°F my car won't start. It is raining and the temperature is below 40°F. Therefore my car won't start.

Tautologies and Contradictions

Section Objective

1. Learn to use truth tables to find out whether any given statement is a tautology, a contradiction, or merely a contingent statement.

Key Term Review

1. Tautology: a truth-functional compound that is necessarily true because of its form.

2. Contradiction: a truth-functional compound that is necessarily false because of its form.

3. Contingent statement: a statement such that its form results in a truth table column containing at least one T and at least one F.

Summary

A truth-functional compound with a statement form that is true in any condition (regardless of the truth value of its components) is a tautology. On a truth table, a tautology results in a column that is made up entirely of Ts. Probably the most obvious tautology is "$p \lor {\sim}p$"; it is called the law of excluded middle:

p	${\sim}p$	$p \lor {\sim}p$
T	F	T
F	T	T

Other simple and well-known tautologies are "$p \supset p$" and "$p \equiv p$," which are known as the laws of identity:

p	$p \supset p$		p	$p \equiv p$
T	T		T	T
F	T		F	T

And "${\sim}(p \,\&\, {\sim}p)$" is known as the law of noncontradiction:

p	${\sim}p$	$p \,\&\, {\sim}p$	${\sim}(p \,\&\, {\sim}p)$
T	F	F	T
F	T	F	T

Of course, all the transformation rules in the previous chapter are tautologies. For example, here is a truth table for divergence:

p	q	$p \equiv q$	${\sim}q$	${\sim}(p \equiv q)$	$p \equiv {\sim}q$	${\sim}(p \equiv q) \equiv (p \equiv {\sim}q)$
T	T	T	F	F	F	T
F	T	F	F	T	T	T
T	F	F	T	T	T	T
F	F	T	T	F	F	T

Truth-functional compounds that are always false are known as contradictions. The obvious contradiction "p and not p" will serve as an example:

p	${\sim}p$	$p \,\&\, {\sim}p$
T	F	F
F	T	F

You should note that the negation of any contradiction is a tautology and that the negation of any tautology is a contradiction. Let us construct a truth table for the denial of one of De Morgan's laws.

$$ {\sim}[\,{\sim}(p \lor q)] \equiv ({\sim}p \,\&\, {\sim}q) $$

p	q	$p \lor q$	$\sim(p \lor q)$	$\sim p$	$\sim q$	$\sim p \, \& \sim q$	$\sim(p \lor q) \equiv (\sim p \, \& \sim q)$
T	T	T	F	F	F	F	T
F	T	T	F	T	F	F	T
T	F	T	F	F	T	F	T
F	F	F	T	T	T	T	T

$$\sim[\sim(p \lor q)] \equiv (\sim p \, \& \sim q)$$

F
F
F
F

Any compound whose form is neither a contradiction nor a tautology is a contingent statement. A column of a truth table for such a form has at least one T and at least one F.

If we think of a valid argument as a conditional that says if the premises are true then the conclusion must be true, we realize that this is always true. Therefore every valid argument can be conceived of as a tautology. Conjunctive simplification asserts "if both p and q are true, then p is necessarily true": $(p \, \& \, q) \supset p$.

p	q	$p \, \& \, q$	$(p \, \& \, q) \supset p$
T	T	T	T
F	T	F	T
T	F	F	T
F	F	F	T

Somewhat strange things sometimes occur when contradictions or tautologies are parts of arguments. One of the exercises in the previous section had premises that contradicted each other and a conclusion that had nothing to do with the statements in the premises:

p
$\sim p$
$\therefore q$

p	q	p	$\sim p$	q
T	T	T	F	T
F	T	F	T	T
T	F	T	F	F
F	F	F	T	F
		premise	premise	conclusion

If one premise is true the other is false, so there cannot be any case of all true premises and a false conclusion. This paradox ceases to be so puzzling when we realize that, although valid, no argument of this form can be sound.

Similarly, an argument with a tautologous conclusion is valid regardless of the premise or premises. An invalid argument must be capable of having true premises and a false conclusion, and a tautologous conclusion will never be false.

Formal Deductions, or Deviations

Section Objective

Learn to prove arguments valid by constructing a formal deduction or derivation or a formal proof based on the rules of inference and on transformation rules.

Summary

Because truth tables are impractical for arguments with many statements, we will develop a system of proving an argument to be valid by deducing its conclusion from the premises via (a series of) simple arguments, each of which has been proved to be valid by a truth table. We will begin by using the eleven rules of inference introduced earlier.

A formal proof using these simple arguments will be contained entirely on numbered lines. Each of the earliest lines will contain a premise. Any line following the premise will contain something that can be derived from one, two, or three lines above it using one of the eleven rules of inference or a transformation rule. Each premise line will be labeled as such, and all other lines will also contain an explanation of how they were derived. The simple argument used will be named, and the line(s) that were used as premise(s) will be listed by line number. The proof is completed if and when the conclusion of the original argument is derived.

Suppose we know that chain argument is valid and we have this argument:

$$A \supset B$$
$$B \supset C$$
$$C \supset D$$
$$D \supset E$$
$$\therefore A \supset E$$

A formal proof would begin with lines one through four listing the premises. It is helpful to list, following a virgule (slash) and the "therefore" symbol, the conclusion we hope to derive. It will be placed on the last premise line to remind us what our goal is. From the first two premises we can deduce "$A \supset C$" by chain argument:

$p \supset q$	$A \supset B$
$q \supset r$	$B \supset C$
$\therefore p \supset r$	$\therefore A \supset C$

Because "$A \supset C$" follows necessarily from the given premises, it has to be true if they are, so it can now be used just like a premise. From it and the third original premise we can deduce "$A \supset D$."

$p \supset q$	$A \supset C$
$q \supset r$	$C \supset D$
$\therefore p \supset r$	$\therefore A \supset D$

From "$A \supset D$" and the fourth original premise, we can deduce "$A \supset E$," so we know the original argument is valid.

$$p \supset q$$
$$q \supset r$$
$$\therefore p \supset r$$

$$A \supset D$$
$$D \supset E$$
$$\therefore A \supset E$$

The completed proof looks like this:

1. $A \supset B$ Premise
2. $B \supset C$ Premise
3. $C \supset D$ Premise
4. $D \supset E$ $/\therefore A \supset E$ Premise/Desired Conclusion
5. $A \supset C$ From (1) and (2) by chain argument
6. $A \supset D$ From (5) and (3) by chain argument
7. $A \supset E$ From (6) and (4) by chain argument

In constructing formal deductions using the rules of inference, it is important to remember that they may be used only in deriving entire lines from entire lines. For example, the premise "$A \supset (B \& C)$" could <u>not</u> be used to derive "$A \supset B$" or "B" or "C" by conjunctive simplification. In order for us to use simplification, the dominant operator must be the ampersand. From "$(X \supset Y) \& Z$" we <u>can</u> derive "$X \supset Y$" or "Z."

Unlike truth table proofs, which can always be completed by following a finite number of clearly defined steps, formal derivations are more like solving a maze. One must get from here (the premises) to there (the conclusion), and some of the routes lead to dead ends. One may fail to complete the maze because one keeps trying ineffectual routes. There may be no single best strategy for trying to solve formal deductions, but we suggest something similar to working on a maze by working both from the entrance going forward and from the exit going backward. In a derivation, this means taking the premises and seeing where they seem to be leading you and, at the same time, taking the conclusion and attempting to see where it might come from.

Say we are to construct a formal derivation for

$$\sim E$$
$$D \supset E$$
$$D \lor J$$
$$\therefore J$$

We might notice that the first and second premises match the premises of *modus tollens* so that we can derive "$\sim D$."

$$D \supset E$$
$$\sim E$$
$$\therefore \sim D$$

$$p \supset q$$
$$\sim q$$
$$\therefore \sim p$$

The conclusion "$\sim D$" may now be treated as a premise and combined with the third original premise to yield "J" by disjunctive argument.

$$D \lor J$$
$$\sim D$$
$$\therefore J$$

$$p \lor q$$
$$\sim p$$
$$\therefore q$$

These then are the steps in the formal proof.

1. $\sim E$ Premise
2. $D \supset E$ Premise

3. $D \vee J$ $/\therefore J$ Premise/Conclusion
4. $\sim D$ From (1) and (2) by *modus tollens*
5. J From (3) and (4) by disjunctive argument

For most arguments, especially longer ones, most people have better results by working backward from the conclusion.

Let us work on this argument:

$X \supset \sim Y$
$X \vee Z$
$\sim\sim Y$
$\therefore Z$

next-to-last step   last step

These boxes will be used for our guesses about the steps in the derivation, and we know the last line has to be the derivation of "Z."

next-to-last step   last step

I see a premise that has "Z" as the right disjunct, and since there is one rule (disjunctive argument) that has a disjunction as one premise and one of the disjuncts as the conclusion, I guess that this may be the last step.

disj. argument

next-to-last step   last step

To complete the disjunctive argument, we know the second premise would have to be "$\sim X$," so it is written in but circled to indicate that it is "missing."

disj. argument

next-to-last step   last step

Moving to the box preceding the one we have been using, we write "$\sim X$" as the conclusion and proceed, as before, to make a guess about where it could come from.

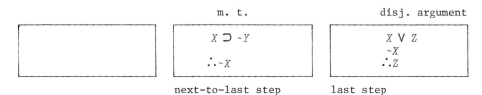

next-to-last step   last step

I see a premise, "$X \supset \sim Y$," that has "X" as the antecedent and realize that *modus tollens* is a rule that derives the denial of an antecedent, so it is a plausible candidate for this step.

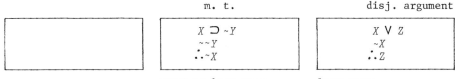

next-to-last step   last step

The other premise, in order to fit the *modus tollens* pattern, must be "$\sim\sim Y$" so it is written in. However, unlike the "last step" box that had a missing premise, both of these premises are given to us in the original argument. This means we do not need the box on the left, because whenever we get to a point where there are no missing parts, we have all the information we need in order to write out the formal derivation. The box furthest to the left that is not empty is the first line after the premises, and all successive boxes to the right of that one are successive lines in the proof.

1. $X \supset \sim Y$ Premise
2. $X \lor Z$ Premise
3. $\sim\sim Y$ $\therefore Z$ Premise/Conclusion
4. $\sim X$ From (1) and (3) by *modus tollens*
5. Z From (2) and (4) by disjunctive argument

Arguments that require transformation rules for their demonstration allow many additional lines of attack. It must be emphasized, however, that transformation rules, unlike rules of inference, allow changes to either whole lines or parts of lines. For example, the premise "$A \supset (B \& C)$" could be used to derive "$A \supset (C \& B)$" by commutation.

Practice Exercises

Construct a formal proof for each of the following. For the first few, the number of additional steps that are required is indicated.

A. 1. $\sim S \& \sim R$ B. 1. X
    2. $\sim S \supset \sim T$ $\therefore \sim T$ 2. Y $\therefore (X \& Y) \lor (Z \& W)$
    3.   3.
    4.   4.

C.
1. $A \supset B$
2. $C \supset A$
3. $\sim B$ $/\therefore \sim C$
4.
5.

D.
1. $A \supset B$
2. $C \supset A$
3. $\sim B$ $/\therefore \sim C$
4.
5.

E.
1. $A \supset B$
2. $\sim A \supset D$
3. $\sim B$ $/\therefore D$
4.
5.

F.
1. $R \supset S$
2. $(R \supset S) \supset T$ $/\therefore T$
3.
4.

G.
1. R
2. $(\sim B \supset C) \ \& \ (\sim X \supset Y)$
3. $R \supset (\sim B \lor \sim X)$ $/\therefore C \lor Y$
4.
5.

H.
1. R
2. $C \lor D$
3. $R \supset \sim C$ $/\therefore D$
4.
5.

I.
1. $X \supset Y$
2. $Y \supset Z$
3. X $/\therefore Z$
4.
5.

J.
1. $X \supset Y$
2. $Y \supset Z$
3. X $/\therefore Z$
4.
5.

K.
1. $X \supset \sim Y$
2. $W \supset Y$
3. X $/\therefore \sim W$
4.
5.

L.
1. $X \supset \sim Y$
2. $X \lor Z$
3. $\sim\sim Y$ $/\therefore Z$
4.
5.

M.
1. $\sim A \lor \sim V$
2. $W \supset V$
3. $\sim\sim A$ $/\therefore \sim W$
4.
5.

N.
1. $\sim(X \ \& \ Y) \ \& \ (A \supset B)$
2. $(J \lor \sim K) \supset (X \ \& \ Y)$ $/\therefore \sim(J \lor \sim K)$
3.
4.

O.
1. $\sim(J \ \& \ K)$
2. $\sim L \supset \sim M$
3. $(J \ \& \ K) \lor (\sim M \supset \sim O)$ $/\therefore \sim L \supset \sim O$
4.
5.

P.
1. $\sim T$
2. $R \supset T$
3. $S \lor U$ $/\therefore (S \lor U) \ \& \ \sim R$
4.
5.

Q.
1. $L \supset M$
2. $(L \ \& \ M) \supset (S \lor T)$ $/\therefore L \ \& \ (S \lor T)$
3.
4.

R.
1. $(J \supset \sim K) \ \& \ \sim(B \lor C)$
2. $\sim K \supset S$ $/\therefore J \supset S$
3.
4.

S.
1. $\sim(X \ \& \ Y) \supset (R \supset T)$
2. $(R \supset T) \supset (J \ \& \ K)$ $/\therefore [\sim(X \ \& \ Y) \supset (J \ \& \ K)] \lor [(L \supset \sim M) \ \& \ A]$

T.
1. A
2. $\sim A$ $/\therefore [B]$

U.
1. $R \lor N$
2. $(R \lor N) \supset \sim N$ $/\therefore R$

V.
1. $(S \supset T) \supset \sim(O \lor P)$
2. $(O \lor P) \lor (Q \ \& \ R)$
3. $S \supset T$ $/\therefore Q \ \& \ R$

W.
1. $(\sim W \lor K) \ \& \ (L \supset \sim V)$
2. $\sim\sim W$ $/\therefore K$

X.
1. $(R \supset T) \supset (J \ \& \ K)$
2. $(X \ \& \ Y) \supset (R \supset T)$ $/\therefore [\sim(X \ \& \ Y) \supset (J \ \& \ K)] \lor [(X \lor L) \supset M]$

Y.
1. $(\sim B \supset C) \ \& \ [(R \ \& \ S) \supset T]$
2. $(G \ \& \ H) \lor [\sim B \lor (R \ \& \ S)]$
3. $\sim(G \ \& \ H)$ $/\therefore C \lor T$

Z.
1. $X \supset \sim Y$
2. $B \lor Q$
3. $\sim Y \supset A$ $/\therefore (B \lor Q) \ \& \ (X \supset A)$

AA. 1. $(R \& S) \vee (A \& B)$
2. $\sim E \vee \sim F$
3. $\sim (R \& S)$ $/\!\!:\!\!.(\sim E \vee \sim F) \& (A \& B)$

BB. 1. $(A \supset R) \supset T$
2. $(A \supset R) \vee (K \& L)$
3. $\sim T$ $/\!\!:\!\!.K \& L$

CC. 1. $\sim J$
2. $J \vee (K \supset L)$ $/\!\!:\!\!.(K \supset L) \& \sim J$

DD. 1. $G \supset (H \& F)$
2. $E \supset (J \& I)$
3. G $/\!\!:\!\!.[E \supset (J \& I)] \& [G \& (H \& F)]$

EE. 1. $(\sim S \& \sim T) \& [(L \& Q) \vee D]$ $/\!\!:\!\!.\sim S \& (\sim S \& \sim T)$

FF. 1. $\sim (J \& K) \& \sim (L \& M)$
2. $(A \& B) \vee \sim C$
3. $(A \& B) \supset (J \& K)$ $/\!\!:\!\!.\sim C$

GG. 1. $[X \supset (X \& Y)] \& (W \supset V)$
2. $(B \vee A) \supset D$
3. $X \vee (B \vee A)$ $/\!\!:\!\!.(X \& Y) \vee D$

HH. 1. $R \supset S$
2. $[L \vee (M \& N)] \supset [(R \& S) \supset T]$
3. R
4. $L \& M$ $/\!\!:\!\!.T$

II. 1. $I \supset (I \& J)$
2. $I \vee (\sim\sim K \& \sim\sim J)$
3. $L \supset \sim K$
4. $\sim (I \& J)$ $/\!\!:\!\!.\sim L \vee \sim J$

8-4

Indirect Proof, or Reductio ad Absurdum

Section Objective

1. Learn to use indirect proof as an aid in proving certain arguments to be valid.

Key Term Review

1. Indirect proof or *reductio ad adsurdum*: a method of proof that a conclusion follows necessarily from the premises (the argument is valid) by showing that assuming denial of the conclusion leads to a contradiction (which is necessarily false).

Summary

Some formal derivations are facilitated by the method of indirect proof. After the premises have been listed, write the denial of the conclusion on the next line and label it as such. Then proceed to try to derive a contradiction. If you can, this proves the conclusion follows from the original premises. The rationale is as follows:

If the original premises plus the negation of the conclusion allow the derivation of a contradiction (a necessarily false statement), then it would be impossible for the premises and the conclusion's negation to all be true, because the false conclusion of a valid argument means that not all the premises are true. Now assume the original premises are true; the conclusion's negation (assumed as an additional premise) must be false, and the conclusion must therefore be true. Hence, any situation that made the premises true would necessarily make the conclusion true, and this is the very definition of a valid argument.

Proving Invalidity: Abbreviated Truth Tables

Section Objective

1. Learn to demonstrate the invalidity of arguments by using a modified (shorter) truth table.

Summary

Although a completed formal derivation proves that a given argument is valid, the mere failure to construct a formal derivation does not tell us whether the argument is invalid or whether we were just not clever enough to find a way to complete the formal proof. Hence, we must return to truth tables for a demonstration of invalidity.

One does not, however, have to construct an entire truth table. A short truth table (equivalent to one row in a full truth table) can quickly be constructed, and it will easily prove an invalid argument to be invalid.

An invalid argument can have all true premises and a false conclusion, so we begin by assigning truth values to the simple statements in the conclusion to make it false. Then we will try to assign truth values to the statements in the premises to make them all true. If we succeed, we have proved the argument invalid.

Consider

$A \supset B$
$B \supset C$
$B \lor C$

For the conclusion to be false, both "B" and "C" must be false. If "B" and "C" are false, then the second premise is true. If "B" is false, the first premise will be true on the assignment of "false" to "A." So, since it is possible for the premises to both be true and the conclusion to be false, the argument is invalid.

In other words, we have just constructed the following truth table row:

A	B	C	$A \supset B$	$B \supset C$	$B \lor C$
F	F	F	T	T	F

Practice Exercises

Using the short truth table method, prove the invalidity of each of the following arguments:

1. p & q
   $p \lor r$
   $\therefore r$

2. $p \supset (q \supset r)$
   p
   $\therefore r$

3. $p \supset q$
   $p \lor r$
   $\therefore q$

4. $p \supset q$
   $q \supset r$
   $\therefore p$ & r

5. $p \supset q$
   $p \lor r$
   $\therefore q \supset {\sim}r$

6. $(p \supset r)$ & $(s \supset q)$
   $r \lor q$
   $\therefore p \lor s$

7. $p \supset q$
   $p \lor r$
   $\therefore q \lor {\sim}r$

8. $(p \supset q) \lor (q \supset r)$
   $p \lor q$
   $\therefore q$ & r

CHAPTER 9
PREDICATE LOGIC

OVERVIEW

Categorical logic (Chapters 5 and 6) can deal with arguments that the truth-functional logic of Chapters 7 and 8 cannot. Conversely, the truth-functional logic of Chapters 7 and 8 can deal with arguments that categorical logic cannot. But predicate logic, or quantification, is a much more fruitful system than either of the others. By dealing with <u>both</u> the internal structure of single statements (as does categorical logic) and the structures of compound statements (as does truth-functional logic), predicate logic allows us to analyze a large number of complicated arguments, many of which could not be evaluated by either of the other logics.

SECTION REVIEWS

Basic Concepts of Predicate Logic

Section Objectives

1. Become familiar with the basic concepts of predicate logic.

2. Identify the subject and the (logical) predicate of simple statements.

3. Determine whether a predicate is monadic or polyadic.

4. Distinguish between singular and general statements.

5. Learn to symbolize statements.

Key Term Review

1. <u>General or Subject term</u>: a word or expression that describes or designates a general class of individuals.

2. <u>Predicate term</u>: an expression, represented by a capital letter, that denotes the properties or relations that are claimed to apply to the subject of the statement (either as a general term or as an individual constant).

3. <u>Monadic predicate</u>: a predicate applying to a single individual.

4. <u>Polyadic predicate</u>: a predicate that refers to some relation between two or more individuals.

5. <u>Propositional function</u>: an expression that contains an individual variable and that becomes a proposition when the individual variable is replaced by an individual constant.

6. <u>Individual variable</u>: a marker to represent any individual whatsoever. Usually the lower-case "x," "y," "z," or sometimes "w" is used for individual variables.

7. <u>Individual constant</u>: the name of an individual (any particular person, object, or entity). Lower-case letters from a through v (or w) are used to symbolize them.

8. <u>Existential quantifier</u>: a symbol used to mean "at least one": $(\exists x)$, $(\exists y)$, and so on.

9. <u>Universal quantifier</u>: a symbol to mean "all": (x), (y), and so on.

10. <u>Singular statements</u>: statements containing predicate terms and names designating specific individuals (individual constants).

11. <u>General statements</u>: statements that contain predicate terms, quantifiers (such as <u>all</u>, <u>no</u>, and <u>some</u>) and general terms as subjects.

<u>Summary</u>

Singular statements will be analyzed into individuals and predicates (the properties or relation that the individuals have). Capital letters will stand for predicates; lower-case letters "a" through "v" will stand for individuals and are placed to the right of predicates. "Elsie is a cat" would be symbolized as "Ce," where "C" is the predicate or property of "catness" and "e" represent "Elsie." Analyzing general statements requires that we use a symbol for the appropriate quantifier. Thus, for example, if one wants to say "something is a cat" or "cats exist" the existential quantifier and an individual variable must be used: $(\exists x)Cx$. $\exists x$, $\exists y$, and so on mean "at least one" or "there exists at least one," so "$(\exists x)Cx$" might be rather literally translated into English as "there exists at least one x such that x is a cat." To make the false statement that everything is a cat requires the universal quantifier "(x)" and an individual variable: $(x)Cx$. In other words, "for every x, x is a cat."

<u>Practice Exercises</u>

A list of singular statements follows. Symbolize each statement.

1. Jane ran.

2. Spot did not jump.

3. If Jane runs, Spot runs.

4. If Dick runs or Jane jumps, then Spot jumps.

5. Trigger is not a dog.

6. Spot is a dog.

7. Spot is a dog with spots.

Quantifiers and Truth-Functional Operators

Section Objectives

1. Learn to distinguish compound statements from compound propositional functions.

2. Gain further skill in symbolizing general statements.

3. Learn to recognize the scope of a quantifier.

4. Learn to tell whether variables are free or bound.

Key Term Review

1. <u>Compound statement</u>: a statement that has one or more simple statements as components.

2. <u>Compound propositional function</u>: a propositional function that has one or more propositional functions as components.

3. <u>Scope of a quantifier</u>: the part of a quantified propositional function to which the quantifier applies. That part of the propositional function is said to be governed by, or bound by, the quantifier.

Summary

"Tarzan is brave and handsome" can be thought of as a compound statement that could be symbolized as *"Bt & Ht."* This is a substitution instance of the propositional function *"Bx & Hx."* This function could be quantified to mean there exists at least one *x* such that *x* is both brave and handsome: (∃x)(Bx & Hx). It is usually best to be as specific as possible in listing predicates. The claim that Tarzan is a brave and handsome man should be translated as *"Bt & Ht & Mt"* where the predicate *"M"* means "is a male."

The scope of the quantifier or the amount of the propositional function that is governed by the quantifier is indicated by parentheses if necessary. The punctuation works like the punctuation for the tilde--the scope of the quantifier is stipulated to be the smallest unit the punctuation allows.

Quantifying Categorical Statements

Section Objective

1. Learn to translate the four categorical forms (the *A*, *E*, *I*, and *O* of categorical logic) into the notation of predicate logic.

Key Term Review

1. <u>Universal affirmative or *A*</u>: a statement in which the entire subject class is said to be included in the predicate class, such as "All Danes are redheads."

2. Universal negative or *E*: a statement in which the entire subject class is said to be excluded from the predicate class, such as "No Danes are redheads."

3. Particular affirmative or *I*: a statement in which some members of the subject class are said to be included in the predicate class, such as "Some Danes are redheads."

4. Particular negative or *O*: a statement in which some members of the predicate class are said to be excluded from the predicate class, such as "Some Danes are not redheads."

Summary

The traditional categorical statements will be symbolized in a standard way in predicate logic. The *A* and *E* forms of statements will be conceived of from the hypothetical point of view. Statements of the form "All *S* are *P*," such as "All cats are mammals," will be interpreted as claiming that, if something (anything) is a cat, then it is also a mammal. This requires a universal quantifier quantifying a hypothetical: $(x)(Cx \supset Mx)$. That is, for any x, if x is a cat, then x is a mammal.

Statements of the form "No *S* are *P*," again from the hypothetical viewpoint, will require us to say that, for any x, if x is an *S*, then x is not a *P*: $(x)(Sx \supset {\sim}Px)$.

Particular statements will always assert the existence of at least one member of the subject class, and the existential quantifier must be used. "Some *S* are *P*" means that at least one thing is an *S* and is also a *P*: $(x)(Sx \& Px)$. And "Some *S* are not *P*" means that at least one thing is an *S* and is not a *P*: $(\exists x)(Sx \& {\sim}Px)$. In summary:

Rule 1: *A* form: $(x)(Sx \supset Px)$

Rule 2: *E* form: $(x)(Sx \supset {\sim}Px)$

Rule 3: *I* form: $(\exists x)(Sx \& Px)$

Rule 4: *O* form: $(\exists x)(Sx \& {\sim}Px)$

Practice Exercises

Translate each of the following.

1. Some students are confused. (Sx, Cx)

2. Some quiet students are not confused. (Sx, Qx, Cx)

3. No pigs fly. (Px, Fx)

4. Some metals are liquid. (Mx, Lx)

5. All wombats are marsupials. (Wx, Mx)

6. Not all birds can fly. (Bx, Fx)

7. Only elephants have trunks. (Ex, Tx)

8. All typists are efficient, kind, and wonderful. (Tx, Ex, Kx, Wx)

9. No teachers are infallible. (Tx, Ix)

10. All creatures that are fallible are mortal. (Fx, Mx)

11. Not all students are omniscient. (Sx, Ox)

12. Some loving persons are unloved. (Lx, Ux)

13. A bat is not a bird. (Tx, Rx)

14. Blessed are the merciful, for they shall obtain mercy. (Mx, Ox)

15. Whosoever shall break one of these least commandments, and shall teach men so, he shall be called the least in the kingdom of heaven. (Bx, Tx, Cx)

16. Whosoever is angry with his brother without a cause shall be in danger of judgment. (Ax, Dx)

17. When thou prayest, enter into thy closet, and when thou hast shut the door, pray to thy Father which is in secret; and thy Father which seeth in secret shall reward thee openly. (Px, Ex, Sx, Fy, Ry)

9-4

Quantifier Negation

Section Objectives

1. Learn equivalences based on the denial of a statement's contradiction.
2. Learn equivalences based on changes affecting quantifiers.

Summary

In the sections on categorical logic we learned that, in both the existential and the hypothetical points of view, A and O statements are contradictories, and E and I statements are contradictories. So of course they are contradictories even if we are translating them into the symbolization of predicate logic.

Because the assertion of an A form is equivalent to the denial of an O form, this means the "$(x)(Sx \supset Px) \equiv \sim(\exists x)(Sx \& \sim Px)$. Similarly, the E form is equivalent to the denial of the I form: $(x)(Sx \supset {\sim}Px) \equiv {\sim}(\exists x)(Sx \ \& \ Px)$. The complete set of equivalences is

All S are P:	A:	$(x)(Sx \supset Px) \equiv {\sim}(\exists x)(Sx \ \& \ {\sim}Px)$	Denial of O
No S are P:	E:	$(x)(Sx \supset {\sim}Px) \equiv {\sim}(\exists x)(Sx \ \& \ Px)$	Denial of I
Some S are P:	I:	$(\exists x)(Sx \ \& \ Px) \equiv {\sim}(x)(Sx \supset {\sim}Px)$	Denial of E
Some S are not P:	O:	$(\exists x)(Sx \ \& \ {\sim}Px) \equiv {\sim}(x)(Sx \supset Px)$	Denial of A

But note that, whereas the A form "$(x)(Sx \supset Px)$" is equivalent to the denial of the O form "${\sim}(\exists x)(Sx \ \& \ {\sim}Px)$," it is also equivalent to "$(x){\sim}(Sx \ \& \ {\sim}Px)$." "For any x, if it's a cat then it's a mammal" is equivalent to "for any x, it's false that it's a cat and not a mammal." To generalize for any formula yields two quantifier negation (Q.N.) tranformation rules.

Q.N. Rule 1 ${\sim}(x)Sx \equiv (\exists x){\sim}Sx$
Q.N. Rule 2 ${\sim}(\exists x)Sx \equiv (x){\sim}Sx$

We can expand the set of earlier equivalences:

A: $(x)(Sx \supset Px) \equiv {\sim}(\exists x)(Sx \ \& \ {\sim}Px) \equiv (x){\sim}(Sx \ \& \ {\sim}Px)$
E: $(x)(Sx \supset {\sim}Px) \equiv {\sim}(\exists x)(Sx \ \& \ Px) \equiv (x){\sim}(Sx \ \& \ Px)$
I: $(\exists x)(Sx \ \& \ Px) \equiv {\sim}(x)(Sx \supset {\sim}Px) \equiv (\exists x){\sim}(Sx \supset {\sim}Px)$
O: $(\exists x)(Sx \ \& \ {\sim}Px) \equiv {\sim}(x)(Sx \supset Px) \equiv (\exists x){\sim}(Sx \supset Px)$

Also, by using the Q.N. rules along with the double negation rule, we find

${\sim}(\exists x){\sim}Sx \equiv (x){\sim}{\sim}Sx \equiv (x)Sx$ and
${\sim}(x){\sim}Sx \equiv (\ x){\sim}{\sim}Sx \equiv (\ x)Sx$

Ignoring the middle step, we have

${\sim}(\exists x){\sim}Sx \equiv (x)Sx$ and
${\sim}(x){\sim}Sx \equiv (\exists x)Sx$

We could expand our earlier equivalences for A, E, I, and O forms even further:

A: $(x)(Sx \supset Px) \equiv {\sim}(\exists x)(Sx \ \& \ {\sim}Px) \equiv (x){\sim}(Sx \ \& \ {\sim}Px) \equiv {\sim}(\exists x){\sim}(Sx \supset Px)$
E: $(x)(Sx \supset {\sim}Px) \equiv {\sim}(\exists x)(Sx \ \& \ Px) \equiv (x){\sim}(Sx \ \& \ Px) \equiv {\sim}(\exists x){\sim}(Sx \supset {\sim}Px)$
I: $(\exists x)(Sx \ \& \ Px) \equiv {\sim}(x)(Sx \supset {\sim}Px) \equiv (\exists x){\sim}(Sx \supset {\sim}Px) \equiv {\sim}(x){\sim}(Sx \ \& \ Px)$
O: $(\exists x)(Sx \ \& \ {\sim}Px) \equiv {\sim}(x)(Sx \supset Px) \equiv (\exists x){\sim}(Sx \supset Px) \equiv {\sim}(x){\sim}(Sx \ \& \ {\sim}Px)$

Practice Exercises

I. Translate each of the following pairs of statements and show how one is equivalent to the other.

  1. a. It is not the case that no pigs swin.
      b. Some pigs swim.

    (Hint: Use conditional exchange.)

  2. a. It is not the case that all spies are double agents.
      b. Some spies are not double agents.

II. Show that the members of each of the following pairs of statements are contradictory by showing that the denial of one can be transformed into the other.

1. a. $(\exists x)\,[(Ax \lor Bx) \lor Cx\,]$
   b. $(x)\sim[\sim Ax \supset (Bx \lor Cx)]$

2. a. $(x)\,(Gx \supset \sim Hx)$
   b. $(\exists x)\,(Gx \,\&\, Hx)$

3. a. $\sim(x)\sim Fx$
   b. $\sim(\exists x)\sim\sim Fx$

4. a. $(x)\,[(Ax \,\&\, Bx) \supset Cx)]$
   b. $(\exists x)\sim[Ax \supset (Bx \supset Cx)]$

5. a. $(\exists x)\sim(Fx \,\&\, \sim Gx)$
   b. $(x)\sim(Fx \supset Gx)$

The Domain of Discourse and Truth-Functional Expansion

Section Objectives

1. Recognize the usefulness of sometimes restricting the domain of discourse.

2. Become familiar with the method of truth-functional expansion of universally quantified and existentially quantified general statements.

3. Learn the meanings of logically true, logically false, and logically contingent formulas in predicate logic.

Key Term Review

1. **Domain**: the universe of discourse or the domain of discourse is the group of all individuals referred to by the statements in an argument.

Summary

The universal quantifier ordinarily makes a claim about all entities, but this universal domain of discourse may be restricted to enable translations to be more easily made. For example, suppose we were dealing with mathematical concepts, were making lots of statements about positive integers, and wanted to assert "All positive integers are either odd or even." If we had no restriction on the domain, we would assert: $(x)\,[(Ix \,\&\, Px) \supset (Ox \lor Ex)]$. If the domain were restricted to integers, we could write $(x)\,[Px \supset (Ox \lor Ex)]$. If the domain were restricted to positive integers, we could simply write $(x)\,(Ox \lor Ex)$.

A truth-functional expansion of universally quantified general statements such as "$(x)Fx$" is the conjunction of all the singular statements represented by that general statement:

$$Fa_1 \,\&\, Fa_2 \,\&\, Fa_3 \,\ldots\, Fa_n$$

A truth-functional expansion of an existentially quantified statement such as "$(\exists x)Fx$" is the disjunction of singular statements:

$$Fa_1 \lor Fa_2 \lor Fa_3 \lor \,\ldots\, Fa_n$$

155

A formula in predicate logic is logically (or quantificationally) true if all possible substitution instances of it are true. A formula is logically false if all substitution instances of it are false. If some substitution instances of a formula are true and some are false, the formula is logically contingent. If two formulas have the same truth values on every interpretation, they are logically equivalent.

We may prove that a formula is not logically true by finding a substitution instance that is false in at least one interpretation. Consider

   $(x)(Fx$ & $\sim Fx)$

Using a two-member domain, we can construct the following expansion:

   $(Fa$ & $\sim Fa)$ & $(Fb$ & $\sim Fb)$

and we can construct a truth table:

Fa	Fb	$\sim Fa$	$\sim Fb$	Fa & $\sim Fa$	Fb & $\sim Fb$	$(Fa$ & $\sim Fa)$ & $(Fb$ & $\sim Fb)$
T	T	F	F	F	F	F

We may prove that a formula is not logically false by finding at least one true substitution instance.

Practice Exercises

Assume a two-member domain and prove that each of the following statements is logically contingent.

1. $(\exists x)(Fx$ & $\sim Gx)$

2. $(x)Hx$

3. $(\exists x)(Fx$ V $Gx)$

4. $(x)(Hx \supset Ix)$

5. $(\exists x)(Hx \equiv Ix)$

Formal Deductions in Monadic Predicate Logic

Section Objective

1. Learn to do formal deductions in predicate logic using all the rules from truth-functional logic, the quantifier negation rules, and four new rules introduced in this section.

Key Term Review

1. <u>Monadic predicate logic</u>: predicate logic restricted to one-place predicates.

2. <u>Universal instantiation</u>: the process of deriving a substitution instance from a universally quantified statement.

3. <u>Existential instantiation</u>: the process of deriving a substitution instance from an existentially quantified statement.

4. Universal generalization: the process of deriving a universally quantified statement from a statement containing an individual constant.

5. Existential generalization: the process of deriving an existentially
quantified statement from a statement containing an individual constant.

Summary

This section presents the remaining rules necessary to yield a sound and
complete deduction system for monadic predicate logic. The complete system
uses

1. The rules of inference and transformation rules from Chapters 7 and 8
   (see Table 8-2).

2. The quantifier negation rules presented in Section 9-4.

3. The four rules of instantiation and generalization presented in
   this section.

The universal instantiation (U.I.) rule states that we may derive from a
universally quantified statement any of its substitution instances. U.I.
cannot be applied to parts of compound statements. The proof that L.C. is
a mammal from "all cats are mammals" and "L.C. is a cat" is as follows:

1. $(x)(Cx \supset Mx)$ Premise
2. C_L $/\therefore M$ Premise/Conclusion
3. $C_L \supset M_L$ 1, U.I.
4. M_L 3, 2 *Modus Ponens*

The existential instantiation (E.I.) rule allows us to derive an instance of
an existentially quantified statement, provided that the individual constant
does not appear in the premises or the conclusion or on a previous line in
the proof. The reason for the restriction is that, if the premise asserts
that there is at least one x such that x is an A, $(\exists x)Ax$, we don't know
which x has the property. If we pick a constant that is mentioned elsewhere, we may erroneously assert that this individual has property x when
it doesn't. We shouldn't be able to derive "Reagan is a Democrat politician"
from "Some politicians are Democrats." Thus, the restriction prevents the
following proof:

1. $(\exists x)(Px \ \& \ Dx)$ $/\therefore Pr \supset Dr$ Premise/Conclusion
2. $Pr \ \& \ Dr$ Wrong use of E.I. from 1

Universal generalization is the rule that allows the derivation of a universally quantified statement from a statement with an individual constant so
long as the constant did not appear in a premise or come from E.I. Thus,
the move from "one" (an individual constant) to "all" (a universally quantified statement) can be made only if that individual constant was obtained
from a universal statement in the first place.

The rule of existential generalization allows us to infer an existentially
quantified statement from any statement with an individual constant.

Practice Exercises

Construct a proof of validity for each of the following.

1. $(x)(Hx \supset Ix)$
   $\underline{Ha}$
   $\therefore Ic$

2. $(y)(Jy \supset Ky)$
   $\underline{Jb}$
   $\therefore (\exists y)Ky$

3. $(z)(Az \supset Bz)$
   $\underline{(z)(Bz \supset Cz)}$
   $\therefore (z)Az \supset Cz$

4. $(x)(Ax \supset {\sim}Bx)$
   $\underline{Bd}$
   $\therefore {\sim}Ad$

5. $(y)(Fy \supset Gy)$
   $\underline{(\exists y)(Hy \ \& \ Fy)}$
   $\therefore (\exists y)(Hy \ \& \ Gy)$

6. $(\exists z)(Lz \ \& \ {\sim}Mz)$
   $\underline{(z)(Lz \supset Oz)}$
   $\therefore (\exists z)(Oz \ \& \ {\sim}Mz)$

9-7

Proving Invalidity

Section Objective

1. Learn to prove the invalidity of arguments in predicate logic by two methods: (a) constructing invalidating natural interpretations and (b) using abbreviated truth tables for model universes.

Key Term Review

1. Model universe: a finite and small set of individuals.

2. Invalidating natural interpretation: an argument with all true premises and a false conclusion and with the same structure as a given argument that has been invented to show that the given argument has an invalid form.

Summary

An invalidating natural interpretation can be used to show the invalidity of an argument. This, of course, can be a complex task for a complicated argument.

Another method, which is similar to the shorter truth table method in Chapter 8, makes use of a model universe. One picks a small number of individuals to represent the statement variables in the argument. If, for a universe of this size, it is possible to construct a truth table to show that the premises could be true while the conclusion was false, then this proves the original argument to be invalid.

Failure to achieve this might occur because the number of individuals chosen is too small. For monadic predicates, however, the largest number of individuals that needs to be considered is 2^n, where n is the number of predicates in the argument.

Practice Exercises

Prove each of the following arguments invalid by (a) an invalidating natural interpretation or (b) a model universe and an abbreviated truth table.

1. $(x)(Cx \supset Mx)$
    Ms
    $\therefore Cs$

2. $(x)(Ax \supset Bx)$
    $(\exists x)(Ax \lor Cx)$
    $\therefore (x)(Bx \supset \sim Cx)$

3. $(\exists x)(Dx \& Ex)$
    $(\exists x)(Dx \lor Fx)$
    $\therefore (\exists x)Fx$

4. $(x)[Rx \supset (Sx \supset Tx)]$
    $(\exists x)Rx$
    $\therefore (\exists x)Tx$

5. $(x)(Vx \supset Wx)$
    $(x)(Wx \supset Yx)$
    $\therefore (x)(Yx \supset Vx)$

6. $(x)(Dx \supset Ex)$
    $(x)(Ex \supset Fx)$
    $\therefore (\exists x)Dx \& Fx$

7. $(x)[(Ax \supset Bx) \& (Cx \supset Dx)]$
    $(\exists x)(Bx \lor Dx)$
    $\therefore (\exists x)(Ax \lor Cx)$

8. $(x)(Bx \supset Qx)$
    $(x)(\sim Bx \lor \sim Rx)$
    $\therefore (x)Qx \lor Rx$

PART THREE: INDUCTIVE REASONING

CHAPTER 10
GENERALIZATION, ANALOGY, AND PROBABILITY

OVERVIEW

The principles for appraising deductive arguments are presented in several preceding chapters. But we also need to understand how to evaluate inductive arguments. Two major kinds of inductive arguments are arguments by generalization and arguments by analogy. This chapter is devoted to a study of the standards for evaluating these two kinds of inductive arguments.

SECTION REVIEWS   *10-1*
Arguing to Probable Conclusions

Section Objectives

1. Distinguish among the various concepts of probability.

2. Identify the kind of probability concept exhibited in various probability statements.

3. Distinguish between the reliability and the strength of an inductive argument.

4. Identify the criteria for assessing the reliability of an inductive argument.

Key Term Review

1. Reliable inductive argument: an inductive argument in which the premises, if supposed to be true, would make the conclusion probable to the degree claimed for it.

2. Rational credibility (of an argument): the degree to which it is reasonable to believe the conclusion.

3. Relative frequency (of an event): the number of (observed) favorable outcomes divided by the number of (observed) outcomes.

4. Statistical probability (of an event): closeness to the mathematical limits toward which the relative frequencies converge as the number of observed outcomes increases indefinitely.

5. "Classical" or mathematical probability (of a statement): the number of possible favorable outcomes divided by all possible outcomes.

6. Modal quantifier: words that indicate the degree of probability claimed for the conclusion, such as possibility and highly likely.

Summary

In Chapter 2 we noted that no inductive argument is valid. And we added
that inductive arguments should not be evaluated in those terms, because
applying deductive standards reveals no difference between the best and
worst inductive arguments. Thus, we need different standards for evaluating
inductive arguments.

We evaluate inductive arguments in terms of their <u>reliability</u> and <u>strength</u>.
Let us consider reliability first. When someone advocates an inductive argument, he tacitly claims a certain degree of probability for the conclusion.
Often (but not always) there will be a word or phrase that indicates the
degree of probability claimed. If someone says the conclusion is "very
likely," he is making a stronger claim than if he were to say there is
"some reason" to believe the conclusion.

When evaluating an inductive argument's reliability, we take into account
the degree of probability the arguer claims for the conclusion. There are
three factors to consider in assessing an inductive argument's reliability:

1. The amount of evidence provided by the premises.

2. The relevance of that evidence to the conclusion.

3. The degree of probability claimed for the conclusion.

Consider this example:

1. Becky defeated Don at tennis last week.
2. So, there is some reason to believe that she'll beat him again.

There is not much evidence (only one match) provided by the premise. However, it is relevant to the conclusion, and only a low degree of probability
is claimed for the conclusion. (This is shown by the words "There is some
reason.") The amount of evidence provided must be considered in relation
to the degree of probability claimed. Because only a low degree of probability is claimed for the conclusion, less evidence is required than if a
higher degree were claimed. Thus, this argument is reliable.

But in Chapter 2 we said that inductive arguments are evaluated in terms of
their strength. Is that inconsistent with evaluating inductive arguments
in terms of reliability? What is the difference between reliability and
strength? Strength is a function of the probability of the conclusion,
given the premises. The difference between reliability and strength, then,
is that the probability the arguer claims for the conclusion is taken into
account only when determining an argument's reliability. It is not taken
into account when determining an argument's strength. There is nothing inconsistent about this. After determining an argument's reliability, we can
ask the further question about its strength. The argument about Becky and
Don, though reliable, is not strong. After all, the probability that she
will defeat him again, given that she defeated him in one match, is not
high. (Remember that we disregard the probability claimed for the conclusion when assessing an argument's strength.)

Contrast the foregoing argument with this one:

1. Becky is an internationally ranked tennis champion.
2. Becky slept 8 hours the night before the match, but Don slept only
    3 hours.

3. Becky defeated Don at tennis last week.
4. Don is a novice at tennis.
5. So, it is very probable that Becky will defeat Don again.

This argument and the first one are equally reliable. That is, they both establish their conclusions with the degree of probability claimed for each. However, they are not equally strong, for the second argument makes a better case for the unqualified conclusion, "Becky will defeat Don again." Since we want to distinguish between better or worse arguments for the same conclusion without modal quantifiers, we retain the criterion of strength in addition to reliability. But strength should not replace reliability. After all, it would be incorrect to say that the first argument is bad. Only a low degree of probability is claimed for the conclusion, so it does establish the conclusion with the degree of probability claimed for it.

Unlike deductive validity, neither the reliability nor the strength of an inductive argument is a consequence of its form alone. We disregard the content of an argument when we consider its form alone. But if we disregard all content, we have no way to figure out whether the premises are relevant to the conclusion, and we have to know whether the premises are relevant in order to determine either the reliability or the strength of the argument. Therefore, neither the reliability nor the strength of an inductive argument is a consequence of its form alone.

Just as the probability of a conclusion can change with the addition or deletion of premises, so the conclusions of inductive arguments can be revised in light of new evidence. The argument in Chapter 2 about the prosecutor's case against Shlomo illustrates this point.

In Chapter 2 we distinguished between empirical and *a priori* statements. This distinction pertains to how a statement is known. Probabilities are ascertained either *a priori* or empirically, depending on the concept of probability used.

Classical (or mathematical) probability is determined independently of empirical evidence. Finding out the classical probability of an event requires two assumptions: (1) all possible outcomes are known, and (2) the outcomes are equally probable. The second assumption, called the principle of indifference, limits the applicability of the mathematical concept greatly. Let us consider a simple case, that of flipping a fair coin. There are three possibilities of how the coin will land: (1) heads up, (2) tails up and (3) on its edge. Note that even in this simple case the principle of indifference does not obtain. If it did, the mathematical probability that the coin would land on its edge would be 1/3. If we disregard the highly improbable possibility that the coin will land on its edge, the mathematical probability that the coin will land heads up (or tails up) is 1/2. Please note that these mathematical probabilities were calculated without flipping a single coin. Our knowledge of the probability is thus *a priori*. Moreover, the argument whereby we calculate the probabilities is deductive. Here is a sketch of the deductive argument:

1. There are two possibilities (heads up or tails up).
2. Both possibilities are equally probable.
3. Therefore, the probability of each is 1/2 (or .5).

There is one probability in the example above, however, that could not be ascertained *a priori*. How is it known that the probability that the coin will land on its edge is much less than 1/3 (or .333...)? Mathematical (or "classical") probability will not help us here. We need to introduce the notion of <u>relative frequency</u> to cover this case and many others.

The reason we know that the probability that a coin will land on its edge is much less than 1/3 is that we have observed several tosses of fair coins (or have appropriate testimonial evidence) and the coins have rarely landed on their edges. That has happened much less frequently than 1/3 of the time. It is noteworthy that relative frequency, unlike "classical" probability, is thoroughly empirical. You must have observed some tosses of fair coins (or read or heard about such findings) in order to ascertain the relative frequency of a coin landing on its edge. There are many probability statements that employ the relative frequency concept.

Relative frequencies change, depending on how many observations have been made and on the outcomes. Suppose we interpret the coin toss case in terms of relative frequency and concern ourselves exclusively with the probability of the coin landing heads up. We toss the coin 10 times and the coin lands heads up 6 times. In that case, the relative frequency of heads is .6. We toss the coin 10 more times, and the result is that 11 of the 20 tosses were heads. The relative frequency of heads is then .55. We toss it 80 more times, and 51 of the results come up heads, making the relative frequency .51. Depending on the number and results of observations, the relative frequencies vary. This means that several different studies can yield different relative frequencies for the same kind of event. Thus, if we <u>defined</u> probability in terms of relative frequency, we would have conflicting results. That is why this kind of probability has been defined more indeterminately as <u>statistical probability</u>. If the sample in each of several studies is sufficiently large, the results will converge on a figure. The statistical probability of an event, then, is defined as a limited range of values that are <u>close to</u> the figure on which the relative frequencies converge as the number of observed outcomes increases indefinitely. The notion of statistical probability plays an important role in science, where there are often several studies of the same topic.

Practice Exercises

I. Identify the kind of probability concept in each of the following statements (relative frequency = RF; mathematical probability = MP; statistical probability = SP; rational credibility = RC). Rational credibility should be the answer only if the probability is more indeterminate than statistical probability. Use the space provided at the left. If necessary, briefly explain your answers.

1. _____ Although she said she would, Pam probably won't be here for dinner tomorrow night.

2. _____ The probability that I will draw a jack from this regular deck of cards is 1/13.

3. _____ Mende's facial expression and tone of voice showed that she was probably telling the truth.

4. _____ The probability that the sun will rise tomorrow is very high.

5. _____ The probability that the law of gravity is true is even greater than the probability that the sun will rise tomorrow.

6. _____ The chance of rain this afternoon is 80 percent.

7. _____ It is much more likely that a smoker will develop lung cancer than that a non-smoker will.

8. _____ The U.S. dollar will probably drop in value, relative to foreign currencies, during the next year.

9. _____ A woman probably will enter the race for President of the United States during the next election campaign.

10. _____ Marie's latest batch of lasagne is almost certainly first-rate.

11. _____ Bob's account of the conversation is probably unreliable, for he frequently distorts such matters.

12. _____ Cathleen will probably enjoy that joke.

13. _____ It is very unlikely that Jerry Falwell will ever vote for Senator Kennedy.

14. _____ It is probable that the U.S.S.R. will never launch a nuclear attack against the United States.

15. _____ The probability that a toss of this die will yield a two or a three is 1/3.

16. _____ There is a one-in-ten chance that any of the ten players will win the chess tournament.

17. _____ Ann-Marie is probably in room 3 teaching class now.

18. _____ It is likely that there will be much more violence in South Africa.

19. _____ Probably relations between the People's Republic of China and the United States will continue to improve.

20. _____ Eduardo will probably pass the exam with flying colors.

II. Indicate whether each of the following statements is true (T) or false (F).

1. _____ An argument can be reliable and not strong.

2. _____ Some inductive arguments are sound.

3. _____ The reliability of an inductive argument is sometimes a function of its form alone.

4. _____ "Classical" probabilities can be ascertained *a priori*.

5. _____ Relative frequencies can only be ascertained empirically.

6. _____ The concept of statistical probability is basically a refinement of relative frequency.

7. _____ Inductive arguments are evaluated only in terms of their strength.

8. _____ The word _relative_ in "relative frequency" means that the probability is relative to all the observations that have been made.

9. _____ The logician evaluates inductive arguments in terms of the reasonableness of believing the conclusion, given the premises.

10. _____ The probability of a conclusion of an inductive argument can change in light of new evidence.

III. The French physiologist Pierre Lecomte du Nouy tried to calculate the probability that a single protein molecule formed (before life on earth began) as the result of the random mixing of atoms. His conclusion was that it was extremely improbable that such an event occurred all at once. Yet Lecomte du Nouy used the _classical_ concept of probability in doing his calculations. What problems arise in using the classical concept in trying to calculate the probability of that event? (Those of you with a little background in chemistry or biology may notice slanted language in Lecomte de Nouy's very description of the event. What is it?)

_____

_____

_____

_____

_____

_____

_____

_____

_10-2_

Inductive Generalization

Section Objectives

1. Apply the criteria for evaluating enumerative and statistical inductions.

2. Identify examples of typical fallacies in enumerative and statistical inductions.

1. Enumerative induction: an inductive argument that has premises that list the observed individuals and characteristic(s), and typically has a conclusion about the whole class of individuals or the next individual that will be encountered.

2. Statistical induction: an inductive argument in which the corresponding inference is from a percentage of observed individuals of a kind (S) that have a property (P) to the conclusion that the same percentage holds for all S's.

3. Sample: (when speaking of inductive inferences) the observed individuals of kind S.

4. Population: the larger group(s) of which the sample is a subset.

5. Positive analogy: the degree of likeness of characteristics (other than being an S) of the sample.

6. Variety of evidence, or negative analogy: the degree of dissimilarity of characteristics (while still having P) of the sample.

7. Random sample: a sample in which only chance determines which individuals are selected.

8. Stratified random sample: a method of sampling in which the relevant subgroups and proportionate size are identified, and a random sample is taken from each subgroup proportionate to its size.

9. Time-lapse sampling: a method of sampling in which two surveys are made, different samples are used, there is a significant lapse of time between the first and the second survey, and the two surveys are compared for consistency.

10. Sweep of a conclusion: the greater the number of possibilities of the falsehood of a conclusion, the greater its sweep; the fewer the number of possibilities of the falsehood of a conclusion, the less its sweep.

11. Hasty generalization: a fallacious argument in which the inference is from a small or unrepresentative sample to a statement about the class the sample supposedly represents.

12. Forgetful induction: a hasty generalization in which the sample is biased or loaded because of failure to consider contrary but readily available evidence.

Summary

Enumerative inductive arguments frequently exhibit one of two patterns. Let the lower case a stand for any individual whatsoever. Let the numerical subscript to a designate a specific individual. Let S designate any class in which individuals fall, and let P designate any property that the individuals have. Let n designate some finite number. Hence a_n means "the finite number of individuals that have been observed." Then the first pattern can be represented this way.

1. a_1, a_2, a_3...a_n have all been observed to be S and to have P.
2. Therefore, probably all S have P.

Only the conclusion of the second pattern is different.

3. Therefore, the next S observed $(a_n + 1)$ will probably have P.

Unless there is only a potentially finite number of S's (for example, "All words on this page are written in black"), it is impossible to observe all the a's that are S.

Thus, two questions arise. How many individuals must be observed for the argument to be reliable? Further, what and how many kinds of S's must be observed?

There is no definite number of individuals that must be observed in every case, because the number of individuals required varies with the argument in question. One factor is the size of the class. For example, if the generalization were about college professors, there would need to be a much larger sample than if the generalization were about college professors of philosophy, because the former class is so much larger. Another factor is what is attributed to the class. Thus, if the generalization were about the political views of college professors of philosophy, the sample would need to be larger than if the generalization were about the marital status of professors of philosophy. The reason is that there are only a couple possibilities for marital status, whereas political views vary more. Of course, our knowledge that political views vary more is itself inductively grounded.

There is a general rule about sample size: The larger the number of observed individuals, the greater the reliability and strength of the conclusion. This general rule has exceptions, so it must be combined with other criteria.

Consider this example:

1. a_1, a_2, a_3...a_{100} have all been observed to be sodium salts and have all burned yellow.
2. Therefore, probably all sodium salts burn yellow.

Suppose that all of your experiments were on specimens of table salt (sodium chloride). Contrast this case with one in which your 100 experiments were on roughly equal numbers of specimens of baking soda (sodium bicarbonate), fluoride (sodium fluoride), and table salt. Baking soda and fluoride are also sodium salts. Although the sample size is the same, the second argument is better. The reason is that there is greater variety of evidence in the second case. Scientists require varied evidence for findings before they are accepted as established. Let us see why variety of evidence is desirable by contrasting the two arguments. It might be the case (as far as the evidence in the first argument is concerned) that table salt burns yellow but that other sodium salts do not. Because all the tests were run on specimens of table salt, there is no test of other sodium salts, yet the conclusion is about sodium salts generally. In the second argument, however, there are also tests of two other kinds of sodium salt. Thus, if it <u>were</u> the case that table salt is the only sodium salt that burns yellow, the second set of experiments would have shown that not all sodium salts burn yellow. The first set of experiments would <u>not</u> have shown this. Variety of evidence, then, puts a conclusion to a more severe test. It increases the likelihood that <u>if</u> the conclusion is false, it will be shown to be so. If the conclusion passes the more severe test, it is better supported by the evidence.

It is important to realize that variety of evidence is not just a matter of <u>counting</u> the number of kinds of S (in this case, sodium salts). Suppose that experiments were run on 100 specimens of sodium carbonate and sodium bicarbonate (baking soda) in one case. Suppose that the experiments were run on 100 specimens of sodium fluoride and baking soda (sodium bicarbonate) in the other case. These two sets of experiments do not make equally strong cases for "All sodium salts burn yellow." This is so even though the numbers of individuals observed (100) and the numbers of kinds (2) are identical. The reason is that sodium carbonate and sodium bicarbonate are more similar to one another than are sodium fluoride and sodium bicarbonate. It might have been the case that the two sodium salts with similar chemical compositions burn yellow, whereas others do not. Only the second set of experiments would test this possibility. Variety of evidence, then, is a matter of the number of dissimilarities between the kinds of things that are S, rather than the number of kinds.

Statistical inductive arguments frequently have the following pattern:

1. n percent of $a_1...a_n$ have been observed to be S and have P.
2. Therfore, probably n percent of all S have P.

Under what circumstances are inferences of this kind reliable? Sample size and variety of evidence apply here, too. It should be pointed out that variety of evidence does not automatically increase with sample size. We could have tested 1,000 specimens of table salt. And the small size of a sample does not preclude reliability. We could have tested two specimens each of all the known sodium salts and have a representative sample. Stratified random sampling is a method used to increase the probability that the sample will be representative without a large sample. Time-lapse sampling is a method used to increase the probability of current accuracy for subjects that are liable to change (such as political opinions). These methods of sampling leave room for a margin of error. Thus, the results of surveys in which these methods are used frequently are expressed in terms of a limited range of percentages.

Sometimes you will observe two things occurring together regularly, and yet it is a mere coincidence that they do so. If their concurrence is a coincidence, then the two things are not relevant to one another. Coincidences provide no basis for inductive inferences. Detecting a coincidence requires background knowledge that is itself inductively grounded. If every college student someone knew had blond hair, he would have little basis to infer that the next college student he meets will have blond hair. We know that it is a coincidence because we know that college students are human beings and that people differ in hair color. But if the observer lived in Iceland, where (I understand) virtually everyone has blond hair, he would have reason to believe that the next college student he meets will have blond hair. It is still a coincidence that the next college student he meets has blond hair, though it is not a coincidence that the next native Icelander (who is a college student) he meets has blond hair.

We must also take the sweep of a conclusion into account when evaluating an inductive argument. "The more sweeping the conclusion, relative to the evidence stated in the premises, the less its probability; and the less sweeping the conclusion, relative to the same evidence, the greater its probability." This is so, because the greater a conclusion's sweep, the greater is the chance that it will be false. Contrast these three conclusions:

(1) All swans are white.

(2) All European swans are nonblack.

(3) All European swans are white.

Conclusion (1) is false if there is a single swan, in Europe or elsewhere, that is not white. Conclusion (3), however, is less sweeping, because it is false only if there is a <u>European</u> swan that is not white. A black Australian swan would not show that (3) is false, although it would establish the falsehood of (1). A purple European swan would show that (1) and (3) are both false. However, it would <u>not</u> show that (2) is false; a purple European swan actually would be evidence for (2). Conclusion (2), therefore, is the least sweeping of the three. Note that the less sweeping a conclusion is, the more cautiously it is stated.

The criteria for reliable inductive conclusions set out thus far are a matter of degree. Conclusions (relative to stated premises) fit the criteria to a greater or a lesser degree. The greater the degree to which a conclusion fits all the criteria, the stronger it is. To summarize:

1. The sample must be representative of the population (referred to in the conclusion) as a whole.

2. The size of the sample must be sufficiently large.

3. The property attributed to a group of individuals should not be a mere coincidence. (This criterion is best viewed as derivative from the others.)

4. The scope or sweep of the conclusion should be proportionate to the evidence on which it is based.

If one or more of these standards is violated to a great degree, the result is a fallacy of <u>hasty generalization</u>. <u>Generalization</u> is perhaps not the best word, because not all the conclusions of such arguments are general. If someone infers that Melissa (who is of English ancestry) reads Shakespeare beautifully because a few other people of English ancestry do likewise, the conclusion is not a generalization. However, there is an <u>implicit</u> connection being made between English ancestry and reading Shakespeare beautifully, which <u>is</u> general in nature.

This fallacy occurs more often than you may think. It occurs when a generalization is inferred on the basis of a sample that is either too small or unrepresentative. It also occurs when rules are formulated on the basis of exceptional cases or when there is a failure to consider contrary but readily available evidence. Prejudices about groups are often defended by citing small or unrepresentative samples. Suppose, for example, that someone defended the opinion that Catholics have a reactionary view on birth control because the Pope, an especially prominent Catholic, has taken a stand against the pill. The problem is that, despite the Pope's position in the Catholic Church, his view may not be representative of Catholics as a group. The sample is much too small.

Practice Exercises

I. Consider the following situations. After each item of information, state whether it makes the inference stronger (S), weaker (W), or neither (N). Consider each item of information separately.

A. Professor Bullgravy reads the student evaluations of Professor Smedley and discovers that 1 of every 25 students complained that Smedley made them afraid to ask questions. Bullgravy infers that Smedley is a bad professor.

1. _____ 15 percent of Smedley's students rated him as either a poor, an unsatisfactory, or a satisfactory professor.

2. _____ 85 percent of Smedley's students rated him as either a good, a very good, or an excellent professor.

3. _____ 10 percent of Smedley's students commented that he is a dynamic and interesting lecturer.

4. _____ Two of the 300 students who completed the forms recommended that Smedley quit teaching and go into another profession.

5. _____ 99 percent of the students rated Smedley as very well-prepared for class.

6. _____ Four students recommended that Smedley part his hair differently.

7. _____ 7 percent of the students complained that Smedley used big words they didn't understand.

8. _____ 40 percent said that Smedley was occasionally hard to understand.

9. _____ 80 percent wrote that Smedley's lectures were "very helpful" in explaining and clarifying the course material.

10. _____ The average mean grade in Smedley's classes is lower than it is in the classes of 90 percent of the other professors at the university.

11. _____ The arithmetic mean response to the question about Smedley's overall performance as a teacher is 3.3, with 3 meaning "good" and 3.5 meaning "very good."

B. _____ Consider items 7, 8, and 9 together.

C. Sally and Jerry purchase a house, believing that it is a good deal because they believe the interest rate is very low and the price reasonable ($60,000).

1. _____ Sally and Jerry discover, after the fact, that the interest rate is $9\frac{1}{2}$ percent, rather than 9 percent.

2. _____ The house is appraised at $65,000 two months after Sally and Jerry move in.

3. _____ A real estate investor offers $70,000 for the house three months after they move in.

4. _____ Sally and Jerry paid $17,000 down, but they discover that other houses require only $10,000 down.

5. _____ The usual interest rate when they bought the house was 13%.

6. _____ The house needed painting when they bought it.

7. _____ Housing is in great demand in the city in which their house is located.

8. _____ Interest rates drop to 11%, and there are signs of a further decline.

D. Julie has just purchased a stereo system for $700 (on sale) and infers that she bought a reliable product for a terrific price.

1. _____ Three of Julie's friends (Charlie, Bob, and Martha) each have the same stereo system, for which they paid $750 each.

2. _____ An advertisement shows a stereo unit of a different brand and inferior quality on sale for $500.

3. _____ Julie learns from her friends that their stereo systems came with a three-year warranty, whereas hers has a one-year warranty.

4. _____ Julie's purchase of the stereo unit means that she must refrain for six months from buying the TV she wanted.

5. _____ Charlie has to take his stereo to the shop for repairs almost immediately after the warranty expires.

6. _____ Julie reads an advertisement in which the same stereo unit she bought is on sale for $725.

7. _____ Julie reads in Consumer Reports that the stereo system she bought has an overall rating of "very good" for quality of sound and "good" for frequency of repairs.

II. Explain why each of the following arguments is fallacious.

1. Sorority girls are so conceited. Margaret and Sarah didn't even speak to me yesterday when they saw me in the hall.

2. I know a guy who runs a very lucrative gambling operation and who drives his new Cadillac downtown every week to collect his welfare check. This just goes to show that welfare programs are unnecessary and are riddled with corruption.

3. Hocker: The people of seventeenth- and eighteenth-century France lived lives of luxurious splendor.
   Bloodworth: On the contrary, most people in France at that time lived in poverty, some of them in squalor.
   Hocker: My dear Bloodworth, to see how wrong you are, just look at the Palace of Versailles, which dates from the time in question.

4. Shlomo: College students these days can't think. Why, in my 10
o'clock class yesterday, not one student formulated a decent argument.

5. The two accounts of creation in "Genesis" are inconsistent with
one another. So, nothing in the Bible can be believed.

Section Objectives

1. Identify and apply the criteria for evaluating inductive arguments by
analogy.

2. Identify some instances of faulty analogy.

Key Term Review

1. Inductive argument by analogy: an inductive argument in which at least
two things are compared in at least one way, and the inference is that
the things being compared share some further (as yet unobserved) characteristic.

2. Statistical argument by analogy: an inductive argument in which it is
inferred that, because a given percentage (N) of individuals mentioned
in the premises share two or more properties, the probability is N that
a new individual that has at least one of those properties has the other
property.

3. Fallacy of faulty analogy: an analogical argument that violates, to a
great degree, one or more of the standards for appraising such arguments.

Summary

Although analogies are sometimes stated non-argumentatively, people commonly
use analogies to formulate arguments. Suppose that Patricia buys a new ball
point pen. She bought two others of the same brand and price; and they have
failed to write before the ink ran out. Patricia infers that this new pen
will fail to write before the ink runs out. Patricia has formulated an
argument by analogy. The pattern of her argument is:

Individuals a, b, and c have properties P_1, P_2, and P_3.
Individual d has properties P_1 and P_2.
Therefore, d probably has property P_3.

Here three individuals are mentioned in the premises, but the number of individuals could have been any finite number and we would still have an argument by analogy. The same is true of the number of properties.

Suppose that not all of Patricia's pens had failed to write before the ink
ran out. Suppose that 7 of the 10 ball point pens she bought failed to
write before the ink ran out, and she infers that the probability is .7
that this new pen will do likewise. She will have formulated a statistical
argument by analogy that has this pattern:

N percent of individuals $a-j$ having properties P_1 and P_2 also have property P_3.

Individual i has properties P_1 and P_2.

Therefore, the probability is N that i has property P_3.

Let us review the criteria for evaluating such arguments:

1. <u>The greater the number of similarities between the individuals mentioned only in the premises and the one mentioned in the conclusion, the stronger the argument</u> (other things being equal).

Suppose that Patricia's new pen, in addition to being the same brand and price, also has an identical construction (is put together in the same way). That would constitute a stronger case for the conclusion. The point of the first criterion is even clearer when it is considered alongside the second:

2. <u>The greater the number of dissimilarities between the individuals mentioned only in the premises and the one mentioned in the conclusion, the weaker the argument.</u>

Suppose that the manufacturers of the pen hear several complaints about their product. They decide to improve the product's construction so that the ink will flow more smoothly. If Patricia's new pen is one of the improved ones and the former ones were made in the old fashion, then the argument is weaker. It is less probable, given this new information, that the new pen will stop writing before the ink is gone.

3. <u>The greater the number of analogous individuals mentioned only in the premises, the stronger the argument</u> (as a general rule).

If Patricia had bought only one pen and swore that she would never buy another because it stopped writing too soon, the inference would be fallacious, an instance of hasty conclusion (generalization). The next pen very well may not share that undesirable feature. But if she had bought seven, then the conclusion would be better supported. It would be stronger still if she knew of a few friends who had been frustrated by the same problem with the pens. The reason for qualifying criterion 3 as a general rule is that variety of evidence must be considered when appraising many analogical arguments.

4. <u>The greater the number of dissimilarities between the analgous individuals mentioned only in the premises, the stronger the argument.</u>

Just as we want to make sure that the individuals being compared are not too analogous when generalizing, so we want the same in arguments by analogy. Suppose you are trying to judge your chances of doing well in logic. You ask some fellow students and discover that all 15 of them made a B or better. They share with you the characteristic of being students at the same university. Furthermore, they all took the course from the same professor with whom you plan to take logic. You infer that you will probably make a B or better.

But suppose that all 15 of these students were economically advantaged people who had had a course in logic in prep school. This similarity between <u>them</u>, rather than the similarities between them and you, probably explains their good grades in logic. The argument would be weakened by this further similarity among the individuals mentioned only in the premises.

Conversely, suppose that the 15 students have varied economic and educational backgrounds. These dissimilarities between them strengthens the argument. This is the point of criterion 4.

Criterion 4 helps to explain criterion 3. The larger the number of individuals being compared, the more probable it is (as a general rule) that the individuals mentioned in the premises only will exhibit dissimilarities among themselves. But the mere presence of a great number of individuals does not guarantee such dissimilarities, as we saw in the previous section.

Note that criteria 2 and 4 are not inconsistent. Criterion 2 pertains to dissimilarities between the individuals mentioned only in the premises and the one mentioned in the conclusion. Criterion 4 has to do with dissimilarities between the individuals mentioned only in the premises. Two different things are being contrasted. If the former logic students were dissimilar among themselves, that would strengthen the argument. But if they are dissimilar to you, that would weaken it.

    5. The similarities between the individuals mentioned in the premises and the individual mentioned in the conclusion must be relevant to the conclusion.

Criterion 1 included the qualification "other things being equal." The reason for this is that the individuals mentioned in an analogical argument can be compared in irrelevant ways. An increase in such similarities would not strengthen an argument by analogy. Suppose that you and the 15 fellow students all have brown eyes. Such a similarity would have no bearing on whether you would be likely to make a B or better in logic.

Judgments about what is relevant (or irrelevant) to an analogically based conclusion are judgments about cause-and-effect relationships. If a similarity is causally connected to the conclusion, it is relevant. Irrelevant factors are mere coincidences. Judgments about cause-and-effect relationships are based on experience. If, for example, the logic professor seriously announced to his classes that he would give a B or better to anyone with brown eyes, then that similarity would be relevant to the conclusion, for it would be causally connected with it. It is because we know from experience that such things rarely (if ever) happen that we know that having brown eyes is (almost assuredly) irrelevant to receiving a B in logic. But how do we distinguish between cause-and-effect relationships and coincidences? We shall address that question in the next chapter.

The last criterion for appraising arguments by analogy is:

    6. The sweep of the conclusion must be proportionate to the evidence in its favor.

This criterion is explained in the previous section.

These criteria are a matter of degree. An analogical argument that violates one or more of these standards to a great degree involves the fallacy of faulty analogy.

Practice Exercises

Put the following arguments into logically proper form and evaluate them, referring to the standards for appraising inductive arguments by analogy.

1. No one would hesitate to infer the existence of a watchmaker from a watch. We know that a watch is designed by someone because its parts are arranged in such a way that they serve a purpose: telling the time. But we find the same ordering of parts in nature, in objects we do not design. Therfore, there is a designer of nature. Thus, God exists.

2. I know that there are bodies because I can observe them. But I cannot observe any mind but my own. So how do I know that there are any other minds? I observe bodies similar to my own. These bodies behave in a way that is similar to the way I behave. I know from my own case that my behavior is accompanied by mental activity. It is reasonable, there-fore, to infer that the similar behavior in similar bodies is also ac-companied by thoughts (mental activity). That is how I know that there are some other minds.

3. Some anti-evolutionists claim that there is no scientific evidence for the theory of evolution because scientists have not seen the past. Sup-pose a detective observes a dead person with a hole in his head. Sup-pose the coroner removes a bullet from his head and examines the body. The coroner testifies that the dead person was in excellent health be-fore his death. The anti-evolutionist would have to say that the detec-tive has no scientific evidence for the claim that the man died from a gunshot wound, because the detective did not see the incident.

4. I probably won't have to have this new car repaired very often, because it is the same model as the one I bought five years ago, and I had that car repaired only rarely.

5. Although the model is the same, there have been important changes in the car over the past five years. The 1978 model you owned has a very different engine from the 1983 model you just bought. The two receive very different ratings for "frequency of repairs" in this consumers' information magazine. The rating for the 1978 model is "very good," but the 1983 model is rated only "fair."

10-4

Numerical Probabilities

Section Objectives

1. Apply the laws of probability in calculating the probability of various events.

2. Identify instances of the gambler's fallacy and the fallacy of unequal chances.

Key Term Review

1. Probability statement: a statement about what proportion or percentage of a population has the property in question.

2. Initial probability (of an event): the ratio of favorable outcomes to the total number of possible outcomes.

3. Odds of success: the ratio of the number of favorable outcomes to the number of unfavorable ones.

4. Law of negation: for any two mutually exclusive events, E and $\sim E$, the probability of either is 1 minus the probability of the other. In other words, $Pr(\sim E) = 1 - Pr(E)$, and $Pr(E) = 1 - Pr(\sim E)$.

5. Independent events: two events are independent of one another if and only if the occurrence or nonoccurrence of either one has no effect on the occurrence or nonoccurrence of the other.

6. Dependent events: two events are dependent if and only if the probability of the second event is no longer what it would have been if the first event had not occurred.

7. Law of conjunction (whether E_1 and E_2 are independent or dependent events): $Pr(E_1 \ \& \ E_2) = Pr(E_1) \times Pr(E_2 \text{ given } E_1)$.

8. Law of restricted conjunction (where E_1 and E_2 are independent events): $Pr(E_1 \ \& \ E_2) = Pr(E_1) \times Pr(E_2)$.

9. Law of exclusive disjunction (where E_1 and E_2 are mutually exclusive events): $Pr(E_1 \lor E_2) = Pr(E_1) + Pr(E_2)$.

10. Mutually exclusive events: two events are mutually exclusive if it is impossible for both to occur at the same time.

11. Law of nonexclusive disjunction (whether or not E_1 and E_2 are mutually exclusive): $Pr(E_1 \lor E_2) = Pr(E_1) + Pr(E_2) - Pr(E_1 \ \& \ E_2)$.

12. Fallacy of unequal chances: drawing a conclusion on the basis of the false premise that the possibilities are equiprobable. (The possibility in question is a dependent event that is affected by available information.)

13. Gambler's fallacy: an error in reasoning about probabilities that is based on the false premise that independent events are dependent and that involves a misapplication of the "law of averages."

Summary

Consider the law of exclusive disjunction and the law of nonexclusive disjunction. The only difference between them is the last term of the right half of the law of nonexclusive disjunction, where the probability of the conjunction of both events is subtracted: $-Pr(E_1 \ \& \ E_2)$. If the two events are mutually exclusive, they cannot both occur at the same time. Thus, the probability of the conjunction of the two is zero (0). Thus when applied to mutually exclusive events, the law of nonexclusive disjunction is numerically equivalent to the law of exclusive disjunction. The last term of the right half of the law of nonexclusive disjunction amounts to subtracting zero. Therefore, the law of exclusive disjunction can be eliminated. If you care to retain it, understanding the relationship between the laws of exclusive and nonexclusive disjunction may help you to remember them both.

Now consider the law of conjunction and the law of restricted conjunction. The difference between the two is in the last term of the right half: The probability of E_2--that is, $Pr(E_2)$--as opposed to the probability of E_2, given E_1--that is, $Pr(E_2 \text{ given } E_1)$. Once again we can eliminate, for the sake of simplicity, the law of restricted conjunction. Note that the law of restricted conjunction applies only to independent events. But if E_1 and E_2 are independent events, the probability of E_2, given E_1 equals the probability of E_2. In other words, when applied to independent events, the law of conjunction yields the same results as the law of restricted conjunction. We may delete the law of restricted conjunction, provided that we retain the law of conjunction.

The applicability of the law of negation presupposes that $Pr(E) + Pr(\sim E) = 1$.

We have formulated the laws of conjunction and nonexclusive disjunction in such a way that they can apply generally. Five laws of the probability calculus have been reduced to three, namely:

1. $Pr(E) = 1 - Pr(\sim E)$; $Pr(\sim E) = 1 - Pr(E)$ law of negation
2. $Pr(E_1 \ \& \ E_2) = Pr(E_1) \times Pr(E_2 \text{ given } E_1)$ law of conjunction
3. $Pr(E_1 \lor E_2) = Pr(E_1) + Pr(E_2) - Pr(E_1 \ \& \ E_2)$ law of nonexclusive disjunction

Practice Exercises

Answer each of the following questions, or assess the argument. Assume in Exercises 1-3 that a child can have one of three possible hair colors: brown, blond, or red. The probability of brown hair is .37 whereas the probability of blond hair is .35.

1. _____ What is the probability that a given child will have either brown or blond hair?

2. _____ What is the probability that a given child will have red hair?

3. _____ Assume that the chances are equal for a boy or girl, and that hair color is independent of sex. What is the probability of a red-haired girl?

Assume in Exercises 4-7 that A and B are mutually exclusive events, $Pr(A) = .42$, and $Pr(B) = .38$.

4. _____ Find $Pr(\sim A)$.

5. _____ Find $Pr(A \lor B)$.

6. _____ Find $Pr(A \ \& \ B)$.

7. _____ Find $Pr(A \ \& \ \sim B)$.

Assume in Exercises 8-10 that each card of an ordinary deck has the same probability of being drawn.

8. _____ What is the probability of drawing a 10 or higher?

9. _____ Find the probability of drawing a jack.

10. _____ Find the probability of drawing a 2 or 3.

11. Consider Lecomte du Nuoy's argument, which is outlined at the end of the exercises for Section 10-1. What fallacy does that argument involve? Explain.

_____

_____

_____

12. The roulette wheel yielded the result "black" eleven times in a row.
So betting on "red" for the next spin is a sure-fire bet. What fallacy
does this argument involve?

_____

_____

_____

CHAPTER 11

HYPOTHESES AND CAUSAL RELATIONS

OVERVIEW

We saw in Chapter 10 that one criterion for a good argument by analogy is that the similarities mentioned in the premises must be relevant to the conclusion. If the similarities are relevant, then there is a cause-and-effect relationship between the similarities mentioned only in the premises and what the conclusion states. If they are irrelevant, then it is a mere coincidence that they occur together. But how do we distinguish between cause-and-effect relationships and coincidences?

A major goal of science is to acquire objective knowledge about the world. We have already considered some scientific procedures for achieving this goal. But we need to refine our study of scientific procedures for justifying and testing hypotheses. This chapter deepens our understanding of science and addresses the question about cause-and-effect relationships.

SECTION REVIEWS

11-1

Hypothetical Reasoning

Section Objectives

1. Identify the common pattern that hypothetical reasoning exhibits, and spot instances of it.

2. Distinguish corroboration from conclusive confirmation, disconfirmation from conclusive falsification, and testing from illustrating a hypothesis.

Key Term Review

1. Narrow inductivism: the claim that (ideal) scientific inquiry begins with gathering facts and generalizing from them without any hypothesis.

2. Hypothesis: any guess or conjecture about what the facts are (or what explains the facts).

3. Hypothetical reasoning: inferring consequences from a hypothesis (and other assumptions).

4. Testing a hypothesis: making observations or conducting experiments to determine whether the consequences of hypothetical reasoning are true.

5. Conclusive disconfirmation (falsification): a deductive demonstration of the falsehood of a hypothesis.

6. Disconfirmation: producing evidence against a hypothesis.

7. Corroboration: producing evidence favorable to a hypothesis.

8. Conclusive confirmation: a deductive demonstration of the truth of a hypothesis.

Summary

Narrow inductivism is a popular belief about scientific inquiry. It may be popular because its advocates believe that it is necessary to preserve the objectivity of science. However, scientific inquiry does not--indeed, cannot--proceed in that way, as will be illustrated below. Moreover, gathering facts without any guesses is not necessary to preserve the impartiality of science. It does not matter by what process someone arrives at a hypothesis. The hypothesis could have occurred to an investigator in a dream. The objectivity of science is a function of the scrutiny a hypothesis is given after it has been proposed. The hypothesis is accepted as part of the body of scientific knowledge only after it has survived rigorous tests--only after it has been corroborated repeatedly. If the hypothesis has been borne out by the evidence, then it is acceptable regardless of how someone thought of it in the first place. If the hypothesis is disconfirmed repeatedly, then it is unacceptable regardless of how someone thought of it in the first place. The weeding out of hypotheses takes place independently of their historical origins. Consider, for example, Semmelweis's search for the cause of the high incidence of childbed fever in the First Division. All sorts of proposals (hypotheses) were put forward: terror induced by the priest, an epidemic, examinations by medical students, and delivery while lying on one's back. Semmelweis was able to disconfirm (rule out) all these hypotheses without considering what prompted people to propose them. And regardless of the steps that led Semmelweis to propose that cadaveric matter was responsible, he was able to corroborate it.

Without a hypothesis, Semmelweis would not have known which facts to investigate. You should note that the investigation depends on the hypothesis. If the hypothesis is that delivery on a woman's back is the cause, it is appropriate to try delivery in a different position. But it would have been pointless to ask the priest to take a different route, given that hypothesis. This illustrates the falsehood of narrow inductivism. Semmelweis's procedure was not less than ideally scientific because he used hypotheses to guide his investigation. That is the only way he could conduct his scientific inquiry. Semmelweis's rejection of hypotheses involved four steps:

1. Formulation of a hypothesis.

2. Elaboration of the consequences of the hypothesis (and auxiliary assumptions--see Section 11-2).

3. Testing of those consequences.

4. Rejection of the hypothesis.

If the testable consequences (predictions) could be deduced from the hypothesis alone, the pattern of reasoning would be

If H, then P.   (step 1-2)
Not-P.   (step 3)
Therefore, not-H.   (step 4)

The form of this argument is *modus tollens*, which is deductively valid. Thus, if the testable consequence (P) could be deduced from the hypothesis alone and P were known to be false, conclusive falsification would be possible.

Unfortunately, testable consequences cannot be deduced from the hypothesis alone. In order for us to deduce testable consequences, there must be at least one auxiliary assumption (AA) in addition to the hypothesis. For example, in order to deduce

Washing with chlorinated lime will reduce the incidence of childbed fever (P)

from the hypothesis

Cadaveric matter is the cause of the great number of cases of childbed fever (H)

Semmelweis had to assume

Washing with chlorinated lime is an effective antiseptic (AA)

This example is not isolated. Other auxiliary assumptions in the Semmelweis case are as follows: this alleged epidemic is like others in not being selective about location; eliminating the cause would eliminate the effect; and 50% of the medical student examiners would not perform nearly as many examinations as the full staff of medical students did. Because auxiliary assumptions are required for deducing testable consequences from hypotheses, the actual pattern of hypothetical reasoning is

If H and AA, then P.
Not-P.
Therefore, H and AA are not both true.

This means that the hypothesis has not been conclusively falsified if the results are negative (that is, if P is false). All that would have been shown is that either the hypothesis or the auxiliary assumption (or both) is false. Sometimes there are several AA's, which complicates matters further, because an error in any one of them can yield negative results. Conclusive falsification of a hypothesis would be possible only if it were possible to identify and conclusively confirm that all the AA's are true. But because conclusive confirmation of the AA's is impossible, so is conclusive disconfirmation of hypotheses.

Consider the typical AA that the instruments used to conduct the test (a microscope, telescope, or scale) are sensitive enough to detect what the scientist is trying to observe. The astronomer Brahe rejected Copernicus's view that the earth moves around the sun. His reasoning was that, if Copernicus's hypothesis were correct, then fixed stars would exhibit "parallactic motions." Brahe watched the fixed stars through a telescope and observed no such motions. Though he was aware of his AA that the stars are close enough for his telescope to detect the fixed stars' motions if there were any, the evidence at the time gave him no reason to doubt it. Naturally, Brahe had not conclusively disconfirmed Copernicus's correct hypothesis, but he had no reason to suspect that his AA was false.

We benefit from taking a historical perspective on Brahe's work, but we do not have that perspective on current scientific inquiry. There may be some false AA's that are currently taken for granted but that we have no reason to doubt at this time. That is why an example from the history of science should not engender smug satisfaction about what we know now.

181

Consider your work in a science laboratory class. Unless the class is advanced, this is not an instance of <u>testing</u> hypotheses but of <u>illustrating</u> well-established statements. Nevertheless, laboratory work can illustrate our point about AA's. Suppose you are mixing chemicals in order to produce a result that fits the following statement:

All mixtures of X and Y in proportion P form crystals with characteristics C_1 and C_2.

Time and again you mix the chemicals and fail to produce the expected results. Under these circumstances you do not tell the lab instructor that the statement is false. What this means is that there is a problem with your AA, namely:

The conditions (that would have been) necessary for a test have been met.

We say "would have been necessary" because laboratory students almost never test hypotheses. It would have been "the conditions necessary for a test" if we had been speaking of a scientist's work. This is a general AA that pervades all scientific inquiry involving hypothetical reasoning and testing. Of course, the particular content of it will vary, depending on the illustration or test. If your results were not as expected, then perhaps you did not mix X and Y in the designated proportions, or perhaps the beakers were not completely clean and the residue prevented the expected result. Perhaps you mistakenly mixed X and Y. The negations of each of the three foregoing statements are AA's. If we assume that those are all the AA's then the argument's pattern is

If H and AA_1 and AA_2 and AA_3 are true, then P is true. Not-P. Therefore H and AA_1 and AA_2 and AA_3 are not all true. (One or more is false.)

Now suppose you are a scientist testing the statement. You cannot rely on anything but fallible memory about a particular test and thus cannot ascertain with certainty that all the test conditions were met. So the idea of <u>conclusive</u> disconfirmation must be given up.

If the results <u>are</u> as expected, on the other hand, that does not constitute conclusive confirmation of the hypothesis either. The form of the argument in that case is affirming the consequent, which is deductively invalid.

If H and the AA's are true, then P is true. P is true. Therefore, H (and the AA's) are true.

Conclusive confirmation is impossible, too.

Granted that an example from the history of science should not engender smug satisfaction about what we know now. But neither should the impossibility of conclusive falsification and conclusive confirmation engender despair about scientific inquiry. Despite that, scientists can corroborate statements to such a degree that the only reasonable course is to believe them. Furthermore, scientists can disconfirm statements to such a degree that the only reasonable course is to reject them. What are the criteria for reasonable belief and disbelief? That question will be addressed in the next two sections.

Practice Exercises

For each description of a scientific investigation below: (a) identify the hypothesis or hypotheses being tested, (b) identify the test implications or predictions, and (c) tell whether the results of the experiment corroborate or disconfirm the hypothesis.

1. F. Redi (1626-1697) had heard that any dead, decaying body by itself causes worms. So he had three snakes killed and put them in an open box. Worms soon appeared and ate the meat. Once they had eaten all the meat, they escaped through a hole in the box. So Redi once again put three snakes in an open box, but this time he sealed every escape route in the bottom of the box. The worms reappeared and ate the meat but, because they could not escape, they eventually assumed an egg shape. Redi placed several of the egg-shaped balls in a glass container and covered it with paper. Eight days later a fly emerged from each "egg."--Based on J. B. Conant, Harvard Case Histories in Experimental Science, Harvard University Press, p. 505.

2. Redi began to suspect that the worms were caused by the dropping of flies rather than by the decay of the dead bodies. So he decided to use two boxes. Both had meat in them, but one was open and the other was closed. Worms soon appeared on the meat in the open box, but there were none in the closed box. Flies had hovered over the box before the worms appeared. The worms in the open box eventually became egg-shaped. Redi put them in a covered glass container. Soon flies emerged from the "eggs."--Ibid., pp. 506-507.

3. The prevailing view of heredity before Mendel's time was a blending theory. According to this view, hereditary material is comparable to a fluid, so that the offspring of a black and a white animal would be gray. Once blended, the hereditary material could not be separated, just as a mixture of black and white paint cannot be separated. Mendel conducted some experiments using garden peas. Some of the plants were tall (6 ft), whereas others were short (1 ft). When Mendel crossed the tall plants with the short ones, the offspring were all tall.--Adapted from J. Crow, Genetics Notes, Burgess Publishing Co., p. 1.

4. If hereditary characters are not determined by blending, they must be determined by segregated (or separate) factors. What happened to the factor for shortness in the tall offspring of the tall and short plants? Did it disappear entirely? Mendel let the tall offspring self-pollinate. The results were 787 tall plants and 277 short plants, roughly a 3:1 ratio. Ibid., p. 2.

5. Lions within the same coalition rarely fight each other for access to a particular female. Some behaviorists believe the explanation is that animals that co-operate with each other are probably related. Two scientists traced the parentage of more than 50 lions in a national park. They found that nearly half of the mating coalitions were composed of lions that were unrelated. Furthermore, these unrelated lions did not fight among themselves any more often than related lions who were members of a coalition.--Adapted from Science 82, July/August, p. 10.

6. "Next time you're seasick, try a teaspoon of ginger. Two psychologists selected 36 volunteers who were highly susceptible to motion sickness and gave them a normal dose of Dramamine, two capsules of powdered ginger root, or two capsules of a placebo. They were blindfolded, put in a motor-driven, revolving chair, and asked every few seconds to describe the feelings in their stomachs by assigning numbers to them. The chair revolved six minutes unless the person vomited, asked it to be

stopped, or reported a three-fold increase in intensity three times in a row. No one asked that it be stopped, but three people on the placebo vomited, and none on Dramamine made it the full six minutes. Half the people on ginger lasted six minutes, and none felt as bad as the other volunteers."--From Science 82, July/August, p. 11.

7. The principle of the conservation of matter is that material substance cannot be created or destroyed. According to the caloric theory of heat, heat is a material substance. Rumford observed that, when the barrel of a brass gun is bored, considerable heat is produced. Weighing the brass before and after boring showed no difference in the amounts of material substance.--Based on W. F. Magie, A Source Book in Physics, Harvard University Press, 1963.

8. A suction pump will lift water no higher than about 34 feet above the surface of the well. Toricelli explained this limitation in terms of the weight of air, which exerts pressure upon the surface of the well. The maximum of 34 feet is thus a function of the total pressure of the atmosphere. The specific gravity of mercury is about 14 times that of water. Toricelli invented the mercury barometer to test his explanation. One uses an open vessel containing mercury and a glass tube sealed at one end. The tube is filled with mercury and the open end is tightly capped. The tube is then inverted and submerged in the open vessel of mercury. The tube is then uncapped. The mercury falls until its length is about 30 inches.--From C. G. Hempel, Philosophy of Natural Science, Prentice-Hall, 1966.

9. Pascal decided to test Toricelli's explanation. He asked his brother-in-law, Perier, to check the length of the mercury barometer at the foot of the Puy-de-Dome, a mountain 4,800 feet high. Perier then carefully carried the barometer to the top of the mountain and measured the length of the mercury column. An assistant kept another barometer at the foot of the mountain; the length of the mercury column there remained unchanged. But the mercury column in the barometer at the top of the mountain was more than 3 inches shorter than at the bottom. --Ibid.

10. Boyle's law states that at constant temperature, the volume of a fixed weight of gas is inversely proportional to the pressure exerted upon it. A fixed weight of a gas, argon, is put inside a container with a movable piston. The temperature is fixed at $100°C$. The initial volume and pressure are measured (given on the first line of the table). The pressure is then increased and the resulting volume is measured. The pressure is measured. The results are as shown in the table.--From Sienko and Plane, College Chemistry, McGraw-Hill, 1961, For the purpose of Exercises 10 and 11, assume that the measurements of pressure can deviate as much as 1.0 from the exact figures Boyle's law would yield and still count as corroborating evidence.

Volume	Pressure
2.000	15.28
1.000	30.52
0.500	60.99
0.333	91.59

11. The temperature is then lowered and kept constant at -50°C. The initial pressure and volume are measured (first line of the table). The pressure is then increased and the resulting volume is measured. The pressure is measured.--Ibid.

Volume	Pressure
2.000	8.99
1.000	17.65
0.500	34.10
0.333	49.50

12. It is commonly observed that a light ray will change direction (angle of refraction) when it passes obliquely (angle of incidence) from one medium to another. This phenomenon is called refraction. In the second century A.D., Ptolemy made some measurements of angles of incidence, (A of I) and angle of refraction (A of R) for the refraction of light in air, water, and glass. Those measurements are as follows:

A of I	A of R	A of I	A of R
10	7	50	30
20	13	60	34
30	20	70	38
40	25	80	42

Ptolemy said that the ratio of the angle of incidence to the angle of refraction is constant. (Assume that the angle of refraction can deviate as much as 1 from the figure Ptolemy's hypothesis yields and still corroborate the hypothesis.--From L. H. Greenberg, Physics for Biology and Pre-med Students, W. B. Saunders Co., 1975.

Section Objective

1. Identify and apply the criteria for justifying and rejecting hypotheses.

Key Term Review

1. Explanatory power of a hypothesis: the degree to which a hypothesis accounts for (previously unexplained) facts; increases with the number and variety of converging statements that support it.

2. Converging statement: a statement that raises the probability of a hypothesis by affirming a consequence that would be expected to be true if the hypothesis were true.

3. Control group: a collection of individuals that differ from the group being studied only in that they are not being subjected to the treatment given as a test to the experimental group.

4. Experimental group: the individuals being subjected to the test.

5. Auxiliary assumption: a premise (other than the hypothesis) that is required in order to deduce a testable consequence of a hypothesis.

6. *Ad hoc* hypothesis: a hypothesis introduced in order to protect another hypothesis against disconfirming evidence.

7. Falsifiability criterion: the requirement that a hypothesis be empirically testable.

8. Testability of a hypothesis: the possibility (in principle, if not in fact) of deducing consequences from a hypothesis (and auxiliary assumptions) that disconfirm the hypothesis.

Summary

What are the criteria for reasonable belief when the argument is inductive? We have already dealt with some of them in Chapter 10 and in the previous section. The first criterion is repeated corroboration. If a single prediction based on a hypothesis and *AA*'s turns out as expected, that does not constitute much evidence for the truth of the hypothesis. But repeated successful predictions afford better reasons, for they can be used as premises in an argument by generalization (see Section 10-2). For example, repeated instances of a sodium salt burning yellow give us more reason to believe that all sodium salts burn yellow than does a single instance.

Repeated corroboration brings us to a criterion for acceptable scientific results: repeatability of evidence. A scientist (or a team of them) may report certain findings and explain how they were discovered. This gives other scientists the opportunity to check their findings. If the results are the same when other scientists test them, that is more reason to believe that the findings are true. But if the results are different than first reported, that is reason to be skeptical. After all, if the results are inconsistent with one another, there is some error in at least one of the two studies. And if several studies yield results that are inconsistent with the first study but are consistent with all the others, that is good reason to believe that the fault lies with the first study. This is why scientists speak of being able (or not being able) to reproduce the results of another's study.

Repeatability of evidence is a criterion for acceptable scientific results; thus, failure of repeatability is grounds for not accepting findings as scientifically established. Sometimes failure of repeatability is a reason for rejecting a study.

But repeated corroboration alone is not sufficient for established results. There must also be sufficient variety of evidence. We saw this point in Chapter 10 when we considered evidence for "All sodium salts burn yellow" (Section 10-2). Increasing the variety of evidence puts the hypothesis to a more severe test. If the statement (or set of statements, as in a theory) passes the more severe test, then that is better reason to believe it, because greater variety of evidence increases the probability that, if the statement is false, the results will show that it is false.

A third criterion is the explanatory range of the hypothesis. Explanatory range increases with the number and variety of converging statements in support of the hypothesis. Not all converging statements need to be the deduced and tested consequences of a hypothesis (and *AA*'s). Semmelweis inferred that washing with chlorinated lime would reduce the incidence of childbed fever and tested that consequence. But there were several converging statements that further corroborated his belief that cadaveric matter caused the high rate of childbed fever, because that hypothesis explained why they were true. For example, there is the fact that examinations in the Second Division, where the rate was much lower, were performed by midwives who did not dissect cadavers. The hypothesis was better supported with each fact surrounding the case that it explained. If the facts had been different, Semmelweis's hypothesis would not have been so well supported. If, for example, the midwives in the Second Division also dissected cadavers and washed in a similar way, yet the rate of childbed fever was lower, that would have been evidence against Semmelweis's hypothesis. The greater a statement's explanatory range, the better supported it is by the evidence.

Controlled experimentation is not possible for all scientific hypotheses. If the hypothesis is a prediction of the next appearance of Halley's comet, the scientist must wait for nature to produce the result. Whenever controlled experimentation is possible, however, it constitutes a criterion for an established scientific result. A control group serves as a test for the effectiveness of the treatment in question. A control group helps to determine whether the result would have occurred <u>without</u> the treatment.

Consider this study: Suppose that you are trying to determine the effectiveness of taking large doses of vitamin C in treating the common cold. You instruct 30 people who just caught colds to take 4,000 mg of vitamin C each day. You ask them each day how they feel, and the second day 8 people report that they feel somewhat better. The fifth day 10 more people report feeling better. Within 10 days everyone is no longer ill. Can we safely infer that the doses of vitamin C were effective for a substantial percentage of the population?

No. One difficulty is that there is no control group. How do we know that these results would not have occurred in the absence of the doses of vitamin C? If we do not know this, we do not know that the vitamin C was effective. The body's own defenses may have caused the reported results. Imagine the same situation, except that this time 30 other people are given a placebo (sugar pills). If the reports of these people do not differ significantly from those of the experimental group, then we do not know that the doses of vitamin C were effective, and we have some reason to believe that the doses were ineffective.

Another difficulty may have to do with the representativeness of the population. If the hypothesis pertains to, say, Americans, then each group must be representative of the American population as a whole, especially with regard to factors relevant to recovery from colds. The 30 people in each group would have to be a stratified random sample (see Chapter 10). A third possible difficulty would be making sure that the control group differs from the experimental group only in that the experimental group takes the vitamin C. For example, if most members of the control group rested more than members of the experimental group, the test results could be rendered practically useless (if rest is a factor relevant to recovery from a cold). Without the appropriate controls, then, results can be practically useless. Whenever possible, <u>controlled experimentation</u> is a fourth requirement for an established result.

These criteria are a matter of degree. A hypothesis can be repeatedly corroborated more than another (or more than itself at an earlier time). The evidence that corroborates it can be more or less varied. A hypothesis can have greater explanatory range than another. A group can better approximate the idea of a control group than another. Since it often is practically impossible to be sure that the control group differs from the experimental group in only one way (the treatment), the goal is to make sure that they differ in no other relevant ways (relevant to the test).

The fifth criterion, precision, is also a matter of degree. The idea is to make the prediction sufficiently specific that it is unlikely to be derived from another hypothesis. Astrology does not meet this criterion. The alleged "predictions" made on the basis of the positions of stars and planets are so vague and general (when they are true, that is) that they could have been made using many different hypotheses. Of course, astrology does not meet other criteria (such as repeatability of evidence) and, most important, many astrological predictions are false.

But precision is not merely a criterion for distinguishing pseudoscience from science. Sometimes it is invoked in order to decide between two actual scientific statements, such as Newton's and Einstein's respective laws of gravitation. In an example in Chapter 1, Bertrand Russell explains that Newton's and Einstein's laws led to predictions of much the same results. But Einstein's law, unlike Newton's, successfully predicted irregularities in Mercury's orbit and is therefore preferable to Newton's. Precision in this case amounts to greater explanatory range.

Once again, however, *ad hoc* hypotheses are not mentioned merely as a means of distinguishing nonscientific (in this case, religious) from scientific statements. *Ad hoc* hypotheses play a role even in science. Second, although falsifiability is in one respect not a matter of degree, in another it is. The reason is that, though a hypothesis may be (conceptually) testable, it may be much less easily testable than alternative hypotheses. That is a matter of degree.

A hypothesis can be rendered less easily testable (but not untestable) by an *ad hoc* hypothesis. The seventh criterion, then, is freedom from *ad hoc* hypotheses that are introduced solely for the purpose of protecting a hypothesis against adverse evidence and that render the hypothesis less easily testable.

Consider the eighteenth century hypothesis that combustion of metals involves the loss of a substance called phlogiston. Lavoisier showed that combustion actually resulted in something that weighed more than the original metal. Some die-hard advocates of the phlogiston theory introduced the *ad hoc* hypothesis that phlogiston has negative weight. This is an example of an objectionable *ad hoc* hypothesis.

Introducing an *ad hoc* hypothesis is not always objectionable. The sixth criterion, falsifiability, is (in one respect) not a matter of degree. A scientific hypothesis must be testable. If it is conceptually impossible for there to be evidence that is unfavorable to the hypothesis, it is not scientific. A hypothesis whose original formulation is testable may be transformed into an untestable formulation by using an *ad hoc* hypothesis. Consider, for example, Francis Galton's investigation of the effectiveness of prayer (Exercise 8 in Section 11-1). The hypothesis under consideration is "Prayer is an effective means of accomplishing what is prayed for." Faced with the adverse evidence about royalty and the babies of the clergy, someone might try to protect the hypothesis by adding the *ad hoc* hypothesis

"God is punishing the congregations, royalty, or clergy." This could be used as an *ad hoc* hypothesis to protect the hypothesis against <u>any</u> disconfirming evidence, thus rendering it untestable. (*Ad hoc* hypotheses are discussed in Section 12-2 of the text.)

Once this is done, however, it cannot be claimed that evidence that would corroborate the hypothesis does count as favorable evidence. For if no evidence could conceivably count against it, then no evidence can count for it. Thus, if members of the royal family should begin living to be older than most other people (something commonly prayed for), that would not constitute favorable evidence if an *ad hoc* hypothesis about God's punishment is used to protect it against all disconfirming evidence. Whether it is depends on the circumstances. If there is a lot of evidence to recommend the hypothesis (or theory), then a little adverse evidence is not sufficient to justify rejecting it. In that event, it may be reasonable to introduce an *ad hoc* hypothesis. Ptolemy's (127-151 A.D.) theory of the solar system, according to which the earth is the stationary center around which the planets and sun revolve, should not have been abandoned the first few times disconfirming evidence was noticed. That theory accounted for many observations, and a theory that works well is quite reasonably not abandoned at the first few signs of trouble. But as the evidence against the theory mounted over the centuries, and Ptolemy's theory became burdened with several *ad hoc* hypotheses, it was time to abandon the theory in favor of Copernicus's (1473-1543). At that point, introducing *ad hoc* hypotheses to save Ptolemy's theory was unreasonable.

When is it unreasonable to introduce an *ad hoc* hypothesis? The criteria are not altogether precise, but some general rules can be formulated. If the *ad hoc* hypothesis is introduced <u>solely</u> for the purpose of protecting the original hypothesis against disconfirming evidence, it is objectionable. An *ad hoc* hypothesis is introduced solely for that purpose if (1) there is no evidence to recommend it, (2) its introduction can yield no new tests of the original hypothesis, (3) it renders the hypothesis untestable altogether, (4) introducing it is merely designed to render the original hypothesis compatible with other scientific results, or (5) there is a lack of background evidence for the original hypothesis. Sometimes the objectionability of an *ad hoc* hypothesis is a matter of how many of them have been used to protect the (theory or) hypothesis. The greater the need for *ad hoc* hypotheses, obviously, the more trouble the hypothesis or theory has accounting for the facts. And freedom from objectionable *ad hoc* hypotheses is our seventh criterion for reasonable belief.

In discussing unobjectionable uses of *ad hoc* hypotheses, we referred indirectly to an eighth criterion for reasonable belief: <u>compatibility with well-established results</u>. There is a presumption in favor of well-established results, since there is a great deal of evidence in their favor. This criterion basically amounts to weighing the evidence for previous results against the evidence for the new hypothesis. If a new hypothesis is incompatible with well-corroborated results, then there must be so much evidence in its favor that it outweighs the previous results. (In other words, there has to be a lot of evidence in its favor.) If a hypothesis is incompatible with well-corroborated results, then there is a strong presumption against it. Presumptions can be defeated, and the ultimate court of appeal is experience.

The eight criteria are as follows:

1. Repeated corroboration (and repeatability of evidence).
2. Variety of evidence.
3. Explanatory range (and converging statements).
4. Controlled experimentation.
5. Precision.
6. Testability (falsifiability).
7. Freedom from (objectionable) *ad hoc* hypotheses.
8. Compatibility with well-corroborated results.

Practice Exercises

I. On a separate sheet of paper, answer the following questions about the indicated problems in the exercises for Section 11-1.

1. (Exercise 1) Did Redi's initial results (before he tried again with a box sealed at the bottom) corroborate or disconfirm the hypothesis he was testing? Specify another hypothesis that Redi could have formulated (other than the one he formulates in Exercise 2), given the evidence at the end of Exercise 1. What standard for scientific results was Redi following by trying a second time (with a box closed at the bottom)?

2. (Exercise 2) What standard for acceptable scientific results is exemplified by Redi's use of a closed box as well as an open box, with meat in both? Explain the point of his procedure. Specify at least two converging statements that corroborate Redi's last hypothesis. The closed box Redi used was airtight. How could a defender of the "spontaneous generation" hypothesis (the hypothesis being tested in Exercise 1) amend his hypothesis to protect it against Redi's observations? How could Redi test that amended hypothesis?

3. (Exercises 3 and 4) Explain why the hypothesis "The hereditary factors occur in separate pairs" explains the offspring of the self-pollinated tall plants. Hint: The first generation of plants were <u>all tall</u> and yet, when they <u>self</u>-pollinated, their offspring were approximately 25% <u>short</u> plants.

4. (Exercise 6) Why did the psychologists choose people who were highly susceptible to motion sickness? Why did they not choose people who were not particularly susceptible? What was the point of giving a placebo to some of the participants?

5. (Exercise 7) Supposing that the principle of the conservation of matter is true, how could an advocate of the caloric theory of heat try to protect it against Rumford's findings?

6. (Exercise 10 and 11) Suppose someone performed only the experiments described in Exercise 10 and inferred that Boyle's law is true. What criterion for acceptable scientific results would have been violated?

7. (Exercises 10 and 11) Suppose someone performed only the experiments described in Exercise 11 and inferred that Boyle's law is useless for understanding the behavior of gases. What more, if anything, would be necessary in order to justify that inference? If something more is required, be <u>specific</u> about what it is.

8. (Exercise 12) How could Ptolemy revise his hypothesis to render it true?

II. Explain any violations of rational scientific criteria that appear in the following passages that contain them. (In the case of Exercise 4, answer the question.)

1. Some people strongly advocate the view that the universe is about 6,000 years old. But it has been well documented that there are visible stars more than 10,000 light-years away. (A light-year is the distance that light travels in a year.)

2. Faced with the evidence given in Exercise 1, these people respond that God created the light "en route" to us. (That is, God made the light begin no more than 6,000 light-years away, although the star is farther away.)

3. Schmuchker: "Pascal's brother-in-law has not proven that the weight and pressure of air alone cause the mercury to rise to different levels (at the foot of the mountain and at the top). I still believe that the mercury rises because nature abhors (hates) a vacuum and thus tries to fill it. Nature's abhorrence of a vacuum simply depends on altitude. It decreases with increasing altitude."

4. What do *ad hoc* hypotheses have to do with testability and the impossibility of conclusive disconfirmation?

5. Shlomo: "A recent survey of 100 heroin addicts shows that 99 of them began by smoking marijuana. Smoking marijuana, therefore, obviously leads to heroin addiction."

11-3

Causal Relations and Mill's Methods

Section Objectives

1. Identify Mill's methods and recognize instances of them.

2. Diagnose examples of causal fallacies.

Key Term Review

1. <u>Necessary condition</u> (for a specified effect): a condition without which the effect cannot occur.

2. <u>Sufficient condition</u> (for a specified effect): a condition the presence of which guarantees that the effect occurs.

3. Method of agreement: a method of identifying a cause that consists in (a) considering several cases in which the effect occurs, (b) identifying the previous circumstances in all those cases that might have produced the effect, (c) eliminating all the previous circumstances except the ones that occur in all the cases, and (d) inferring that the common circumstance(s) is (are) the cause(s).

4. Method of difference: a method of identifying a cause that consists in (a) comparing one case in which the effect is present with another in which it is not; (b) determining that the two cases have every relevant factor in common except one, which occurs only in the one in which the effect is present; and (c) inferring that the factor that is different is the cause or part of it.

5. Joint method of agreement and difference: combining the two methods described above in the same investigation.

6. Method of concomitant variation: a method of identifying cause-and-effect relationships by noting that one factor varies directly or inversely with the other.

7. Method of residues: a method of identifying a cause-and-effect relationship that consists in (a) identifying the part of an effect that is known to be caused by some factor, (b) noting the part of the effect and the part of the previous circumstances that are "left over," and (c) inferring that the part of the previous circumstances is the cause of the remainder of the effect.

8. *Post hoc* fallacy (or fallacy of questionable cause): an error in reasoning that consists in inferring from "*A* occurred before *B*" to "*A* causes *B*."

9. Fallacy of accidental correlation (another variety of the fallacy of questionable cause): an error in reasoning that consists in inferring from "*A* and *B* are regularly correlated" to "*A* causes *B*."

Summary

The method of agreement is based on the idea that nothing that is absent when an effect occurs can be a necessary condition for the effect. Problem 3 on page 403 of your text illustrates this kind of reasoning. The director of the plant's health clinic first considered several cases in which the effect occurred—namely, four employees who were suffering symptoms of food poisoning. The director then identified the previous circumstances (eating in the cafeteria at lunch Monday) that might have produced the effect. The director did this by observing that all the employees suffering from the symptoms noted them several hours after having eaten in the cafeteria. The previous circumstances, then, were the foods eaten in the cafeteria. He interviewed the four employees, which yielded the following information.

Case (Employee)	Previous Circumstances (Foods Eaten)							Effect
1			VS	S	BS	AP			food poisoning
2					BS		CM	F	food poisoning
3		LB	CC		BS			IC	food poisoning
4	IT		VS		BS	AP			food poisoning

192

Because the only thing that all of them ate was the beef stew, the director identified it as the probable cause. Note that, if all four employees had eaten both apple pie and beef stew, the method of agreement would only rule out the other possibilities, yielding the conclusion that either the apple pie or the beef stew, or both, is the probable cause.

The method of difference is based on the idea that nothing that was present when the effect failed to occur can be a sufficient condition for the effect. If something is present and did not produce the effect, then it is not a sufficient condition for the effect. Let us suppose that all four employees ate both apple pie and beef stew. The director might then use the method of difference. Suppose she interviews a fifth employee who suffers from the symptoms and discovers that he did not eat apple pie but did eat beef stew. This means that eating apple pie was not a necessary condition for the effect, and it points to the beef stew as the cause of the food poisoning. This expansion of the example is an instance of a combination of the methods of agreement and difference.

It is noteworthy that the fifth employee with symptoms was, from the standpoint of someone trying to identify the cause of food poisoning, a matter of luck. The director of the health clinic can then take the appropriate measures to ensure that the employees do not suffer again (such as shipping the beef stew back to the company from which it was purchased and demanding a refund).

The method of concomitant variation is used when the intensity of the effect can be positively correlated with the intensity of a single factor. The last paragraph in Problem 7 on page 405 of the text illustrates this method. The increase in blood clots and death rate among the rats in the experimental group is correlated with injection of testosterone. Note the use of a control group to corroborate the hypothesis that the increased number of blood clots would not have happened without the injection of testosterone. Furthermore, a decrease in the death rate of rats injected with testosterone was correlated with being injected with an agent that inactivates testosterone. In both cases, the intensity of the effect (an increase in death rate, a decrease in death rate) was correlated with the intensity of a single factor (injection with testosterone, injection with an agent that inactivates testosterone).

The method of residues, unlike the methods of agreement and difference, explicitly appeals to at least one cause-and-effect relationship that is already known. Suppose you want to know how much your cat weighs but can't get him to stand on the scale. One way to find out would be to stand on the scale by yourself first and note the reading. (Suppose you weigh X pounds). Then you stand on the scale while holding your cat. The scale registers Y pounds. Thus, your cat weights Y minus X pounds. Here you explicitly appeal to two cause-and-effect relationships you know: (1) you standing on the scale caused the scale to register X and (2) you, holding the cat, caused the scale to register Y.

There are fallacious inferences about cause-and-effect relationships. Someone can identify a cause-and-effect relationship correctly and still reason fallaciously. The *post hoc* fallacy has to do with inadequate evidence for the claim that a certain cause-and-effect relationship obtains. The same is true of the fallacy of accidental correlation. When someone commits the fallacy of accidental correlation, the point is that he has sufficient evidence to claim that there is a correlation but inadequate evidence for the conclusion that there is a cause-and-effect relationship. Thus, a good generic name for the two fallacies is questionable cause. For the error is in reasoning: Given the evidence, it is questionable whether the obstensible cause-and-effect relationship actually obtains.

Practice Exercises

I. On a separate sheet of paper, answer each of the following questions, assuming ordinary circumstances. Explain your answers.

1. Is water a necessary condition for life? A sufficient condition for life?

2. Is being an adult a sufficient condition for being a bachelor? A necessary condition?

3. Is needing prescription glasses a necessary condition for not having perfect vision? A sufficient condition?

4. Is having a XX chromosome a necessary condition for being a human female? A sufficient condition? (restricted to class of humans)

5. Is the car starting a necessary condition for there being fuel in the tank? A sufficient condition?

6. Is being a cat a necessary condition for having fur? A sufficient condition?

7. Is getting the majority of popular votes in a U.S. presidential election a necessary condition for becoming president? A sufficient condition?

8. Is being an atheist a necessary condition for being amoral? A sufficient condition?

9. Is the tangibility of something a necessary condition for being able to prove its existence? A sufficient condition?

10. Is believing a statement a sufficient condition for the statement's truth? A necessary condition?

II. Explain why each of the following passages involves a causal fallacy. Specify what evidence the arguer would need in order to establish the cause-and-effect relationship. Occasionally you will also need to specify the fallacious inference you are invited to make.

1. "Soon after assuming this office, inflation dropped from approximately 13% to 4%."--Ronald Reagan, who was listing his accomplishments when he made this statement.

2. Having body lice promotes good health. This unexpected fact is proved by what anthropologists discovered among the members of a South Seas tribe. Healthy members of the tribe invariably had some lice, whereas most sick members had none.

3. The last time I had a cold, I took Virex cold tablets every four hours. Within a week I was feeling much better, Virex certainly did a job on my cold, and I recommend it enthusiastically.

4. Ever since President Johnson instituted the surtax in 1968, the stock market prices have been declining. Let's put the blame for the stock market's troubles where it belongs--squarely on the last Democratic president.--Argument formulated in 1973.

5. A recent study shows that among the youth of our city, 80% of those who contracted venereal disease last year had taken sex education classes in high school. The conclusion is obvious: If we want to reduce the incidence of venereal disease among our young people, we must get rid of those sex education classes.

6. I think that Furtwangler was more worried about his daughter's marriage than he ever admitted. She was his only daughter, you know. He never said anything about it, but I noticed that his hair began to turn white after the wedding.

7. If you project a curve showing the increase in behavioral disturbances and learning disabilities over the past 25 years, you will find that it parallels the increase in the dollar value of food additives over that time. Judicious readers will draw their own conclusion from this striking correlation.

8. The increasingly frequent and brazen sale of pornographic literature to persons 18 and under is paralleled by an alarming increase in the incidence of juvenile crime. Let's put a lid on this type of crime. Let's put the filth peddlers out of business!

9. "A new study shows that overweight people may be America's largest unprotected minority. The study, by Robert Half Personnel Agencies, reveals that of all executives earning $25,000 to $50,000, only nine percent were more than ten pounds overweight, but in the $10,000 to $20,000 range, 39 percent were more than ten pounds overweight. These figures, compared with a study done four years ago, show that discrimination against fat executives is increasing."--From Oklahoma Journal, 7 April 1974. (The first sentence of the passage is simply a pun and should be ignored.)

10. "At San Francisco State there were some demonstrations against the Vietnam war in the late 60's. The university president discovered that the grades of those students who participated in the demonstrations were up one full point, so those students were rewarded for being liberal, rewarded for activities unrelated to their coursework."--Max Rafferty, 17 May 1976, on the program "Good Morning America."

CHAPTER 12

FALLACIOUS REASONING

OVERVIEW

We have identified several kinds of fallacious reasoning in previous chapters. The "straw man" fallacy was discussed in Chapter 2. Chapter 3 explained loaded questions and the fallacies of suppressed evidence and false
dilemma. Chapter 4 includes a discussion of the fallacies of equivocation
and slippery slope. In Chapter 10 the fallacies of faulty analogy and hasty
conclusion (generalization) are identified. Two varieties of the fallacies
of questionable cause are explained in Chapter 11: accidental correlation
and the *post hoc* fallacy. In the course of identifying the principles for
determining that an argument of a given kind establishes its conclusion, it
has been useful to point out violations of those principles. However, there
are several kinds of fallacious reasoning that have not yet been identified.
Moreover, the ability to identify and analyze instances of fallacious reasoning is a very useful skill. Thus, this chapter is devoted to some kinds
of fallacious reasoning.

SECTION REVIEWS

12-1 and 12-2

Fallacies of Inconsistency
Begging the Question

Section Objectives

1. Identify and analyze passages that contain the fallacy of inconsistency,
    begging the question, or invincible ignorance.

2. Distinguish the various ways in which the fallacies of begging the ques-
    tion and invincible ignorance are committed.

Key Term Review

1. Fallacy or fallacious argument: any argument that does not establish
    its conclusion because it contains an error in reasoning.

2. Fallacy of inconsistency: an argument in which either the premises or
    a premise and the conclusion contradict each other, or the premises are
    inconsistent.

3. Inconsistency (of statements): when two or more statements imply pairs
    of consequences that are contradictories.

4. Fallacy of begging the question: an argument in which there is an at-
    tempt to use the conclusion (almost always in disguised form) as a
    reason for believing the very same conclusion.

5. **Question-begging expression**: a way of begging the question in which a term or phrase is used that implies a position on the very question at issue.

6. **Circular reasoning**: a way of begging the question in which the conclusion is (usually implicitly) stated as one of the premises.

7. **Complex or "loaded" question**: a way of begging the question in which a question is formulated to create the impression that a prior question has been settled, but the context is such that the questioner needs to prove that the answer to the prior question is what he presumes.

8. **Invincible ignorance**: a form of begging the question in which someone argues that evidence need not be considered because he "knows" in advance that the evidence has no bearing on the truth or falsity of the belief.

Summary

Although several fallacies have been covered in previous chapters, we have not paid enough attention to the all-important question "How do you analyze passages containing fallacious arguments?" These follow some rules of procedure and also have some advice on what not to do. The procedural rules are not complete and do not apply to the analysis of every passage. Consider them as useful guidelines.

1. **Read the passage carefully.**

You may have to read it a few times in order to understand just what is being said. If you become emotional about the passage, try to set aside those emotions. You may want to replace emotion-laden words with neutral ones, so that the emotion-laden words will not impede your impartial assessment of the passage.

2. **Determine just what is being argued.**

Sometimes the conclusion is not stated explicitly. In that case, you must supply it. The same goes for premises. Make sure that the conclusion (or premise) that you say is suppressed in the passage is clearly justified by the context. Occasionally a suppressed conclusion is something you are invited to infer.

3. **Put the explicit (or tacit) argument into logically proper form.**

If you take the time to do this, it will deepen your understanding of the passage.

4. **Ask yourself the following questions:**
   a. Is the evidence sufficient to justify the conclusion?
   b. If not, then would more evidence of the same kind make the argument better? Specify what that evidence would be.
   c. Or is the evidence (are the premises) irrelevant to the conclusion drawn?
   d. If the evidence is irrelevant to the conclusion, for what conclusion are the premises relevant? What conclusion should have been inferred from the premises? Specify the conclusion.
   e. If the evidence is irrelevant to the conclusion, what would the evidence for the conclusion actually drawn have to be? What

would be required in order to justify the conclusion drawn? Describe it (at least in general terms).

By thinking directly about what would make the argument a good one, you become aware (by contrast) of just what is lacking in the passage. Of course, you will occasionally have to think of what a good case would be for something you disbelieve. This is all to the good; those who can think impartially about a good case for beliefs they do not share may be more likely to be objective about their own beliefs. If you make that a habit of mind, you are on your way to becoming rational.

5. Write your analysis, addressing yourself to the above questions.

6. Apply the best label (or labels) to the passage.

The order of the rules is not arbitrary. Following them in the order in which they are listed helps to avoid common pitfalls in student responses. Here are a few common problems with such responses:

1. Immediately (or merely) slapping a label on the passage. Sometimes only a superficial understanding of the passage will make it fairly clear what kind of error it is. But mere classification does not take much thought, and the ideal here is to think well and carefully. Sometimes a person can apply the appropriate label without being able to specify just how the particular passage fails to prove its conclusion. What is required is a careful analysis of the passage.

2. Redefining the fallacy. Sometimes a student will slap a label on the passage and offer as an "analysis" a mere definition of the fallacy. But knowledge of the definitions is presupposed when analyzing passages. Furthermore, a definition of the fallacy, is not a diagnosis of just how the particular argument fails to prove its conclusion. It is not a specification of what would be required for the argument to be a good one.

3. Emotional reactions. Some of the passages you read will be arguments for conclusions you consider obviously false, even upsetting. This is probably what prompts such uncritical responses as "Who says that X?" or "That's just irrelevant." These responses do not exhibit any careful thought. The issue is not who said X, but whether the argument for X is any good and, if not, exactly why not. The second response leaves open the question "Irrelevant to what?" Further, to what is it relevant? Why is the premise irrelevant to the conclusion? The questions listed under Rule 4 above need to be addressed carefully in order to formulate an analysis and develop rational thought.

4. Merely denying the truth of a claim. Some of the passages you read will contain statements you consider obviously false, or even upsetting. This is probably what prompts some students to offer as an "analysis" of the passage a mere denial of one or more statements. But nothing is achieved by denying what someone else believes. He believes X; you believe non-X. So what? We are still left with the question "Has the author made a good case for X?"

Although the truth (of falsity) of premises is relevant to whether the arguer has proved the conclusion, denying the truth of a premise is not usually the first step in assessing an argument. In Chapter 2 we analyzed the question "Does this deductive argument prove its conclusion?" into three issues:

(1) Is it valid?

(2) Are all the premises true?

(3) Are all the premises known to be true?

Similarly, we analyzed the question "Does this inductive argument establish its conclusion?" into

(1) Granting the premises, do they establish the conclusion to the degree claimed for it? (question of reliability)

(2) Granting the premises, how probable is the conclusion? (question of strength)

The other two questions about inductive arguments are the same as questions (2) and (3) about deductive arguments.

The essential point to note is that the question about the truth of the premises in either case occurs after the question of the argument's worth, disregarding the truth (or falsity) of the premises. There are two related reasons for this order. First, if you claim that an arguer's premise is false, then the burden of proof shifts to you. You must prove that the premise is false. Second, there may be no need to broach that question. If a deductive argument is invalid, or an inductive argument is unreliable, then the argument does not establish its conclusion regardless of whether all the premises are true. The point of studying logic is to improve your reasoning skills. Denying someone else's statement (by itself) shows no skill in reasoning. Proving that someone else's statement is false does. Accordingly, professors of logic are (as logicians) not interested in a mere statement of your beliefs, but in whether you can defend them. When it comes to informal fallacies, the professor is interested in whether you can prove that the fallacious argument does not prove its conclusion. Therefore, you usually should address the question "Are the premises true?" after you have assessed the argument in terms of reliability, strength, or validity.

5. Labeling a statement "an opinion." This maneuver should be avoided. Labeling a statement "an opinion" is not a substitute for proving that the statement is questionable, dubious, or false. In a way, it is obvious that the arguer is expressing his opinion. But that would settle the matter only if all opinions were equally indefensible, and not all opinions are equally indefensible. Some are well founded; others are ill founded. Some are better defended (and more defensible) than others.

These statements may appear to be undemocratic and dogmatic, but they are not. Suppose we agree that everyone has a right to her or his opinion. That does not commit us to saying that everyone's opinion is right. Such an argument commits the fallacy of equivocation. The word right means "moral entitlement" in the first statement, but it means "true" in the second. Even if we agree that everyone is morally entitled to her or his opinion, it is nevertheless impossible for everyone's opinion to be true.

The false belief that labeling a statement and opinion closes all rational inquiry into its truth is sometimes buttressed by a false dilemma: either a statement is proved beyond a reasonable doubt or believing it is a matter of arbitrary choice. However, a statement can be better defended than its competitors without being proved beyond a reasonable doubt. For example, a prosecuting attorney may have made a better case for the defendant's guilt than a defense attorney made for the defendant's innocence without proving that the defendant is guilty "beyond a reasonable doubt." (Given the presumption of innocence, the verdict in such a case would be "not guilty on grounds of insufficient evidence.")

The fact that not everyone is persuaded of an opinion does not show that it is a matter of arbitrary choice whether it should be adopted. We need to distinguish between proving a conclusion and persuading others of it. Unfortunately, one can persuade others of a conclusion without proving it. More important, one can prove a conclusion without persuading others of it. This can happen even when the evidence proves the conclusion beyond a reasonable doubt. For example, someone who is bigoted about an issue or did not understand the proof may not be persuaded. Therefore, a lack of universal agreement does not show that adopting an opinion is a matter of arbitrary choice.

We are left with the task of weighing arguments and evidence when one side or the other is not proved beyond a reasonable doubt. Criticizing the case for someone else's opinion, lastly, is not to deny his moral entitlement to believe it. To criticize the case for someone else's opinion is to argue that the evidence does not warrant believing it. Labeling a statement an opinion is not a substitute for proving that the statement is dubious, questionable, or false.

The fallacies of inconsistency and begging the question are peculiar in that arguments that commit either fallacy are deductively valid. What, then, makes them fallacious? Unlike our approach to the analysis of other fallacies, we must immediately turn to consider questions about the truth or knowability of the premises.

Although every argument with inconsistent premises is valid, no such argument can be sound. And if the argument cannot be sound, it cannot prove its conclusion. If the premises of an argument are inconsistent, they cannot all be true. But all the premises of sound arguments are true.

The "validity" of arguments that commit the fallacy of inconsistency is peculiar. No matter what the conclusion is, the argument is "valid." But if any conclusion whatsoever can be derived from the premises, they cannot "justify" any particular conclusion.

The analysis of passages that commit the fallacy of inconsistency may seem to be an exception to our decision to avoid merely denying the truth of one or more statements in the passages. But it is not, because you must still prove that the statements are inconsistent and thus cannot all be true.

"Arguments" that beg the question are also valid. But their validity is also peculiar. The only reason such "arguments" are valid is that a premise is identical with the conclusion. It is possible for a question-begging "argument" to have all true premises. Thus, it is possible for a question-begging "argument" to be sound. What, then, is objectionable about question-begging "arguments"?

You will notice that we have put the word arguments in quotation marks when referring to so-called question-begging "arguments." This is because a question-begging "argument" can be called an argument only if we stretch the meaning of the word. An argument, strictly speaking, is a set of statements in which an attempt is made to establish one statement on the basis of another statement. But in a question-begging "argument," the "other" statement is identical to the conclusion and thus is not <u>another</u> statement. To beg the question, then, is to restate the claim being made rather than to justify it. But the restatement of the claim being made is put forward as though it were an independent reason for believing the statement. And <u>that</u> is a logical error.

The relationship of support between premises and conclusion is asymmetrical. That is, the premises support the conclusion, but not vice versa. Thus, the premise of a question-begging "argument" does not support the conclusion, because the conclusion implies the premise. The relationship is thus symmetrical, rather than asymmetrical. The premises of every non-fallacious argument, on the other hand, support the conclusion.

The point of an argument is to establish that something is the case. But if it is impossible to know that the premises are true without already knowing that its conclusion is true, then the argument does not establish the conclusion. In a question-begging "argument," it is impossible to know that the premises are true without already knowing its conclusion. (Complex questions are discussed in Chapter 3.)

Practice Exercises

On a separate sheet of paper, put each of the following arguments into logically proper form. Then explain exactly why the passage is fallacious. Do not merely slap a label on the passage, redefine the fallacy, or use a quick slogan. Rather, dissect the passages carefully.

1. No sane person would commit murder. I know that some murderers have been certified sane by psychiatrists, but they couldn't really have been sane or they wouldn't have committed murder.

2. Kubichek argued that no intelligent person believed in the existence of God. In response to examples of people who were both alleged to be intelligent and known to believe in the existence of God, he responded that they weren't really intelligent or they wouldn't believe in the existence of God.

3. During a discussion of the forthcoming election with a Republican friend, Sturdley said, "Are you going to vote for the Democrats in the next election, or have you decided that the rich should get richer and the poor poorer?"

4. The Bullhorns are the outstanding team in the conference, because they have the best players and the best coach. We know they have the best players and the best coach because they will win the conference title. And they will win the conference title because they deserve to win the conference title. Of course they deserve to win the conference title, for they are the outstanding team in the conference.

5. Bullgravy: "That new student says that I am his favorite professor. He must be telling the truth, because no student would lie to his favorite professor."

6. From an exam: "I feel God is the first cause and everything is caused. Therefore, God exists."

7. I. M. Pious: "There aren't any universal moral truths. We have no right to judge people in other cultures. Everyone is obligated to be tolerant of the beliefs of others. So, your claim that there are some universal moral truths is just dogmatic, intolerant, and narrow-minded."

8. Jerry Allswell: "As Christians, we believe that sinners will fry in hell."

   I. T. Endswell: "Wait a second! There are lots of Christians who believe that an all-forgiving God wouldn't condemn people to hell. Many don't believe in hell at all."

   J. F. Allswell: "Well, they can't be true Christians. Otherwise they'd believe God's word."

9. Concerning Pope Paul VI's decree barring women from the Roman Catholic priesthood: "Reserving the priesthood for men is no more discriminatory than restricting women singers to the soprano section of a choir," the Pope said. (Oklahoma Journal, 31 January 1977.)

10. Sturdley: "Capital punishment should be abolished."

    Schmucker: "What reason do you have for saying that?"

    Sturdley: "Because it is not the right of the state to continue its policy of putting human beings to death, no matter how awful their crime."

12-3

Nonsequiturs: Unwarranted Assumptions

Section Objective

1. Identify and analyze passages that contain a fallacy of unwarranted assumption.

Key Term Review

1. <u>Fallacy of unwarranted assumption</u>: an argument in which at least one premise is unsupported and has been shown by experience to be generally unsupportable.

2. <u>Fallacy of false dilemma</u>: an argument in which one reduces the alternatives to fewer than there are (usually to just two), rejecting all but one alternative, and inferring that the remaining alternative must be accepted (also known as the "black-and-white fallacy"). (Discussed in Chapter 3.)

3. <u>Fallacy of moralism</u>: an argument in which it is inferred that simply because something <u>is</u> (or is not) the case, it <u>ought</u> (or ought not) be the case.

4. <u>Wishful thinking</u>: an argument in which it is inferred that something <u>is</u> the case from premises that express wishes, hopes, desires, and beliefs about right and wrong (basically the reverse of the fallacy of moralism).

5. <u>Fallacy of negative proof</u>: an argument in which it is claimed that the

inability to demonstrate that a statement is true constitutes proof that
the statement's contradictory is true.

Summary

The Key Term Review and the discussion in the text constitute a good summary
of this section. The fallacy of negative proof consists in a failure to distinguish between "These arguments do not prove that the conclusion is true"
and "The conclusion of these arguments is not true." That distinction is
discussed in Section 2-4.

Practice Exercises

I. Analyze each of the following passages, using the procedural rules discussed in this chapter. Some passages may contain more than one fallacy.

   1. A Winston ad in response to the criticism that the company should have
      said, "Winston tastes good as a cigarette should" rather than "Win-
      ston tastes good like a cigarette should": "What do you want?
      Good grammar or good taste?"

   2. Sturdley: "I believe that some provisions of our criminal laws
      give the police authority to do things that are both dangerous and
      unconstitutional."

      Schmucker: "Oh, well, if you want to disarm and handcuff the
      police and turn the country over to thugs, fags, and hippies, we'd
      better all pack up and go to Australia."

   3. Smedley: "These 55 milies-per-hour speed limits are just plain
      idiotic."

      Sturdley: "Don't you think that such restrictions reduce the num-
      ber of accidents?"

      Smedley: "Oh, well, if you want us to crawl along at 5 m.p.h.,
      then no doubt there wouldn't be any accidents, barring the old
      women who step onto the highway sideways in front of the car."

   4. It hasn't been proved that God exists. This is the most compelling
      case for atheism.

   5. No one has proved that there is no God. This must be because there
      is a God.

   6. Of course there is a God. Why, life would have no purpose if
      there were no God.

   7. People in other cultures have moral beliefs that differ from those
      of people in our culture. So, we should not judge their beliefs.

   8. A newspaper in Pittsburgh, Kansas stopped printing "Doonesbury"
      recently. There was an outcry from the readers. The newspaper re-
      sponded with a ballot, asking the readers to vote either to con-
      tinue "Doonesbury" or to replace it with "The Far Side," another
      popular comic strip.

II. Below are several passages that contain one or more fallacies. Most of them contain fallacies discussed in previous chapters. (The overview for this chapter tells you where to find the textual explanation.) Analyze the following passages. Concentrate more on explaining just what is fallacious about the passage than on assigning a label.

1. Congress shouldn't bother to consult the Joint Chiefs of Staff about military appropriations. As members of the armed forces, they will naturally want as much money for military purposes as they think they can get.

2. Isn't it true that students who get all A's study hard? So if you want me to study hard, Professor, the best way to do it is to give me A's in all of my courses.

3. The wives of successful men wear expensive clothing, so the best way for a woman to help her husband become a success is to buy expensive clothing.

4. Of course socialism is desirable. Look at the facts. At one time all utilities were privately owned, but now more and more of them are owned by the government. The Social Security laws embody many of the principles socialists have always espoused. We are well on our way to socialism; its complete triumph is inevitable.

5. Senator Muskie: "If it means the re-election of Richard Nixon, then I am opposed to putting a Negro on the Democratic ticket."

   News bulletin (based on the foregoing statement by Senator Muskie): "Senator Muskie today expressed opposition to putting a Negro on the Democratic ticket."

6. The Golden Rule is basic to every system of ethics ever devised, and everyone accepts it in some form or other. It is therefore an undeniably sound moral principle.

7. From an ad for Sears barbells: Exercise with weight is considered by authorities in and out of the medical profession as having great therapeutic value. Dr. Paul Dudley White, the famous heart specialist, is quoted as saying, "I, myself, have found that exercise in moderation is one of the best ways to treat many of my convalescent cardiac patients. The establishment of a good program of regular exercise, I find, is often more important than many medicines."

8. Car advertisement: "We will give a brand new color TV, absolutely free, to anyone who buys a car from us."

9. From a news story in the Daily Oklahoman (December 10, 1975) about an attempt to outlaw steel hunting traps: Witt (vice president of the Oklahoma Trappers Association) said the leghole steel trap, which is opposed by the anti-trappers, "is not cruel like this group claims it to be. The leghole trap is one of the most efficient means of controlling predators and of harvesting fur-bearing animals. It's been used ever since 1823 and all of a sudden these humane groups show up, stating their opposition and protesting." (Note: There are two fallacies to be identified in this exercise.)

10. Smedley gargled with Micro antiseptic one morning, and only two hours later made the biggest sale of his career. Never underestimate the power of a sweet breath!

11. Sweden has many of the trappings of a socialist country--socialized medicine, guaranteed wage, etc. It also has one of the highest suicide rates in the world. So, if you want an epidemic of suicides, just let your country go socialistic.

12. Newspaper reporters should have the right to report the facts as they find them and to express their opinion without fear of reprisal. Jack Anderson was justified, therefore, in publishing unsubstantiated reports that Senator Eagleton was arrested four times for drunken driving.

13. "The University of Oklahoma certainly made a wise choice and did the right thing in dumping art education from its curriculum.... Cutting out the frills and getting back to basics mean the removal of all courses that don't pay off in good citizenship or dollars and cents. And this includes those silly, dangerous classes that teach 'art appreciation' to normal American children. Who are these artistic 'geniuses' whose work the little ones are forced to study? Edgar Allen Poe was an alcoholic dope fiend who died in the gutter; Vincent Van Gogh cut off his ear and shot himself; Virginia Woolf was crazy everyday of her life before she too took the coward's way out; Gertrude Stein was a lesbian, etc., etc. Are these the people we want our children to emulate? Of course not. But everyday of the school year one cultural criminal or another is held up for respect and admiration." (From a letter in the Oklahoma Journal, 22 September 1977.)

12-4

Non Sequiturs: Fallacies of Irrelevance

Section Objective

1. Identify and analyze passages that contain a fallacy of irrelevance.

Key Term Review

1. Fallacy of irrelevance: an argument based on a premise that has no bearing on the truth or fallacy of the conclusion.

2. *Ad hominem* fallacy: occurs when it is inferred that someone's claim is false or unworthy of attention because of that person's character or situation.

3. Abusive *ad hominem*: an *ad hominem* fallacy in which the premise is an attack on a person's character or ability rather than the claim at issue.

4. Circumstantial *ad hominem*: an *ad hominem* fallacy in which an attempt is made to undercut a person's claim by pointing out that his circumstances are such that he would be expected to accept the claim (suggesting that the claim is self-serving).

5. *Tu quoque*: an attempt to undercut a claim by calling attention to an alleged weakness or wrongdoing of the opponent (or others generally).

6. Appeal to inexpert authority: an attempt to get others to accept a conclusion by citing the veiws of someone who is not an expert on the issue in question.

7. Appeal to tradition: inferring that X is true (or should be done) from the popularity of a belief (or common practice).

8. Genetic fallacy: an attempt to dismiss a belief by making disparaging remarks about how the belief arose (or arises).

9. Poisoning the well: an attempt to dismiss an opponent's point of view by setting up the controversy in such a way that any response can be regarded as false, misguided, or not altogether honest.

Summary

Ad hominem arguments range from unconvincing cases of name calling to (unfortunately) persuasive suggestions that a claim is self-serving. The latter kind of case is fallacious because it bypasses the issue—namely, whether the case for the claim, regardless of the person's circumstances, is a good one. The fact that a claim would benefit the person making it does not alone justify disregarding the claim. For example, if some college professors argue that the size of classes should be reduced, the claim needs to be considered on its own merits. The fact that a reduction in class size would benefit those professors does not justify disregarding the claim or rejecting it, for there may be adequate reasons for making the claim.

Practice Exercises

Analyze each of the following passages and identify the major fallacy (or fallacies).

1. The Daily Oklahoman included an editorial calling for the resignation of Carl Albert. Somebody on the news responded to that editorial by saying that "I'd just like to point out that the Daily Oklahoman stuck by Richard Nixon to the bitter end."

2. "Mr. Sparkman and Mr. Stephenson (the Democratic vice-presidential and presidential nominees, respectively) should come before the American people, as I have, and make a complete financial statement as to their financial history, and if they don't, it will be an admission that they have something to hide."--Richard Nixon, during the 1952 presidential campaign.

3. Those who condemn the killing of civilians at My Lai should remember that the Viet Cong engaged in similar practices.

4. It is unfair for S.M.U. to be punished for violating NCAA rules. All the big football schools-Nebraska, Alabama, Texas, O.U., U.S.C., Notre Dame--are guilty of equally serious violations, maybe more serious.

5. Speeder to patrolman: "I don't see what's wrong with going 70 m.p.h.-- almost everybody does it."

6. "Of course it's all right to take (shoplift) these clothes. Big business rips us off all the time."

7. Ronald Reagan, in response to George McGovern's criticism of the number of tax loopholes allowed for big businesses, remarked, "Those same loopholes are the ones he (McGovern) takes."

8. Sturdley: "Of course Nixon's policy with the People's Republic of China is a bad one. What do you expect from a power-hungry politician who authorized burglary of the Democratic headquarters? Besides, that two-faced so-and-so has been a rabid anti-communist for years. So why is he being so friendly?"

9. "I just can't understand," fumed Sturdley, "why everyone is raising so much commotion about the C.I.A.'s illegal activities. Do they think that foreign governmental agencies follow the letter of the law?"

10. There must be a God, since a large number of people believe in God.

11. Argument against giving up the language requirement for majors in arts and sciences: If we give up the language requirement, why not give up the English requirement? We might as well give up the government requirement too. Pretty soon nothing will be required. Besides, we've always had a language requirement; and if it is good enough for your fathers and your fathers' fathers, it is good enough for you. Of course, some people don't mind being illiterate. Note: There are three fallacies to be identified in this passage. Some are discussed in previous chapters.

12. You can't believe what Professor Fizzbee says about the importance of higher salaries for teachers. As a teacher himself, he would naturally be in favor of increasing teachers' pay.

13. It is clear that Richard M. Nixon should not have been forced to resign the presidency. Why, some of his loudest critics were guilty of the same things they were accusing Nixon of. Furthermore, several of Nixon's predecessors in the White House--Johnson, Kennedy, and FDR-- had misused presidential power in much the same way Nixon did.

14. Norman Transcript, April 13, 1975, reporting an argument against outlawing cockfighting: "Cockfighting has a great history in the United States and the world," declared Representative John Monks, Democrat-Muskogee, noting that American patriots such as George Washington, Benjamin Frnaklin, and Abraham Lincoln were cockfighting fans.

15. From the same news story: Monks warned that countries outlawing cockfighting have turned from great powers to meek nations. "Look at the British Empire," he said. "King Henry VIII had a royal cockfighting pit. Now look at England...a toothless pussycat." (The fallacy involved here is discussed in a previous chapter.)

16. Nothing can be said on behalf of belief in God. After all, Freud pointed out that belief in God arises from the fear of the unknown and a need for a father figure as protection. (This is not an appeal to inexpert authority.)

CHAPTER 13
LEGAL REASONING

OVERVIEW

This chapter discusses the way logical principles and methods have been adapted to meet the practical needs of courts in solving the problems that come before them. The discussion focuses on the structure of arguments in judicial opinions of the appellate courts--that part of the legal system that shapes legal reasoning the most. Attention is paid to the nature of courts and trials and to how adversary proceedings in courts have influenced the character of legal reasoning. And special attention is given to reasoning by example, which is the predominant part of legal reasoning.

SECTION REVIEWS

Law as a Forum for Argument

Section Objective

1. Learn the nature of the adversary process and the kind of problems that legal reasoning must solve.

Key Term Review

1. <u>Question of fact</u>: the descriptive question of what actually happened.

2. <u>Question of law</u>: the problem of determining which rule of law should be applied in a particular situation.

Summary

The primary function of reasoning in the law is concerned with questions of law rather than questions of fact. The concrete case at hand must be placed within a line of precedents, and a ruling must be made in accordance with those precedents. The opposing lawyers in the adversary process both try to show why the given case fits better into one line of precedents than another. The appellate judge, or whoever is called on to make the decision, must try to decide which group of arguments best represents the situation.

Practice Exercises

1. Show the difference between questions of fact and questions of law by "inventing" a case that might come to trial and raising both kinds of questions.

2. Explain why it may be difficult to decide whether a certain law applies to a given case.

3. Reflect on the laws with which you are familiar. Does there appear to be a general purpose or function to all the laws? If so, what is it?

4. Reread Question B1 at the end of Exercise 13-1 in the text (regarding the local law prohibiting citizens from taking a vehicle into the public park) and rule on each of the following cases:

   a. The two brothers Phil and Throp, who gave the park to the city under the agreement that they may live there and use the grounds until their deaths, have been driving their Duesenburg out of the park for groceries.

   b. A student named Fleur Tasious has been roller skating through the park to the community college on the other side.

   c. Beginning hang-gliders practice on the embankment on the west side of the park under the supervision of an advanced flyer.

   d. Mr. and Mrs. Rivalry have allowed their twins, Sib and Ling, to ride their tricycles on the outdoor basketball court when it is not in use.

   e. Clara Nette, Suzy Fone, and Barry Tone from the high school band were maneuvering a powered bandstand into the amphitheater area for the annual Fourth of July concert when arrested by a police officer.

13-2

Logic and Legal Reasoning

Section Objective

1. Become familiar with the perspective of the legal realists, and understand how it affected the popular view about the relationship between legal decisions and logic.

Summary

The legal realists reacted to the view that judges could find a law that addressed a particular set of facts and could derive the proper conclusion by deductive argument. Because cases are specific and in some respects unique, and laws are general, there can be no mechanical application of laws to cases. The legal realists held that legal decisions have very little to do with logic.

Realism meant opposition to the illusion of law as a complete and logically consistent set of rules and their application. Realism meant recognizing that certainty was neither attainable nor important. Realism meant being aware that social responsibility and desirable consequences were the important concern of the law. Realism meant understanding that judges sometimes base their decisions on hunches, prejudices, emotions, desires, and social concerns.

The realists brought a breath of fresh air to the halls of justice. These revolutionaries attempted to supplant a strict and incorrect view of the legal process at the same time Dewey and the education reformers supplanted a strict view of the educational process.

These moves were important, valuable, and influential. But like most revolutionaries and iconoclasts, the legal realists overreacted, overstated their case, and broke too many idols. The truth lies somewhere between the extreme of the completely deductive model of law and the completely non-rational model of law.

Practice Exercises

1. Rewrite the "law" about vehicles in the park from Section 13-1 to be as precise as possible about the vehicles you will exclude from the park. If you wish, you may also list any "vehicles" that would be allowed in the park.

2. Now see whether you can come up with a possible situation that your "law" did not foresee.

3. Discuss whether or not it is possible in principle or in practice to write laws that will cover all possible future situations.

4. Now that you appreciate the difficulty of writing all-inclusive laws, discuss the adequacy of the view that the legal realists were reacting to.

13-3

Reasoning by Example

Section Objective

1. Understand the use of analogy in legal reasoning.

Summary

Legal reasoning is neither deductively mechanical nor entirely free and open. There are laws in existence, precedents in other cases, and a public expectation of a certain rationality in the courts. Hence judges are scarcely free to make any decision to which they might be inclined. But on the other hand, there are few laws so encompassing and few facts so obvious that there is no question about what must be decided.

As the text so ably points out, there may be many laws and precedents favorable to one interpretation of the case, but there may be an equal number favorable to another interpretation. The reasoning involved in dealing with such situations is reasoning by analogy. This is certainly not deductive reasoning. Although many might think of it as inductive reasoning, it does differ from the more common inductive moves from "some" to "all" or from observed cases to unobserved cases. Reasoning by example does not involve inferences about new facts; rather, it involves inferences about the proper way to classify a case.

As has been said, there may be laws and precedents on both sides of a legal issue. The role of the opposing lawyers is to try to show why "their" set of precedents applies correctly to the issue. The judge must then "judge" these arguments to determine whether the facts that would bring the decision under one set of precedents are more important than the facts that would bring the decision under another set of precedents. In other words he is deciding whether the analogy between the present case and one set of rulings is stronger than the analogy between this case and another set of rulings.

Some considerations that may be taken into account are (1) the intention of the lawmakers who adopted a particular statute, (2) the purpose that the ruling or act was designed to achieve, and (3) the social implications of various possible rulings. After reflecting on these things, the judge may formulate a rule that could be applied immediately and directly to the case at hand.

This rule might be a modification of a previous rule to make it fit the present (but possibly unforeseen) case, or it might be a modification or clarification of vague language in an existing rule. Applying the modified rule to the present case is merely a deductive analysis.

Practice Exercises

Examine the following passage from the 1896 Supreme Court ruling *Plessy v. Ferguson* and the passage from the 1954 decision *Brown v. Board of Education*. (a) List the previous cases and rulings that are given as having a bearing on the Supreme Court's 1954 decision. (b) Discuss whether you think the Thirteenth and Fourteenth Amendments would require the ruling that was made in 1954.

Plessy v. Ferguson

163 U.S. 537 1896.

Mr. Justice Brown delivered the opinion of the Court.

This case turns upon the constitutionality of an act of the general assembly of the state of Louisiana, passed in 1890, providing for separate railway carriages for the white and colored races.

The information filed in the criminal district court charged in substance that Plessy, being a passenger between two stations within the state of Louisiana, was assigned by officers of the company to the coach used for the race to which he belonged, but he insisted upon going into a coach used by the race to which he did not belong....

The petition for the writ of prohibition averred that petitioner was seven eighths Caucasian and one eighth African blood....

...The constitutionality of this act is attacked upon the ground that it conflicts both with the 13th Amendment of the Constitution, abolishing slavery, and the 14th Amendment, which prohibits certain restrictive legislation on the part of the states.

1. That it does not conflict with the 13th Amendment, which abolished slavery and involuntary servitude, except as a punishment for a crime, is too clear for argument....

Indeed, we do not understand that the 13th Amendment is strenuously relied upon by the plaintiff in error in this connection.

2. By the 14th Amendment, all persons born or naturalized in the United States, and subject to the jurisdiction thereof, are made citizens of the United States and of the state wherein they reside; and the states are forbidden from making or enforcing any law which shall abridge the privileges or immunities of citizens of the United States, or shall deprive any person of life, liberty, or property without due process of law, or deny to any person within their jurisdiction the equal protection of the laws....

The object of the amendment was undoubtedly to enforce the absolute equality of the two races before the law, but in the nature of things it could not have been intended to abolish distinctions based upon color, or to enforce social, as distinguished from political, equality, or a commingling of the two races upon terms unsatisfactory to either. Laws permitting, and even requiring their separation in places where they are liable to be brought into contact do not necessarily imply the inferiority of either race to the other, and have been generally, if not universally, recognized as within the competency of the state legislatures in the exercise of their police power. The most common instance of this is connected with the establishment of separate schools for white and colored children, which have been held to be a valid exercise of the legislative power even by courts of states where the political rights of the colored race have been longest and most earnestly enforced....

So far, then, as a conflict with the 14th Amendment is concerned, the case reduces itself to the question whether the statute of Louisiana is a reasonable regulation, and with respect to this there must necessarily be a large discretion on the part of the legislature. In determining the question of reasonableness it is at liberty to act with reference to the established usages, customs, and traditions of the people, and with a view to the promotion of their comfort, and the preservation of the public peace and good order. Gauged by this standard, we cannot say that a law which authorizes or even requires the separation of the two races in public conveyances is unreasonable or more obnoxious to the 14th Amendment than the acts of Congress requiring separate schools for colored children in the District of Columbia, the constitutionality of which does not seem to have been questioned, or the corresponding acts of state legislatures.

We consider the underlying fallacy of the plaintiff's argument to consist in the assumption that the enforced separation of the two races stamps the colored race with a badge of inferiority. If this be so, it is not by reason of anything found in the act, but solely because the colored race chooses to put that construction upon it. The argument necessarily assumes that if, as has been more than once the case, and is not unlikely to be so again, the colored race should become the dominant power in the state legislature, and should enact a law in precisely similar terms, it would thereby relegate the white race to an inferior position. We imagine that the white race, at least, would not acquiesce in this assumption. The argument also assumes that social prejudices may be overcome by legislation, and that equal rights cannot be secured to the negro except by an enforced commingling of the two races. We cannot accept this proposition. If the two races are to meet on terms of social

equality, it must be the result of natural affinity, a mutual appreciation of each other's merits and a voluntary consent of individuals.
As was said by the court of appeals of New York in *People v. Galla-
gher*, "this end can neither be accomplished nor promoted by laws
which conflict with the general sentiment of the community upon whom
they are designed to operate. When the government, therefore, has
secured to each of its citizens equal rights before the law and
equal opportunities for improvement and progress, it has accomplished
the end for which it is organized and performed all of the functions
respecting social advantages with which it is endowed." Legislation
is powerless to eradicate racial instincts or to abolish distinctions
based upon physical differences, and the attempt to do so can only
result in accentuating the difficulties of the present situation.
If the civil and political rights of both races be equal, one cannot
be inferior to the other civilly or politically. If one race be inferior to the other socially, the Constitution of the United States
cannot put them upon the same plane....

Brown v. Board of Education

347 U.S. 483 1954

Mr. Chief Justice Warren delivered the opinion of the Court.

These cases come to us from the States of Kansas, South Carolina,
Virginia, and Delaware. They are premised on different facts and
different local conditions, but a common legal question justifies
their consideration together in this consolidated opinion.

In each of the cases, minors of the Negro race, through their legal
representatives, seek the aid of the courts in obtaining admission
to the public schools of their community on a nonsegregated basis.
In each instance, they had been denied admission to schools attended
by white children under laws requiring or permitting segregation according to race. This segregation was alleged to deprive the plaintiffs of the equal protection of the laws under the Fourteenth Amendment. In each of the cases other than the Delaware case, a three-
judge federal district court denied relief to the plaintiffs on the
so-called "separate but equal" doctrine announced by this Court in
Plessy v. Ferguson. Under that doctrine, equality of treatment is
accorded when the races are provided substantially equal facilities,
even though these facilities be separate. In the Delaware case, the
Supreme Court of Delaware adhered to that doctrine, but ordered that
the plaintiffs be admitted to the white schools because of their superiority to the Negro schools.

The plaintiffs contend that segregated public schools are not "equal"
and cannot be made "equal," and that hence they are deprived of the
equal protection of the laws. Because of the obvious importance of
the question presented, the Court took jurisdiction. Argument was
heard this Term on certain questions propounded by the Court....

In the first cases in this Court construing the Fourteenth Amendment,
decided shortly after its adoption, the Court interpreted it as pro-
scribing all state-imposed discriminations against the Negro race.
The doctrine of "separate but equal" did not make its appearance in
this Court until 1896 in the case of *Plessy v. Ferguson* involving
not education but transportation. American courts have since labored

with the doctrine for over half a century. In this Court, there have
been six cases involving the "separate but equal" doctrine in the
field of public education. In *Cumming v. County Board of Education*
and *Gong Lum v. Rice* the validity of the doctrine itself was not
challenged. In more recent cases, all on the graduate school level,
inequality was found in that specific benefits enjoyed by white students were denied to Negro students of the same educational qualifications. In none of these cases was it necessary to re-examine the
doctrine to grant relief to the Negro plaintiff. And in *Sweatt v.
Painter* the Court expressly reserved decision on the question whether
Plessy v. Ferguson should be held inapplicable to public education.

In the instant cases, that question is directly presented. Here, unlike *Sweatt v. Painter*, there are findings below that the Negro and
white schools involved have been equalized, or are being equalized,
with respect to buildings, curricula, qualifications and salaries of
teachers, and other "tangible" factors. Our decision, therefore,
cannot turn on merely a comparison of these tangible factors in the
Negro and white schools involved in each of the cases. We must look
instead to the effect of segregation itself on public education.

In approaching this problem, we cannot turn the clock back to 1868
when the Amendment was adopted, or even to 1896 when *Plessy v. Ferguson* was written. We must consider public education in the light
of its full development and its present place in American life
throughout the Nation. Only in this way can it be determined if
segregation in public schools deprives these plaintiffs of the
equal protection of the laws.

Today, education is perhaps the most important function of state
and local governments. Compulsory school attendance laws and the
great expenditures for education both demonstrate our recognition
of the importance of education to our democratic society. It is
required in the performance of our most basic public responsibil-
ities, even service in the armed forces. It is the very foundation
of good citizenship. Today it is a principal instrument in awaken-
ing the child to cultural values, in preparing him for later professional training, and in helping him to adjust normally to his
environment. In these days, it is doubtful that any child may reasonably be expected to succeed in life if he is denied the opportunity of an education. Such an opportunity, where the state has
undertaken to provide it, is a right which must be made available
to all on equal terms.

We come then to the question presented: Does segregation of children in public schools solely on the basis of race, even though the
physical facilities and other "tangible" factors may be equal, deprive the children of the minority group of equal educational opportunities? We believe that it does.

In *Sweatt v. Painter* in finding that segregated law school for
Negroes could not provide them equal educational opportunities,
this Court relied in large part on "those qualities which are incapable of objective measurement but which make for greatness in
a law school." In *McLaurin v. Oklahoma State Regents* the Court,
in requiring that a Negro admitted to a white graduate school be
treated like all other students, again resorted to intangible considerations: "...his ability to study, to engage in discussions
and exchange views with other students, and, in general, to learn

his profession." Such considerations apply with added force to children in grade and high schools. To separate them from others of similar age and qualifications solely because of their race generates a feeling of inferiority as to their status in the community that may affect their hearts and minds in a way unlikely ever to be undone. The effect of this separation on their education opportunities was well stated by a finding in the Kansas case by a court which nevertheless felt compelled to rule against the Negro plaintiffs:

> Segregation of white and colored children in public schools has a detrimental effect upon the colored children. The impact is greater when it has the sanction of the law; for the policy of separating the races is usually interpreted as denoting the inferiority of the negro group. A sense of inferiority affects the motivation of a child to learn. Segregation with the sanction of law, therefore, has a tendency to retard the educational and mental development of negro children and to deprive them of some of the benefits they would receive in a racially integrated school system.

Whatever may have been the extent of psychological knowledge at the time of *Plessy v. Ferguson*, this finding is amply supported by modern authority. Any language in *Plessy v. Ferguson* contrary to this finding is rejected.

We conclude that in the field of public education the doctrine of "separate but equal" has no place. Separate educational facilities are inherently unequal. Therefore, we hold that the plaintiffs and others similarly situated for whom the actions have been brought are, by reason of the segregation complained of, deprived of the equal protection of the laws guaranteed by the Fourteenth Amendment....

13-4

Evaluating Judicial Decisions

Section Objective

1. Become familiar with the contemporary points of view and issues involved in evaluating the reasonableness of judicial reasoning.

Key Term Review

1. *Stare decisis*: Literally "let the decision stand;" the policy of following precedents in establishing new rulings.

2. Judicial activism: the view that courts should take a leading role in advancing individual rights and shaping public policy.

3. Judicial restraint: the view that the courts should take little or no initiative in public policy matters but should follow the lead of legislative bodies insofar as possible.

Summary

The model of reasoning by analogy or reasoning by example presented in this chapter sees the judicial process as allowing the law to live and grow and adapt at the same time that it is a product of the past. Both stability and growth are extremely important elements.

The *stare decisis* ("let the decision stand") rule of applying principles to later cases as they have been applied to earlier ones promote reliability and stability for the system. Without it, many more cases would come to trial because it would be so hard to anticipate how any ruling would be made. But at the other pole is the fact that new issues, new facts, new attitudes, and new interests can mold rulings into new shapes.

Judicial activists believe that courts should take an active role in shaping public policy, whereas those who advocate judicial restraint believe that the courts should leave any policy changes to the legislative bodies.

Practice Exercises

1. Re-read the *Plessy v. Ferguson* and *Brown v. Board of Education* cases.
   (a) Do you think the 1896 court could be described as either exhibiting judicial activism or exhibiting judicial restraint? (b) What about the Kansas court (see the quotation near the end of the *Brown v. Board of Education* case)? (c) What about the 1954 Supreme Court?

2. Suppose that thorough long-term psychological studies show that no emotional or psychological harms ever come to those who have been unwillingly segregated. Discuss whether or not you think the Supreme Court could still rule that "in the field of public education the doctrine of 'separate but equal' has no place."

CHAPTER 14
THE PRACTICE OF ANALYZING ARGUMENTS

OVERVIEW

Many of the previous chapters concentrate on specific principles and techniques for appraising arguments. Comparatively little attention has been
paid to the problem of how systematically to analyze an argument. How do
you put a passage into such a form that you can apply the principles for
appraising arguments? Some techniques for doing so were discussed in Chapters 2 and 12, among others. But in this chapter the procedures are sys-
tematized. Moreover, this chapter introduces a diagramming technique for
exhibiting the structure of arguments.

SECTION REVIEWS

14-1

The Six Steps of Argument Analysis

Section Objectives

1. Identify and apply the six steps of argument analysis.

2. Identify and apply the subsidiary steps of argument analysis.

Key Term Review

1. Main conclusion (of an extended argument): the major point the author
   tries to establish (or prove).

2. Extended argument: a complex argument consisting of one main conclusion supported by premises that are the conclusions of subsidiary arguments.

3. Subsidiary argument (in an extended argument): an argument whose conclusion is a premise from which the main conclusion is (at least in
   part) inferred; an argument that indirectly helps to make the main
   point (or conclusion).

4. Supposition: a statement that is hypothetically assumed in order to
   show that certain consequences follow from it, but that, unlike a
   premise, is not affirmed to be true.

5. *Reductio ad adsurdum* argument: an argument in which (a) the arguer
   begins with the supposition of the contradictory of what the arguer intends to prove; (b) a contradiction or an obvious falsehood is inferred
   from that supposition (and perhaps other statements assumed to be true);
   and (c) what the arguer intends to prove is concluded.

6. Tacit assumption: a premise or conclusion that the author of the pass-

age does not state explicitly but that is accepted by the author, as shown by the context of the passage.

7. Leading argument (in an extended argument): an argument whose premises are the conclusions of subsidiary arguments and whose conclusion is the main conclusion.

8. Cause of a belief: whatever explains the fact that someone has a belief, which may not or may not consist in evidence for the belief.

9. Provisional acceptance (of an argument): regarding an argument as establishing its conclusion, provided that its questionable premise is true.

10. Counterexample: an example that shows that a generalization is false.

11. Refutation by analogy: an argument designed to show that another argument is invalid, and that has (a) the same form as the argument being refuted, (b) easily recognizable true premises, and (c) an easily recognizable false conclusion.

Summary

Let us consider each step briefly.

1. Identify the main conclusion. Doing this presupposes that the passage under consideration is an extended argument. If it is an argument, but not an extended one, identify the conclusion. The conclusion may be unstated, in which case you will have to supply it. You may have to revise your initial identification of the conclusion, if further analysis shows that your first guess is not correct.

2. Clarify meaning and formulate tacit assumptions. This step involves three procedures.

    a. Reducing ambiguity and vagueness. This is accomplished by replacing unfamiliar terms with familiar synonyms and reformulating sentences to bring out their informative content. If synonymous terms occur, use the same term throughout. The reformulation of sentences and the substitution of synonyms must not distort the author's intended meaning.

    b. Standardizing statements: In Chapter 2 we discussed paring a passage down to the argument only. This involves crossing out everything that is repetitious or neither premise nor conclusion. You should also delete digressions, mere examples, personal recollections, exclamations, and phrases such as "on the other hand" and "as a matter of fact."
        In a *reductio ad absurdum* argument, the supposition with which the arguer begins is the contradictory of what he intends to prove. Accordingly, you should not interpret the supposition as something the arguer believes to be true. If you did, then you would attribute to the arguer the belief that a statement and its contradictory are both true. Thus, the supposition should be interpreted as the antecedent of a conditional statement.

    c. Formulating tacit assumptions. Before doing this, you must have identified all the explicit statements, deleted statements that are neither premises nor conclusions, deleted extraneous phrases from the premises and conclusions, and eliminated ambiguities. Then you

218

are prepared to formulate tacit assumptions. But you must be cautious in doing so. The statements attributed to the arguer must be ones that it is reasonable to believe he would accept. Generally, they should be plausible and consistent with the explicit premises. Only on very rare occasions is it legitimate to attribute an implausible tacit assumption to the arguer.

If the argument is deductive, your knowledge of formal logic can help you formulate tacit assumptions. If the conclusion is explicit, ask yourself, "What must the tacit premise be in order to render the explicit argument formally valid?" Of course, there is an infinite number of premises that would fit. But you should choose the one that is most plausible and most clearly suggested by the explicit statements. Suppose, for example, that the deductive argument is correctly symbolized as "A/Therefore, B." The conclusion would be formally valid if a tacit assumption were either "R & B" or "If A, then B." There are other possibilities, but let us concentrate on the choice between these two. There are a couple of reasons (other things being equal) for preferring "If A, then B." If "R & B" were the tacit assumption, then the explicit premise, "A," would play no role in the derivation of the conclusion, and you would be faced with the problem of explaining why the arguer stated it. But "A" would play a role in deriving the conclusion if the tacit premise were "If A, then B." Second, if the tacit premise were "R & B," the argument would be open to the criticism that it is question-begging; not so if the tacit premise were "If A, then B." Third, "R" would play no role in deriving the conclusion if the tacit premise were "R & B."

A couple of general rules for formulating tacit premises based on formal considerations, then, are (1) interpret the tacit premise in such a way that all the plausible explicit premises must be used to derive in such a way that the argument is not informally fallacious. The second rule is an instance of the principle of charity (Chapter 3). Occasionally there are exceptions to this rule, because some arguments are fallacious.

3. <u>Portray the structure.</u> You are in a position to do this only if you have followed steps 1 and 2. For simple arguments, we display the structure by underlining the conclusion and putting brackets around the premises. We display the structure of extended arguments with tree diagrams, which will be explained in the next section.

4. <u>Evaluate the inference.</u> Let us speak of the evaluation of simple arguments. Because an extended argument is an interrelated set of simple arguments, the evaluation of inferences in extended arguments is largely a matter of applying to each constituent argument the principles for appraising simple arguments.

If the argument is inductive, then it should be evaluated in terms of reliability and strength (Chapter 10). When appraising an inductive argument's strength, you are considering the probability of the conclusion, given the premises. If the probability (given the premises) is sufficiently high, then the conclusion is the best explanation for the evidence stated in the premises. This points to a way to appraise inductive arguments. Try to think of alternative explanations of the premises (that is, other possible conclusions). Compare them with the conclusion and rank them in terms of how well they account for the premises. If the conclusion in the passage fares better than all of its competitors, then the argument is a strong one. But if the conclusion provides no better an explanation than at least one of its competitors, then the argument is inconclusive. Worse still, if one of its competitors is a better explanation of the premises, then the argument is weak.

If the argument is deductive, you can symbolize the argument and test its validity. Sometimes a very effective way of demonstrating an argument's invalidity is to formulate a refutation by analogy (Chapter 2). A common error that students make in constructing refutations by analogy is that they use premises that few people know to be true and a conclusion that few people know to be false. The premises of a refutation by analogy must be statements that are clearly true and statements that your audience will recognize as clearly false. Otherwise you will not succeed in showing to your audience that an argument with the same form, having all true premises and a false conclusion, can be constructed. Now this does not mean that the argument that you are trying to refute must have clearly true premises and a clearly false conclusion. If it did, there would be no need to refute it; the argument would be clearly invalid in that event. Thus, even if the premises and conclusion of an argument you are trying to refute are not known to be true or false, the argument with which you refute it must have clearly true premises and a clearly false conclusion. If an argument that is part of an extended argument is weak, inconclusive, or invalid, then that has ramifications throughout the extended argument. If a subsidiary argument does not establish its conclusion, then the leading argument does not do so either. The reason is that the leading argument's premises are the conclusions of the subsidiary arguments.

5. Assess the premises. Even if the conclusion of an inductive argument is the best explanation of the premises, it may still be criticizable. Even if a deductive argument is valid, it may still be unsound, or it may not be known to be sound. This is the case if a premise is false, questionable, ill supported, or unsupported altogether.

It is impossible to prove every premise, since the arguments for each premise would contain premises that would need to be proved by arguments that contain premises, and so on. However, there are many premises that require an argument in their favor. When is it reasonable to require proof of a premise? There are no mechanical procedures, but it is possible in many cases to detect questionable claims even when you do not have sufficient information to judge their truth or falsity.

Classifying statements can help you determine what sort of evidence would be necessary to establish their truth. A first step would be to classify the statements as necessary or contingent. If a statement is necessarily true, it is unobjectionable and need not be considered further unless a contingent statement is inferred from it (or a set of necessarily true statements). The reason is that no contingent statement is a deductive consequence of a necessarily true statement alone. (But this is an evaluation of an inference, rather than the premises.) If a statement is necessarily false, that alone is sufficient to justify inferring that the argument does not prove its conclusion.

If a statement is contingent, a more refined classification is usually necessary. If the statement is statistical, then the corroborating evidence would consist of a study of a sufficiently large and representative sample. If the statement is historical, then the evidence would consist of the historical records, their internal consistency, and consistency with other things that are known or justifiably believed. The credibility of the statement would depend on these factors. If the statement is a report of an observation (such as a crime), such factors as the lighting, the witness's vision, consistency with the reports of other witnesses, and distance from the scene would have to be considered. If the statement is an inference based on an observation, we must evaluate the inference and determine that it is reliable before assessing it further.

Let us review the steps thus far: (1) Identify the main conclusion. (2) Clarify meaning and formulate tacit assumptions by (a) reducing ambiguity and vagueness, (b) standarizing statements, and (c) formulating tacit assumptions. (3) Portray the argument's structure. (4) Evaluate the inference. (5) Assess the premises. Once you have done these things, you are prepared to take the final step.

6. Make an overall assessment. This is largely a matter of noting what you have done already. If an argument is unreliable, weak, or invalid, then it does not establish its conclusion. If at least one premise is false or quite dubious, then the argument does not establish its conclusion. If, on the other hand, an argument passes these tests, then it establishes its conclusion.

There will nevertheless be occasions where you are not sure whether an argument has established its conclusion. This may happen, for example, when a premise requires support that is not provided, but you are not sure whether the proof could be produced. In that case you will need to consider

Whether there are other arguments on the same issue that support the opposite or different conclusions and, if there are, how good they are (in comparison to the argument under consideration).

Whether there are other arguments that support the same conclusion and, if so, how good they are.

Whether you know if there is any new or previously unnoticed evidence that has a bearing on the issue and, if so, whether it supports the argument under consideration or its competitors.

Making an overall assessment is sometimes a matter of weighing the evidence. In the absence of a sufficiently strong case for a particular conclusion to warrant confident belief in it, we must determine which conclusion is the most plausible, given the evidence. Our degree of belief in the most plausible conclusion should be proportionate to the evidence in its favor. That is, the better the evidence, the less confident we should be about the conclusion. That is what it means to be rational. It is not the case that the only alternative to conclusive proof of a conclusion is arbitrary choice.

Practice Exercises

Answer the following questions in your own words.

1. What is the difference between an extended argument and the leading argument in the same passage?

2. What is the point of formulating subsidiary arguments?

3. Why is it important to distinguish between deductive and inductive arguments before evaluating them?

4. What is the relationship between a subsidiary argument and a leading argument?

5. Explain what, if anything, is wrong with the following argument: "Professor, this argument that you want me to refute by analogy does not have clearly true premises and a recognizably false conclusion. So, I can refute it effectively by using premises that only I recognize as true and a conclusion that only I know is false."

14-2

Tree Diagrams for Extended Arguments

Section Objective

1. Portray the structure of arguments with tree diagrams.

Key Term Review

1. Tree diagram: a drawing that shows the logical relationship between the main conclusion and every other statement integral to an argument.

2. Primary premises (of an extended argument): the premises of the leading argument; premises that directly support the main conclusion.

3. Secondary premises (of an extended argument): the premises of a subsidiary argument; premises that support the primary premises.

4. Dependent support: a premise supports the conclusion only in conjunction with at least one other premise.

5. Independent support: a premise by itself supports the conclusion (independently of any other premise).

Summary

Before you can diagram an argument, you must label the parts of the passage as follows:

1. Underline the main conclusion and label it *"MC."* (Label it *"MC*"* if it is not stated explicitly.)

2. Put the primary premises in brackets; label and number each one *"P₁," "P₂,"* etc. Put an asterisk between the *P* and the number of the premise if it is tacit. (Of course, tacit premises and conclusions will have to be written out in full.)

3. Put the secondary premises in parentheses; label and number each one *"SP₁," "SP₂,"* etc. Follow the same directions for tacit secondary premises as for tacit primary premises.

Make sure that the parts of the passage thus marked contain only premises and conclusion. You have then completed the preliminaries and are prepared to diagram the argument according to the following rules:

1. Each premise is connected to the conclusion it supports by a straight line.

2. Each tree diagram has only one main conclusion (or base), and branching occurs only in an upward direction.

3. A statement that supports the conclusion dependently is joined to the other dependently supporting premise by a brace.

4. An implicit premise can be designated with an asterisk and added to any part of the tree diagram above the main conclusion. (If the main conclusion is implicit, it is designated with an asterisk.)

5. A statement that weakens or diverges from another claim is attached by a broken line to the statement it affects.

Consider these examples from the text:

1. (*MC*) <u>Voluntary euthanasia ought not to be legalized</u>. In the first place, (*SP₁*) (it is difficult to ascertain whether the consent of the patient is really voluntary). Thus, (*P₁*) [there is substantial danger that the law will be abused]. Second, (*SP₂*) (the judgment that a person is incurably ill may be wrong on two counts: the diagnostic judgment may be in error, and the judgment that no cure will be available within the life expectancy of the patient may be in error). Thus, (*P₂*) [there is substantial risk that some will die unnecessarily]. Finally, (*P₃*) [to legalize voluntary euthanasia is to accept the "thin edge of the wedge," thus preparing the way for the legalization of involuntary euthanasia]. The diagram of this argument is

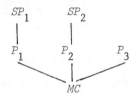

Statement (*P₃*) is a conditional statement: if voluntary euthanasia is legalized, then the "thin edge of the wedge" is accepted and the way is prepared for legalization of involuntary euthanasia. The primary premises independently support the *MC*, and this fact is reflected by separate lines connecting each to the *MC* and by the lack of a brace connecting P_1, P_2, and P_3. The statements that follow the colon in SP_2 are elaborations of the statement before the colon, rather than premises that support the statement before the colon.

2. The principle I wish to attack is this: There is no natural difference between the sexes that makes the male-dominated society inevitable. (*P₁*) [There is such a difference.] (*SP₁*) (Owing to hormonal differences, males are inherently more aggressive than females.) (*P₁*) [This greater aggressiveness assures male domination of the high-status roles in society.] Moreover, (*MC*) <u>if society does not socialize women to reject competing with men, then most women will be condemned to failure and unhappiness</u>. (*SP₁*) (Given the innate-aggression advantage of men over women,) consider what would happen (*P₂*) [if society did not socialize women to reject competing with men for society's high-status positions. Some women would be aggressive enough to succeed. The vast majority

would be failures,] however--socialized to desire high-status positions but incapable of attaining them.

You will note that I have labeled two statements "P_1" and two sets of words "SP_1." This is because they both make the same statements. Ordinarily you should delete the repetition of the same statement. The first occurrence of P_1 and the second appearance of SP_1 would be deleted, since those do not express the statement as clearly as the other formulations. It is noteworthy that the second occurrence of SP_1 is a sentence fragment, which illustrates the fact that there is not a one-to-one correspondence between sentences and statements. Another example of this point is that P_2 encompasses parts of two sentences and the entirety of a third. It can be paraphrased as "If society did not socialize women to reject competing with men for society's high-status positions, then some women would be aggressive enough to succeed, but the vast majority would be failures." The last part of the passage ("socialized to desire high-status positions but incapable of attaining them") merely repeats P_2.

It is arguable that the main conclusion is unstated and that there is a suppressed premise. The arguer could be interpreted as arguing for the wisdom of the "status quo" as follows:

> If society does not socialize women to reject competing with men, then most women will be condemned to failure and unhappiness. (MC)
>
> It is undesirable for most women to be condemned to failure and unhappiness. ($P*_3$)
>
> Therefore, it is desirable for society to socialize women to reject competing with men. ($MC*$)

This would, in effect, reduce the status of the stated MC to a primary premise, the primary premises to secondary premises, and the secondary premises to third-order premises. In order to avoid labeling everything again, I shall use the same labels. The diagram is

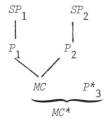

MC and $P*_3$ support $MC*$ only in conjunction with one another. This dependent support is represented in the diagram by a brace that connects MC and $P*_3$. It is also reasonable to interpret the stated passage as

having two main conclusions, the one I have not identified heretofore being "There is a natural difference between the sexes that makes the male-dominated society inevitable." Assessing this argument represents a real challenge, particularly since many people are likely to be emotional about the thesis defended. What evidence would be required in order to show that P_1, for example, is false (alternatively, ill founded)?

Practice Exercises

On a separate sheet of paper, label and then diagram each of the following passages as shown above.

1. How do we explain the existence of things that began to exist? Either things that began to exist are causes of themselves or were caused by something else. If anything that began to exist were its own cause, it would have to exist before it began to exist. But that's impossible. So, everything that began to exist is caused by something else (that existed beforehand). We know we have to turn to the past to find the causes of things that began to exist, but how far back can we go? There cannot be an infinite regress of causes. In other words, there must be a beginning of the chain of causes. If so, then there is a first cause, which (a) does not begin to exist and (b) is not caused but (c) causes everything else. Thus, there is a first cause, which everyone calls "God." Therefore, God exists. Why must there be a beginning of the chain of causes? If there were no beginning of the chain of causes, then there would be no first cause. But if there were no first cause, then, since to take away the cause is to take away the effect, nothing thereafter would have existed, and nothing would exist now. However, something exists. (Based on Aquinas's "second way.")

2. Aquinas's "second way" does not even prove that there is a first cause, much less God's existence, for the subsidiary causal argument (SCA) commits the fallacy of equivocation. Consider the first premise of the SCA: "if there were no beginning of the chain of causes, then there would be no first cause." In order for that statement to be true, "there is no first cause" must mean "everything is caused." Now consider the second premise, "if there were no first cause, then nothing thereafter would exist." If that premise is true, "there is no first cause" cannot mean "everything is caused." For if everything is caused, then there is always something or other that began to exist and causes subsequent things to begin to exist. And that is compatible with things existing now. The second premise is translated as "if at one time nothing existed, then nothing would exist now." Only that interpretation renders the premise true. This fits with Aquinas's statement that "to take away the cause is to take away the effect." Aquinas has in mind taking away the existence of things, which would make it impossible for things to exist now. However, the supposition that everything is caused does not imply that at one time nothing existed. Thus, "there is no first cause" means two different things in the premises of the SCA. However, the argument would be valid only if the meaning were the same in both premises.

3. A religious text (such as the Bible, the Koran, or the Torah) sometimes is offered as proof of God's existence. But the major premise of such arguments--namely, "Every statement in the religious text is true"-- stands in need of justification. There are basically four responses to

this challenge: (a) refuse to acknowledge the justice of the challenge by declaring that the fact that a statement is in the book by itself makes it true; (b) attempt to prove all the statements; (c) make a case for the major premise by establishing a subset of the book's statements; or (d) argue for the major premise by claiming that God inspired (or wrote) the religious text. Now (a) is absurd. If the fact that a statement occurred in a book by itself made it true, then contradictory statements would both be true. We are given no reason to prefer the statements in the religious text to statements in a book in which atheism is advocated. Of course, (d) may be offered as a reason for preferring the religious text. But if it were, the argument would be question-begging. After all, the argument is supposed to prove God's existence, and (d) presupposes God's existence. If the attempt described in (b) were successful, then God's existence would have been proved. But if it had been proved, then there would be no need to argue from the authority of the book. Furthermore, the proof of God's existence would be preferable to an argument from the authority of the religious text. In order to know whether the argument from authority is any good, a direct argument for God's existence must be considered. But one does not need to consider the authority of the religious text in order to assess direct arguments for God's existence. The degree of success of maneuver (c) is a function of the evidential or logical connection between the statements established and God's existence. If the appropriate connection does not obtain, the defense is unsuccessful. But if the connection is there, then an independent argument for God's existence can be formulated thereby (independent, that is, of the authority of the book). Therefore, if either (b) or (c) is successful, then the book's authority is _irrelevant_ to the proof of God's existence. And neither (a) nor (d) is successful. Therefore, no argument from the authority of a religious text proves God's existence.

4. If God is all-knowing, God knows about all pain, suffering, and wrongdoing. If God is all-powerful, God is capable of eliminating those things. If God is completely good and benevolent, God wants to eliminate those things. By definition, God is all-knowing, all-powerful, completely good, and benevolent. But if God knows about all pain, suffering, and wrongdoing and is capable of and wants to eliminate those things, then there should be considerably less pain, suffering, and wrongdoing than there is. The only way God could allow <u>any</u> pain, suffering, or wrongdoing is if some instances of them were necessary for some greater good. Although some suffering may promote a greater good, this is simply not true of many cases. Therefore, there is no individual that is all-knowing, all-powerful, completely benevolent, and good. Therefore, God does not exist.

5. Even an atheist understands what "God" means. "God" means "the being that is perfect in every possible way." But the being that is perfect in every possible way must actually exist. Therefore, God actually exists. Suppose that the being that is perfect in every possible way were only a product of thought. Only something that actually exists could exist independently. No product of thought could exist independently. Existing independently is a perfection. Thus, if the being that is perfect in every possible way were only a product of thought, it would not be perfect in at least one way. But that's impossible. Thus, the being that is perfect in every possible way is not a mere product of thought but also actually exists.

6. Some believers try to solve the problem of evil by changing the definition of "God." The problem arises, after all, only on the assumption
that there is an all-powerful, all-knowing, and completely benevolent
and good God. They have the impression that the definition is arbitrary
and dispensable. But that impression is an illusion. The definition is
not arbitrary, and the attempted solution amounts to abandoning beliefs
that are essential to religious practices. Denying God's omniscience
in order to solve the problem of evil amounts to explaining evil's existence in terms of God's ignorance of it. God would be ignorant of a lot
in that event. But the believer has "thrown the baby out with the bath
water" by leaving open the possibility that God may not know that human
beings exist. Belief in God would lose its significance if that possibility were left open. Only an omniscient God rules out that possibility. Saying that God is not completely good and benevolent would account
for evil. But it would amount to saying that God does not care about
pain, suffering, and wrongdoing. That also is not an acceptable consequence for a believer. One might try to account for evil by denying
God's omnipotence. But in order to account for all pain, suffering,
and wrongdoing, God would have to be considerably less than all-powerful.
After all, this is an attempt to account for evil by saying God cannot
control any of it. Often human beings can control pain, suffering, and
wrongdoing, which means that God would be less powerful than people.
Again, this would not be a God worth worshiping.

7. One popular attempt to solve the problem of evil is the "contrast proposal," which runs as follows: There has to be some evil in order for
there to be good. It is better for there to be good and some evil than
neither good nor evil. So, God can allow the evil there is and still
be completely good and benevolent. The problem with this proposal is
that a false dilemma is embedded in it. The only two possible universes
in the proposal are (a) good with all the pain, suffering, and wrongdoing there is and (b) neither good nor evil. But there are other possible universes, such as (c) the same amount of good with somewhat less
evil, or (d) the same amount of good with much less evil. Even if the
contrast proposal included an argument against the possibility of an
all-good universe, that does not mean that God could have created a
universe with as much evil as there is. The "contrast proposal" would
at best justify only a small amount of pain, suffering, and wrongdoing.

14-3

Analyzing Moral Arguments

Section Objectives

1. Identify and apply the ways of appraising a moral judgment, argument,
or standard.

2. Distinguish between various kinds of "ought statements."

3. Construct arguments for various moral judgments.

Key Term Review

1. Moral judgment: an assertion either that an action is right or wrong,
or ought or ought not to be taken; or that either a person or some

trait of a person, or an object or some quality of an object, is good or bad.

2. **Moral judgment**: a claim that pertains to a person's fair relations with others and usually includes one of the following concepts: permissibility, impermissibility, or obligation.

3. **Moral argument**: any argument that has a moral judgment as its conclusion and that (at least tacitly) often has a moral standard as a premise.

4. **Natural Law standard**: moral actions are those that are in harmony with nature or with universal laws of nature.

5. **Divine Command standard**: moral actions are those commanded by God.

6. **Subjectivist standard**: moral actions are those one personally likes or approves of or that make one feel good or happy.

7. **Egoistic standard**: moral actions are those that maximize the individual's own long-term interests or well-being.

8. **Relativist standard**: moral actions for a given society are those that a majority of the members of that society accept as right or obligatory.

9. **Intuitionist standard**: moral actions are those that are consistent with the individual's conscience or that the individual intuits as a duty or obligation.

10. **Act-Utilitarian standard**: moral actions are those that produce the greatest amount of happiness or well-being for the greatest number of people.

11. **Rule-Utilitarian standard**: moral actions are actions consistent with rules that maximize the overall happiness or well-being of those to whom the rules apply.

12. **Kantian standard**: moral actions are those for which the maxim, or rule, governing the individual's action could be willed to become a universal law for all rational beings.

Summary

Because many students find it difficult to distinguish moral judgments from other statements, it is worthwhile to discuss the nature of moral judgments.

Generally, moral judgments are evaluations of conduct that pertain to a person's fair relations with others. Moral judgments generally include at least one of the following three concepts: permissibility, impermissibility, or obligation. A statement is a moral judgment **regardless** of its truth or falsity. A moral judgment may, if noncognitivism is correct, be neither true nor false. Here are some examples:

1. Within the first three months of pregnancy, obtaining an abortion is a woman's prerogative. (That is, it is morally permissible for her to have an abortion under those circumstances.)

2. It is wrong to perform an abortion unless the mother's life is in danger.

The examples above are general rules. Sometimes moral judgments are not general rules, such as

3. It was wrong for Shlomo to vandalize Snurdley's car last night.

228

Of course, one might construe this judgment as an application of a general rule about the permissibility of vandalism.

It is noteworthy that circumstances are specified in statements 1 and 2. Sometimes the circumstances are not specified but are taken for granted. Suppose, for example, that someone says

4. An individual has an obligation to return what he has borrowed.

Suppose Shlomo borrowed a gun from Snurdley, who demands its return so that Snurdley can murder Klotzmeier. Shlomo is not obligated to return the gun, even if he believes statement 4, because statement 4 is an elliptical statement. What is unstated, but taken for granted, is "unless there are overriding moral considerations." And there are such considerations in the example. Sometimes the circumstances are unspecified because we cannot foresee all the possible exceptions to the general rule.

Sometimes, however, people state rules to which they believe there are no exceptions:

5. It is reprehensible to abuse children physically.

Here are a few more moral judgments:

6. It is okay to make false claims to an insurance company.

7. Other things being equal, a person should be considerate of the feelings of others.

8. An individual has no obligation to pay his taxes.

9. It is immoral to prohibit organized prayer in the public schools.

Some statements are not moral judgments. For example,

10. God exists.

is _not_ a moral judgment. Some people misidentify it as a moral judgment, I think, because they think God's will is a foundation for moral obligation. However, the statement "God exists" _itself_ is not a statement in which conduct is evaluated. It is not a statement in which moral permissibility, impermissibility, or obligation is the topic. Contrast statement 10 with

11. It is obligatory to obey God's will.

which _is_ a moral judgment, because it says something about a person's moral obligations.

Moral judgments are not rules of etiquette. Thus,

12. A person should not say "congratulations" but "best wishes" to the bride.

is _not_ a moral judgment.

Although statements about legality often encode moral beliefs, they are not moral judgments. Thus,

13. Shoplifting is a crime.

is _not_ a moral judgment. It is possible for something to be morally permissible but illegal or to be legal but morally impermissible. Most importantly, statement 13 is a statement about something that is illegal. Contrast statement 13 with the following two statements:

14. Shoplifting is immoral.

15. Shoplifting is not immoral.

both of which are moral judgments.

We frequently use the word should when we express moral judgments. However, we also use the word should in statements that are not moral judgments but statements about what it is prudent to do.

16. You should proofread what you have written.

is not a moral judgment.

A moral argument (if it does not embody a confusion) tacitly appeals to a moral standard as a premise. Several moral standards appear in the Key Term Review. But what makes them moral standards? Here are some general features of moral standards:

1. The standard has a preemptory character: it is supremely authoritative and overrides any nonmoral standards that conflict with it.

2. The standard applies to the whole range of human activity, rather than to a specific segment of it, such as the rules of order in legislative debates, the rules of games, or the canons of professional ethics.

3. The standard takes a prescriptive form: it is primarily intended to guide action and not to describe states of affairs.

4. The standard is concerned with human well-being; it thus makes direct reference to the welfare of persons or, at the very least, is concerned with harm and benefit to them, including the arguer.

5. The standard can be universalized; it can be applied in a similar way to all people situated in relevantly similar circumstances.

There are several ways in which a moral standard (and, by implication, a moral argument) can be criticized:

1. Its vagueness or generality.

2. Internal inconsistency.

3. Inadequacy or irrelevance of the standard as a justification for the moral judgment in question.

4. Equivocation in the moral argument.

5. Producing an actual or hypothetical counterexample to the moral standard.

Practice Exercises

Each of the following claims is a moral judgment. Cite at least one moral standard that could be used in an argument for the judgment, and formulate that argument. Then cite another standard and formulate an argument against the moral judgment.

1. It is okay to make false claims to an insurance company.

2. Premarital sex is okay if you're in love.

3. Premarital sex is okay whether or not you're in love.

4. Experimenting on animals is immoral when the research can be conducted using volunteers or plants.

5. It is wrong to pass judgment on others.

6. Everyone is obligated to be tolerant of the beliefs of others.

7. A person should keep his promise only if doing so will produce the best consequences.

8. It is wrong to work on Sunday.

9. Homosexuality was permissible in ancient Greece but is now wrong.

10. A person is obligated to take care of his pet.

SOLUTIONS TO EXERCISES

CHAPTER 1

Section 1-1

1. Q.

2. D.

3. I.

4. F. The answer "C" is defensible; people sometimes say "Happy Birthday!" to strangers because it is expected of them.

5. I. "N" is defensible because the sentence constitutes a promise.

6. E. The speaker is evaluating the listener's behavior. The speaker may also express feeling, thereby, but that is not the sentence's primary function. The answer "I" is arguable; a parent may be informing a child of a moral rule by using that sentence.

7. I.

8. D. The vice president is politely telling the faculty to wear academic regalia.

9. "I" or "D." The warning conveys information, but it is also intended to discourage smoking.

10. C. "F" is also defensible.

11. D.

12. Q.

13. E.

14. I.

15. N. Unless taken as metaphorical, this grammatical sentence makes no sense.

16. D.

17. D.

18. I.

19. D. The answer is not "I" because the listener is being asked to suppose that something is so.

20. I.

Section 1-2

1. A. (1) The Bible says there is a God.
       (2) I know that everything the Bible says is true (suppressed premise).
       (3) So I know that there is a God.

2. A. The argument is just as it appears in the exercise, except that
        a suppressed premise (If Miss New Mexico is the first runner-up,
        she is not Miss U.S.A.) would have to be supplied to make the
        argument formally valid.

3. NA. Simone de Beauvoir is explaining why she hesitated to write a book
         on woman, rather than trying to prove that she hesitated.

4. NA. Freud is stating his convictions about obsessional ideas and
         dreams, but he is not trying to establish their truth.

5. A. (1) If Einstein's law of gravitation had not yielded nearly the
            same results as Newton's when applied to the calculation of
            the orbits of planets and their satellites, it could not have
            been true.
        (2) But Einstein's theory does yield nearly the same results.
        (3) Einstein's theory accounts for the empirical fact of the
            perihelion of Mercury, whereas Newton's does not.
        (4) Thus, Einstein's theory is superior to Newton's, and the
            reasons for preferring Einstein's are partly empirical.

6. A. (1) We regard ourselves as free even though people who know us
            well can predict accurately what we will do.
        (2) We regard doubt about what we will do as a sign of ignorance
            of the kind of person we are, and sometimes even resent the
            doubt as if it amounted to saying we had a different character
            trait.
        (3) Thus, the certainty that others' acts are thoroughly predic-
            table if we have thorough knowledge does not conflict with
            our feeling of freedom.

7. A. The argument would be set out in the order it appears on the page,
        the last sentence being the conclusion.

8. A. (1) In an article I described the outmoded nineteenth-century
            belief that the perfection of creation was the best evidence
            of a creator.
        (2) This description was reported in creationist literature as
            evidence of my rejection of evolution.
        (3) I am an evolutionist and was not advocating that outmoded be-
            lief in the article (suppressed premise).
        (4) Therefore, sometimes creationists plunge more deeply into dis-
            honesty by taking statements of evolutionists out of context
            to make them say the opposite of what was intended.

9. A. (1) Some acts are not premeditated but are responsible.
        (2) Some acts are premeditated but are not responsible.
        (3) Therefore, responsibility is not determined by the presence
            or absence of premeditation.

10. A. (1) Evolution is a theory of the development of life-forms.
        (2) Evolution is not a theory of the creation of the universe.
        (3) Therefore, the theory of evolution is not inconsistent with
            the belief that God created the universe.

11. NA. This is an explanation of the fact that there is water all over
         the garage floor, not an attempt to prove that there is.

12. A. (1) The number 119 is evenly divisible by (the whole numbers) 7
            and 17.
        (2) Any number that is evenly divisible by a whole number other
            than itself and 1 is not prime (suppressed premise).

(3) The numbers 7 and 17 are not the same as either 1 or 119 (suppressed premise).

(4) Thus, the number 119 is not prime.

13. NA. Mill is explaining how the capacity for nobler feelings can be killed easily.

14. A. (1) A contractual democracy is founded upon the citizens' promise to obey its commands.

(2) Thus, a contractual democracy is legitimate.

(3) But such states achieve their legitimacy only because the citizens forfeit their autonomy.

(4) The fundamental problem of political philosophy is to reconcile the autonomy of individuals with the state (suppressed premise).

(5) Therefore, contractual democracy is not a solution to the fundamental problem of political philosophy.

15. NA. This is probably not an argument, because what might be construed as a premise is the same as the conclusion, only expressed in different words.

Section 1-3

1. A. (1) Several other brands of diet soft drink could not beat diet 7-Up for taste.

(2) So, many people believe diet 7-Up has the best taste. (C&P)

(3) So, you should buy diet 7-Up.

2. A. The argument is just as it appears in the text.

3. NA. Freud is offering a psychological explanation of religious belief. He is not arguing for the truth of the explanation or for any other conclusions.

4. A. The argument is just as it appears in the text.

5. A. The first two sentences are premises, whereas the last one is the conclusion.

6. A. (1) The knowledge of the principles of demonstration has its origin in sense experience.

(2) Thus, whatever transcends all sense experience cannot be demonstrated (proven). (C&P)

(3) The statement "God exists" transcends all sense experience.

(4) Thus, the statement "God exists" cannot be demonstrated.

It may <u>seem</u> that lines (1) and (2) are the antecedent and consequent of a conditional statement, rather than two separate categorical statements. But the phrase "as is shown" shows that the statements are categorical. Aquinas is reporting an argument that he does not advocate.

7. A. This is a report of an argument. The argument itself is:

(1) The existence of a physical object is dependent upon its being perceived; that is, a physical object <u>is</u> a construct made up of percepts.

(2) Thus, the physical world is completely dependent on some perceivers for its existence. (C&P)

(3) Therefore, if all perceivers were to cease to exist, so would the physical world.

Actually, (3) is a consequence of either (1) or (2). A suppressed premise is: The physical world is a collection of physical objects.

8. A. This passage contains two arguments, one quoted, the other advocated. The quoted argument is:
   (1) Opponents of abortion are against the taking of human life unless someone else's life is in danger.
   (2) The death penalty consists in taking a human life even though no one's life is endangered, since the convict is in prison (suppressed premise).
   (3) Thus, opponents of abortion should oppose the death penalty.
   (4) Thus, (some) opponents of abortion inconsistently support the death penalty.

   The advocated argument is:
   (1) Opponents of abortion oppose the taking of innocent human life.
   (2) Whereas an embryo or fetus is innocent of wrongoing, someone who (in their opinion) merited the death penalty would not be.
   (3) Thus, opponents of abortion have a means for distinguishing between embryos and convicted felons (suppressed conclusion). (C&P)
   (4) So, those opponents of abortion who support the death penalty are not being inconsistent (for the reason cited).

9. A. (1) Opponents of abortion have given no good reason for opposing only the taking of innocent <u>human</u> life.
   (2) Animals are innocent.
   (3) Thus, killing animals for food constitutes the taking of innocent (animal) life (suppressed conclusion). (C&P)
   (4) Opponents of abortion could survive on plants and animal by-products.
   (5) So, it is not a question of needing to kill animals for food (suppressed conclusion). (C&P)
   (6) Thus, unless opponents of abortion can give a good reason for singling out human life for special consideration, they should be vegetarians.

10. A. (1) Street crimes are more frequently and severely punished than "white-collar" crimes.
   (2) Street crimes are most frequently committed by people of the lower economic classes.
   (3) So, law breakers of economic classes lower than "white-collar" workers are the victims of injustice. (C&P)
   (4) The only way to eliminate such injustice is to change the economic system so radically that society becomes classless.
   (5) Thus, we should take Marx's advice.

Sections 1-4 and 1-5

I. 1. (1) Every compatibalist is a determinist.
   (2) Professor Klotzmeyer is a compatibalist. (SP)
   (3) Thus, Professor Klotzmeyer is a determinist.

   2. (1) Whoever makes things in which there is evil, which could have been made without any evil, or the making of which could have been omitted, does not choose the best.
   (2) God has made a world in which there is evil, a world which could have been made without any evil, or the making of which could have been omitted.
   (3) Therefore, God did not choose the best. (SC)

236

(4) Whoever does not choose the best is lacking in power, knowledge, or goodness.
(5) Therefore, God is lacking in power, knowledge, or goodness.

3. (1) If we know that there are trees, then we know that there is not an invisible demon who prompts us to believe, falsely, that there are trees.
(2) There is no way to rule out the possibility of the invisible demon.
(3) If there is no way to rule out the possiblity of the invisible demon, then we do not know that there is not an invisible demon who prompts us to believe, falsely, that there are trees.
(4) Thus, we do not know that there are trees.

4. (1) If you know that you are reading a logic text now, then you know for certain that you are awake.
(2) But it is possible for you to be dreaming that you are reading a logic text.
(3) You cannot specify the differences between dreaming that you are reading a logic text and actually reading it.
(4) If premises (2) and (3) are true, then you do not know for certain that you are awake. (SP)
(5) Therefore, you do not know that you are reading a logic text. (SC)

5. (1) If you knew a thing's properties by seeing it, then this straight stick would not appear to be bent when immersed in water.
(2) But this straight stick does appear to be bent when immersed in water. (SP)
(3) Therefore, you do not know a thing's properties by seeing it.

6. (1) All cats are mammals.
(2) Merlin is a cat. (SP)
(3) So, Merlin is a mammal.

7. (1) No argument is true or false.
(2) This enthymeme is an argument. (SP)
(3) Accordingly, this enthymeme is neither true nor false.

8. (1) Some arguments are valid.
(2) No argument is true.
(3) So, there is a difference between validity and truth. (SC)

9. (1) A human being's existence is an issue for him.
(2) A person's existence could not be an issue for him unless he had some understanding of his existence.
(3) So, a human being has some understanding of his existence. (SC)

10. (1) Every statement is either true or false.
(2) No argument is either true or false.
(3) Therefore, no argument is a statement. (SC)

II. 1. E.

2. N. Austin is giving advice. The broader context of the passage shows that this passage can be contrued as a rationale for Austin's way of philosophizing. But the passage given merely constitutes advice.

3. A and E. In this passage Quine and Ullian cite a generalized argument:

(1) This theory (any thesis that lies or is beyond the fringe of believability) cannot be disproven.
(2) So, the theory should be believed.

Then Quine and Ullian proceed to explain why these "theories" cannot be conclusively disproven. The reason is that the "theories" are cast in such cloudy terms that it is hard to know what would constitute a refutation of them.

4. A. There are two interrelated arguments in this passage. Quine and Ullian indirectly cite an argument they reject:
(1) It is not absolutely certain that cigaret smoking causes lung cancer.
(2) So, you can be confident that cigaret smoking does not cause lung cancer.

Then they rebut the argument as follows:
(1) When the advertisement appeared, evidence for a causal connection between cigaret smoking and lung cancer was overwhelming and should have been accepted as such.
(2) So, these advertisers were magnifying the less than reasonable residual doubt into a proclamation of confidence in the opposite claim.
(3) Therefore, it is not just false science (but false advertising as well) that wantonly exploits the fact that many theories do not admit of absolute proof or disproof.

5. E.

6. E. This is an explanation of the fact that the lower parts of a ship appear after the upper parts when it appears on the horizon. If the passage <u>had</u> included something about the "flat earth" theory, so that the passage was a reply to that claim, then this explanation, <u>though not itself an argument</u>, would form a part of an argument, as follows:
(1) The "spherical earth" hypothesis can explain the appearance of a ship on the horizon much more easily than can the "flat earth" hypothesis.
(2) So, it is reasonable to believe that the earth is spherical.
As the passage stands, however, it is an explanation only.

7. E. This is an explanation of Freud's knowledge that he would be reviled for publishing case histories.

8. E. This is an explanation of the fact that the heavenly body does not twinkle.

9. N. Although combative, this passage is not an argument but merely a series of threats.

10. A. This passage consists of interrelated arguments.
(1) There are no (I cannot imagine) potential data that could lead creationists to abandon their beliefs.
(2) So, creationism is an unbeatable system that cannot be falsified. (C&P)
(3) Unbeatable systems are dogma, not science.
(4) Therefore, "scientific creationism" is a self-contradictory, nonsense phrase.

This alone consists of two interrelated arguments, because line (2) is both a conclusion and a premise. But Gould uses another argument in support of lines (1), (2), and (4) above:

(5) Creationism's leading intellectual, Duane Gish says, "we cannot discover by scientific investigations anything about the creative processes used by the Creator."

(6) Yet so-called scientific creationism consists of a number of statements about the Creator's creative processes. (a likely suppressed premise)

(7) If Gish's statement is true, then there are no potential data that could lead creationists to abandon their beliefs, and creationism is an unbeatable system that cannot be falsified.

(8) If Gish's statement and line (6) are true, than "scientific creationism" is a self-contradictory, nonsense phrase.

(9) So, lines (1) and (2) are true, from (5) and (7).

(10) So "scientific creationism" is a self-contradictory, nonsense phrase, from (5), (6), and (8).

Though it is not part of his central point, Gould tacitly formulates another argument:

(11) Any evolutionary theory can be falsified.

(12) Creationism cannot be falsified.

(13) Thus, evolutionary theories can be scientific, whereas creationism cannot.

CHAPTER 2

Sections 2-1 and 2-2

I.
1. I.	8. D.	15. Probably I.
2. I.	9. D.	16. I.
3. D.	10. D.	17. D.
4. D.	11. D.	18. I.
5. D.	12. Probably I.	19. Probably D.
6. D.	13. I.	20. D.
7. D.	14. I.	21. D.

The following comments apply to the foregoing exercises indicated.

7. The word "cannot" shows that the arguer regards the premise as conclusive evidence for the conclusion.

12. The classification of this argument depends on the unstated premises, and it is impossible to know exactly what they are. If a suppressed premise is "Becky was in Montreal all day" or "Becky was in Montreal at the same time as the break-in," then we have reason to say the argument is deductive. But it is noteworthy that three witnesses testified, which calls attention to the probability of the truth of what was said. This probability affects the conclusion. Thus, the argument is best classified as inductive.

15. If the suppressed premise is "Everyone who has AIDS is either a Haitian, a homosexual, or an intravenous drug user," then the argument is deductive. But if the premise is "Most (or almost all) people...," then the argument is inductive. Since the first interpretation yields a clearly false statement, it is more charitable to attribute the second claim to the arguer.

19. This probably is a bad deductive argument. The arguer is probably reasoning that, since the male parent has apricot eyes and is not the female parent, the male offspring will not have apricot-colored

eyes. Naturally, the female parent could have apricot-colored eyes also, thus producing male offspring with apricot-colored eyes.

II. In this exercise, the arguments given in Chapter 1 are to be identified as either deductive or inductive.

Exercise 1.2: Some of the passages in this exercise are not arguments at all and thus are neither deductive nor inductive. Such passages are designated as NA.

1. D.	6. D.	11. NA.
2. D.	7. D.	12. D.
3. NA.	8. D.	13. NA.
4. NA.	9. D.	14. D.
5. D.	10. D.	15. NA.

Exercise 1.3: In some of the following passages there are two arguments. They have been indicated.

1. D and I.	5. Probably D.	9. D and D.
2. D.	6. D and D.	10. D and D.
3. NA.	7. D and D.	11. D and D.
4. Probably I.	8. NA.	

Exercise 1.4/1.5

I.
1. D.	3. D.	5. D.	7. D.	9. D.
2. D and D.	4. D.	6. D.	8. D.	10. D.

II.
1. NA.	4. I and D.	7. NA.	10. 1- 2: D
2. NA.	5. NA.	8. NA.	2- 4: D
3. D and NA.	6. NA.	9. NA.	5- 9: D
			9-10: D
			11-13: D

10. 1- 2: D
2- 4: D
5- 9: D
9-10: D
11-13: D

References are to line numbers in solutions to exercises for Chapter 1.

4. C. The cigarette advertisers' argument is inductive, whereas Quine's and Ullian's two interrelated arguments are deductive.

Section 2-3

1. NT, E.	8. NF, AP.	15. C, E.	22. C, E.	29. C, E.
2. C, E.	9. NT, AP.	16. C, E.	23. NT, AP.	30. C, E.
3. C, E.	10. C, E.	17. NF, AP.	24. NF, AP.	31. NT, AP.
4. C, E.	11. C, E.	18. C, E.	25. C, E.	32. NF, AP.
5. C, E.	12. C, E.	19. NT, AP.	26. NT, AP.	33. NT, AP.
6. NT.	13. C, E.	20. NT, AP.	27. NT, AP.	34. C, E.
7. C, E.	14. NT, E.	21. C, E.	28. NT, AP.	35. NT, AP.

Some of the answers given require some justification. A few are controversial.

1. To understand the statement, "Mark Twain is identical with Samuel Clemens" is not to know that it is true. Thus, the statement is known not *a priori* but empirically. Although the individual named by those names might have had a different name, the individual himself could not

be identical with anyone but himself. And the names in the statement are used to refer to that person, who must be identical with himself. Thus, the statement is necessarily true.

2. Samuel Clemens might have had a different pseudonym, but he could not have been identical with anyone but Mark Twain. Thus, although item 2 is contingent, item 1 is necessary.

12. Contrast this statement with "The winner of a U.S. presidential election receives the majority of electoral votes."

13. This is a contingent truth of which too few students are aware.

14. The rationale is the same as for item 1.

22. Imagine a library of films. Although this statement may seem to be necessary, it is contingent.

24. The two components of this compound statement contradict one another, though many students do not recognize that fact. Try to prove that the two components contradict one another.

26. Items 26 and 19 show that some statements about existence (non-existence) are necessarily true.

32. It is arguable that "The square root of two went to the football game" is nonsensical and thus neither true nor false. The square root of two is not the sort of entity that could go to a football game (or not go, for that matter). Yet we understand the sentence. Thus it makes sense, which is a reason for saying that the statement is necessarily false.

Section 2-4

1. It is noteworthy that instances of the "straw man" fallacy have a remote connection with what the opponent said, although it is distorted. In this case, Julian Bond referred to a particular brand of patriotism as stupid. The idea is that it is stupid to be first in war, etc. But Bond's opponent misrepresents Bond as repudiating patriotism itself.

2. Senator Ted did not say that the handgun legislation would make walking outside at night "completely safe," as though the legislation were a panacea. He said the legislation would make life safer. To point out that the legislation would not render a walk at night completely safe is not to show that the bill is undesirable. In order to show that the bill is undesirable, Senator Snort would have to show that the undesirable consequences of the bill (restricting the freedom of individuals who own or want to own handguns) outweigh the undesirable consequences of not passing the bill (fear, increased numbers of murders, and increased danger of being a crime victim.)

3. Senator Snuff has distorted Senator Ted's position, thus making it an easy target to knock down (a man of straw). Senator Ted's proposed legislation pertained to "Saturday night special" handguns, not to hunting rifles. Again, establishing the undesirability of the proposed legislation would require what is specified in the answer to Question 2.

4. Senator Swine has not presented the reasons behind Senator Snort's position. The reasons make it clear that Senator Swine's statement is a distortion. Senator Snort apparently views ratifying the treaty as the least undesirable of two undesirable alternatives. At any rate, there is no indication that Senator Snort wants to "give away" the Panama

Canal. This is a matter of inference from what Senator Snort Said. But the fact that he thinks there are only two alternatives probably means that he thinks the Panama Canal could not be sold. And, the attempt in Snort's estimation, to sell it would only lead to a futile effort to defend it against terrorist attacks. Of course, it is possible to dispute this estimation of the situation. But Swine's attack is an attempt to bypass the need for analysis and argument.

5. The author of the letter to the editor did not attack the small amount of objectivity in the editorial. He attacked the slanted coloring of the few facts with emotionally charged words.

CHAPTER 3

Sections 3-1 and 3-2

I. 4. "Happy Birthday!" can express the speaker's wish for the hearer (F) and thus constitute wishing someone happiness on his birthday (P). It can also be a merely ceremonial utterance (C).

5. "I shall return your exams Friday," when spoken by a professor to students, informs them when the exams will be returned (I) and is a promise to return the exams on that date (P).

8. "The faculty will wear academic regalia at commencement" is a polite order to wear regalia (D) and informs the faculty of what to wear (I).

10. "I'm pleased to meet you" can inform the hearer of the speaker's pleasure at meeting him (I) and, if the circumstances are right, express the speaker's feeling (F). Occasionally this utterance is merely ceremonial and expresses no particular feeling.

16. "Abandon hope, all ye who enter here" constitutes a warning (P) and informs the hearer or reader that his situation is hopeless if he enters (I).

17. "Working men of all countries, unite!" expresses fervor, as the exclamation point shows (F). Likewise, it directs behavior (D), as the sentence and its context show. (It is the last line of The Communist Manifesto, in which Marx argues that revolution is the necessary and inevitable solution to the problems with "pure" capitalism.)

19. This sentence is purely directive (D), because the reader is being told to suppose something. He is not being informed that there are several accidents; he is merely asked to suppose there are.

II. 1. "Have you stopped beating your wife?" is a classic example of a loaded question, since it is not a mere request for information (Q). It makes at least two statements as well: (a) the hearer has a wife, and (b) the hearer has beaten her.

2. "Why did you lie about your age?" is also a loaded question. It is not a mere request for information, since it makes a couple of tacit statements: (a) the hearer's age is different from what he said it was, and (b) the hearer believes or knows that his age is different. Imagine a policeman trying to elicit a confession from

a teenager who illegally consumed liquor by asking that loaded question. In that event, the loaded question would be directive (as
well as informative and a request for information).

3. This sentence clearly is informative. It is also directive, since
    a student would say this to a professor in order to be allowed to
    take a make-up exam.

4. I, D, and P. Clearly, this sentence conveys information; we can
    imagine a professor informing his students of a rule in a course
    by making this statement. The utterance is also directive; the
    professor intends to discourage students from attempting to take
    a make-up test without a good and documented reason. The utterance
    is also performative; if a professor says that at the beginning of
    a course, what he says becomes a rule.

5. I, F, and D. Because it is addressed to the person found attrac-
    tive, this utterance could be directive as well as informative in
    many circumstances. It could be an attempt to elicit a similar
    response from the hearer or play a role in seduction. It is (or
    can be) expressive as well.

6. F and I. (See item 7.)

7. E and I. "Renoir is one of my favorite painters" expresses the
    speaker's enjoyment of Renoir's works, but does not, unlike
    "Renoir is one of the world's greatest painters," evaluate the
    worth of those works. Statement 6 conveys information about the
    speaker's tastes, whereas statement 7 is a statement about the
    paintings. Accordingly, it is appropriate to invoke standards for
    good art to assess statement 7 but not to assess statement 6.

8. I and F. Because statement 8 is not addressed to the person found
    attractive, it is not directive in most ordinary circumstances.

9. I, F, and D. "I love you" conveys information, even if the infor-
    mation is not new. When the information is not new (such as when
    it is said among married couples), the expressive and directive
    functions overshadow the informative.

III. 1. Pig--(a) any swine or hog; (b) a person of piggish character or
         habits; (c) a police officer.

     2. Cat's meow--(a) the sound a cat makes; (b) the best, especially
         the epitome of style.

     3. Joint--(a) the place or part in which two things, or parts of
         one thing, are joined or united either rigidly or so as to admit
         of motion; (b) a dirty or disreputable place of public accommoda-
         tion, especially a cheap restaurant or night club; (c) a marijuana
         cigarette.

     4. Clown--(a) a jester or buffoon in a circus; (b) a coarse, ill-bred
         person.

     5. Stuffy--(a) oppressive from lack of freshness, as the air; (b)
         dull, self-important, or strait-laced.

Section 3-3

1. Botha claims that universal suffrage ("one-man, one-vote") would pro-
    duce faction, strife, chaos, and poverty. He tacitly claims that white

minority rule causes the absence of those things. After all, that is the rationale offered for keeping white minority rule. The first causal claim is not supported with any evidence, and the presence of relatively orderly and prosperous democratic countries constitutes *prima facie* evidence against it. Botha would need to show that countries similar to South Africa had committed "suicide" by allowing every adult to vote. He would also need to show that South Africa has characteristics that relatively orderly and prosperous democracies do not, characteristics that would lead to chaos if there were universal suffrage.

The second causal claim (that white minority rule produces the absence of faction, strife, chaos, and poverty) is at best questionable and at worst false. South Africa seems to have strife despite—or, more precisely, <u>because of</u>—white minority rule. The right to vote is a matter of fairness to <u>black</u> and other nonwhite adults. Thus, P. W. Botha would have to prove that so much <u>more</u> chaos, strife, faction, and poverty would result from universal adult suffrage that white minority rule is morally justified.

2. This argument for the conclusion that the worries are exaggerated includes a slanted description of 25% of the U.S.'s budget as "uncontrolled spending." It is as though there were no alternative between a 20% ceiling and no ceiling at all, which is literally what "uncontrolled spending" means.

3. Mazola will give you $2 if you check "Mazola is the best way to fry" and $1 if you refuse. Then the advertisers will report that Mazola beat the other leading oils in taste tests. This is a questionable inference, because it is probable that most people check "Mazola is the best way to fry" in order to receive an extra dollar in refund.

The Mazola people probably would insist that they offer $2 in Mazola coupons or $1 in cash, so choosing the coupons does show a preference for Mazola.

But the evidence would not establish that conclusion, because it is consistent with people believing that Mazola is much the same as other vegetable oils and preferring a $2 savings on a comparable product to $1 in cash. The evidence is even consistent with people believing that Mazola is slightly inferior, but not sufficiently worse to justify bypassing the extra savings. In either case, the extra spending power, and not Mazola's superiority, would explain checking "Mazola is the best way to fry." Naturally, you are not reminded of the nature of the "survey" on TV commercials for Mazola. The Mazola people would have to establish that extra spending power is not the real motivation. Imagine what the results would be if the offer were $1 in Mazola coupons or $1 in cash.

4. There is a false dilemma in Butz's argument. Even if it is objectionable for a family earning $12,000-$15,000 per year to receive food stamps, that does not mean that it is objectionable for a family of four earning $5,001 per year to receive food stamps. Yet the plan Butz defended would prohibit a family of four earning $5,001 per year from receiving food stamps. Because Butz argued from extreme, unusual cases, he did not adequately defend the plan.

5. This is a case of distortion by quoting out of context. Phanthene Brampton clearly panned the movie. But the quotation makes it sound as though Brampton highly praised the film.

6. The Crisco advertisement does not inform you of the fact that there are all-vegetable shortenings that are cheaper than Crisco. This

suppressed evidence is damaging to the conclusion, "Crisco's worth the difference because you can taste the difference." Revealing the suppressed evidence also shows that the commercial presents the viewer with a false dilemma: either a bargain-brand shortening with part animal fat that makes foods taste greasy, or Crisco, which is an all-vegetable shortening that does not make foods taste greasy.

7. This is a classic case of slanting. The Nixon ad uses words with disagreeable connotations to create an impression about Douglas's candidacy that is not warranted by the evidence. Douglas would not have described herself as "tolerating Communist conspiracies within U.S. borders, condoning bureaucratic profligacy, or appeasing totalitarian aggression." In order to prove that Douglas tolerated Communist conspiracies, for example, Nixon would have to prove that (a) there had been such conspiracies, (b) Douglas had every reason to believe there had been such conspiracies, and (c) Douglas did nothing.

8. This is a slanted description of abortion. No one would describe himself as permitting "slaughter" or "the murdering of babies." The advocate of this argument has to establish that abortion constitutes slaughter or the murder of babies, rather than arguing from that premise, since the claim that abortion constitutes murder is itself the anti-abortionist's position.

9. This is a slanted description of the embryo. The advocate of this argument has to establish that the embryo is a part of a woman's body that she is morally entitled to do with as she pleases. (This is not questioning an abundantly evident fact: that the fetus develops inside of and depends on its mother's body.) After all, the premise describes the "pro-choice" position. Considered as an argument, therefore, this presupposes precisely what it is supposed to prove. It is a case of using a question-begging expression (see Section 12-1). The words reactionary and legislate morality are also slanted. It is a misrepresentation of the anti-abortionist's position to say that he believes he can force others to conform to his morals, as the words legislate morality imply. Anti-abortionists do think that, if an anti-abortion amendment is passed, those who perform or obtain abortions will face (discouraging) penalties.

10. This passage includes a slanted description of "voluntary" school prayer and a corresponding misrepresentation of Congresswoman Smith as being against the right of students to pray. This misrepresentation constitutes a "straw man" fallacy.

The school prayer debate is about organized prayer. There is no serious debate about whether a student may (voluntarily) decide to pray. The debate is about whether taxpayers should support organized religious activities. Thus, the identification of Congresswoman Smith's opposing state-supported, organized school prayer with opposing the right of students to pray is a distortion of her position (a "straw man"). It is easy to attack opposition to basic religious freedom. It is not so easy to attack opposition to state-supported, organized school prayer.

CHAPTER 4

Section 4-1

1. Amphiboly. Is the owner or the house unbelievable?

2. Equivocation. Protestants consider themselves members of the holy catholic (universal) church but not, of course, of the Roman Catholic church.

3. Amphiboly. Who was looting? The mayor?

4. Equivocation on "independent existence."

5. Amphiboly.

6. Equivocation on "raise."

7. Amphiboly.

8. Equivocation on "man."

9. Equivocation on "discrimination."

10. Equivocation on "gambling."

11. Equivocation on "right."

12. Accent.

13. Equivocation on "fast."

14. Amphiboly.

15. Amphiboly.

16. Accent.

17. Accent.

18. Accent.

19. Accent.

20. Equivocation on "senses deceive us."

Section 4-2

Student responses will vary.

Section 4-3

II. 1. Disagreement in attitude and possibly also a verbal dispute.

2. Verbal dispute.

3. Disagreement in attitude.

4. Verbal dispute.

Section 4-4

III. 1. Object of furniture used by one person for sitting.

2. A writer of poetry.

3. A performing artist who acts a part.

4. A human female related to another by having the same parents.

5. A sound that has no musical qualities.

6. A construction that is vertical and serves to enclose space or as a barrier.

7. A color between red and yellow in hue.

8. The finger next to the thumb.

9. A self-propelled vehicle designed for carrying a small number of passengers.

10. An institution of higher learning serving students who have completed high school and usually offering bachelor's degrees.

11. An institution of higher learning offering both bachelor's degrees and other (graduate, professional) degrees.

CHAPTER 5

Section 5-1

1. All cats are mammals.

2. No bats are birds.

3. Some students are students who make all A's.

4. All dogs are creatures that bark.

5. Some dogs are creatures that bark.

6. All guppies are ferocious fish.

7. All persons who passed are persons who studied.

8. Some students are persons who study too much.

9. Some flutes are not wooden instruments.

Section 5-2

I. 1. Passenger pigeons don't exist.

2. The Loch Ness monster exists.

3. Nothing is said about the class of students.

4. B's exist.

5. Nothing is said about the class of C's.

6. There are no D's.

II. 1.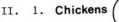

2.

3. **Computers** **Pieces of electronic equipment**

4.

5.

6. "All R are J."

7. "All wombats are mammals."

Section 5-3

	a.		b.		c.
1.	False	b.	Unknown	c.	Unknown
	True	b.	Unknown	c.	Unknown
	False	b.	False	c.	True

Section 5-4

I.
1. No A are non-B.   All A are B.

2. All C are non-D. , No C are D.

3. Some E are not non-F. . Some E are F.

4. Some G are non-H. . Some G are not H.

5. No non-I are non-J. . All non-I are J.

6. All non-K are non-L. . No non-K are L.

7. Some non-M are not non-N . Some non-M are N.

8. Some non-O are not non-P . Some non-O are P.

9. No Q are R.   All Q are non-R .

10. All S are T.   No S are non-T. .

11. Some V are not T. Some V are non-T .

12. Some W are not X. Some W are non-X .

13. No non-Y are Z.   All non-Y are non-Z .

14. All non-A are B.   No non-A are non-B. .

15. Some non-C are not D. Some non-C are non-D. .

16. Some non-E are not F. Some non-E are non-F .

II.
1. No objects usable for building materials are house plants. Equivalent.

2. All non-smokers are healthy persons. Not equivalent.

3. Some non-smokers are healthy persons. Not equivalent.

4. Some mechanisms designed for washing windows are machines. Equivalent.

5. Some B are non-A. Equivalent.

6. No non-D are C. Equivalent.

7. All non-F are non-E. Not equivalent.

8. Some non-H are not G. Not equivalent.

III. 1. All smokers are non-healthy persons. Equivalent.

2. Some non-smokers are not non-students. Equivalent.

3. Some O are non-M. Not equivalent.

4. Some non-B are non-A. Not equivalent.

5. No persons who don't spend their lives indoors are non-cowboys. Not equivalent.

6. Some persons not over seven feet tall are persons who are not basketball players. Not equivalent.

7. Some problems that are not extremely difficult are problems that are not contrapositions.

Section 5-5

1. All persons who can vote are citizens.

2. All persons who can vote are citizens.

3. All persons inducted into the Hall of Fame are good players.

4. All persons identical to Reagan are Presidents.

5. No assignments identical to this assignment are easy assignments.

6. All assignments identical to this assignment are important assignments.

7. All things that end well are well things.

8. No bats are birds.

9. Some things that glitter are not gold things.

10. All persons who don't study are persons who fail.

11. Some persons are hungry persons.

12. Some dogs are dogs that bark all night.

13. Some cats are friendly creatures.

14. All bats are mammals.

15. All persons identical to Socrates are mortals.

16. All war heroes are brave persons.

17. All persons who live by the sword are persons who shall perish by the sword.

18. Some students are persons who are able to understand this material.

19. No days identical to today are Sundays.

20. No good furniture is cheap furniture.

21. All places identical to the basement are damp places.

22. All persons identical to John are pusillanimous persons.

23. All times identical to now are times it is raining.

24. All places identical to this place are places with trash.

25. No times before exams are times Betty studies.

26. All persons who study are persons who improve their grades.

27. No plants identical to this plant are rare plants.

28. Some marriages are not marriages that end in divorce.

29. All persons who would engage in that activity are fools.

30. All situations of having no friends are situations that are better than having dishonest friends.

31. All persons who sow injustice are persons who will reap calamity.

CHAPTER 6

Section 6-1

I.   1. *EIO*-1   2. *AAA*-1   3. *AAA*-3

     4. *IAI*-2   5. *EAO*-4   6. *AOO*-2

     7. *AII*-3   8. *EOO*-1   9. *OAO*-3

    10. *AEE*-1   11. *AII*-2   12. *IOO*-2

II. 1. No   2. Yes   3. No   4. No   5. No

III. 1. Some *A* are *F*.   2. All *B* are *N*.   3. Some *P* are not *O*.
        All *A* are *I*.   All *S* are *N*.   Some *C* are not *P*.
        Some *I* are *F*.   Some *S* are *B*.   Some *C* are not *O*.
        IAI-3   *AII*-2   *OOO*-1

     4. All *C* are *P*.   5. Some zealots are not young persons.
        Some *M* are not *P*.   All zealots are winners.
        Some *M* are not *C*.   Some winners are not young persons.
        AOO-2   *OAO*-3

IV. 1. All *M* are *P*.   2. All *P* are *M*.   3. No *P* are *M*.
        All *S* are *M*.   All *M* are *S*.   Some *S* are *M*.
        All *S* are *P*.   All *S* are *P*.   Some *S* are not *P*.

     4. No *M* are *P*.   5. Some *P* are *M*.
        All *M* are *S*.   All *M* are *S*.
        Some *S* are not *P*.   Some *S* are not *P*.

Section 6-2A

I.   1.   2.   3.

II. 1. No *C* are *V*; No *V* are *C*.
     2. No *X* are *N*; No *N* are *X*.
     3.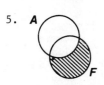
     4.

     5.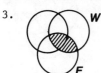

     6.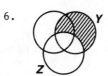

     7.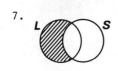

     8.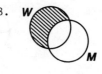

     9.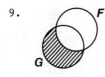

III. 1. All *S* are *L*.   2. All *B* are *Z*.
      3. All *D* are *F*.   4. All cats are mammals.

Section 6-2B

  I. Diagrams 5, 6, and 7 are correct.

 II. 1.   2.   3.

III. Diagrams 4 and 6 are correct.

IV. 1.   2.  3.

Section 6-2C

I.   1. Invalid   2. Invalid   3. Invalid
     4. Invalid   5. Invalid   6. Valid
     7. Valid   8. Invalid   9. Invalid
    10. Invalid   11. Valid   12. Valid

II. 1.   2. 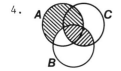   3.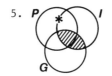

     4. 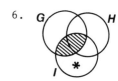   5. 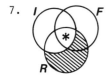   6.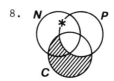

     7. 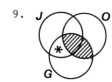 8. 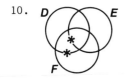 9.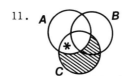

    10. 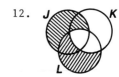 11. 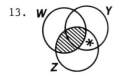 12.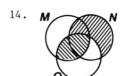

    13. 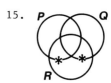 14.  15.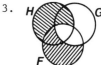

16. 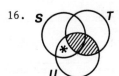 17.  18.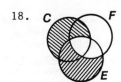

19. 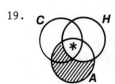 20. 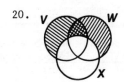 21.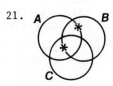

The arguments given in Exercises 3, 4, 7, 9, 11, 12, 14, 16, and 18 are valid. The rest are invalid.

Section 6-3

I. 1. Rule 1 2. Rule 2
    3. Rule 2 4. Rule 1

II. 1. Rule 3 2. Rule 3 3. Rule 3

III. 1. Rule 2 2. Rule 3 3. Rule 1
     4. Rule 2 5. Rule 4 6. Rule 3

Section 6-4

I. 1. No *F* are *E*.   2. Some *H* are not *I*.   3. Some *L* are not *K*.
   Some *F* are *D*.   Some *I* are *G*.   All *J* are *L*.
   Some *D* are not *E*.   Some *G* are *H*.   No *J* are *K*.

   Valid   Rule 1   Rule 1

II. 1. No *N* are *O*.   2. All *G* are *I*.
    Some *M* are not *O*.   All *I* are *H*.
    Some *M* are not *N*.   All *G* are *H*.

    Rule 3   Valid

III. 1. Some *S* are not *H*.   2. All *C* are *B*.   3. All *M* are *C*.
     All *D* are *S*.   All *A* are *C*.   All *A* are *M*.
     All *H* are *D*.   All *A* are *B*.   All *A* are *C*.

     Rule 1   Valid   Valid

IV. 1. All compatibalists are determinists.
       (All persons identical to Professor Klotzmeyer are compatibalists.)
       All persons identical to Professor Klotzmeyer are determinists.

    2. All persons who make things with evil...are persons who do not
       choose the best.
       All persons identical to God are persons who make things with
       evil....
       (All persons identical to God are persons who do not choose the
       best.)

253

All persons who do not choose the best are persons lacking in power, knowledge, or goodness.
All persons identical to God are persons who do not choose the best.
__(conclusion from previous argument)__
(All persons identical to God are persons lacking in power, knowledge, or goodness.)

3. All cats are mammals.
   __(All animals identical to L.C. are cats.)__
   All animals identical to L.C. are mammals.

4. All philosophers are persons who know Kant's ethics.
   __(All persons identical to Dr. Acre are philosophers.)__
   (All persons identical to Dr. Acre are persons who know Kant's ethics.)

   (All persons who know Kant's ethics are persons who can tell you something about the categorical imperative.)
   __All persons identical to Dr. Acre are persons who know Kant's ethics__
   All persons identical to Dr. Acre are persons who can tell you something about the categorical imperative.

CHAPTER 7

Section 7-1

I.   1. U is not true.   II.   1. $\sim U$

      2. If L then W.   2. $L \supset W$

      3. S if P.   3. $P \supset S$

      4. S and W.   4. S & W

      5. P.   5. P

III.   1. A & B 16. $B \supset A$

      2. A & B 17. $B \supset A$

      3. A & B 18. $(A \supset B)$ & $(B \supset A)$

      4. A & B 19. $B \supset A$ or $\sim A \supset \sim B$

      5. $\sim B$ 20. $(A \lor B)$ & $\sim (A$ & $B)$

      6. $\sim (A$ & $B)$ 21. $(A$ & $B) \supset C$

      7. $\sim A$ & $\sim B$ 22. $A \supset (B$ & $C)$

      8. $A \lor B$ 23. $(A \lor B)$ & C

      9. $A \lor B$ 24. $A \lor (B$ & $C)$

    10. $\sim (A \lor B)$ or $\sim A$ & $\sim B$ 25. $A \lor B$ or $\sim B \supset A$

    11. $A \supset B$ 26. $B \supset A$

    12. $A \supset B$ 27. $A \supset B$

    13. $A \supset B$ 28. $B \supset A$

    14. $A \supset B$ 29. $\sim (A$ & $B)$

    15. $A \supset B$ 30. $\sim A$ & $\sim B$

31. ~(~A & ~B)   or   A ∨ B   34. ~(A ∨ B) ⊃ (~C & ~D)

32. ~A & ~B   35. S & [J ∨ (A & B)]

33. I ⊃ (M ⊃ C)   or   (I & M) ⊃ C

IV. 1. False   3. False   5. True   7. False
     2. True   4. False   6. False   8. True

Section 7-2

1.

p	q	r	$q \lor r$	$\sim p$	$(q \lor r) \supset \sim p$
T	T	T	T	F	F
F	T	T	T	T	T
T	F	T	T	F	F
F	F	T	T	T	T
T	T	F	T	F	F
F	T	F	T	T	T
T	F	F	F	F	T
F	F	F	F	T	T

2.

p	q	r	$p \supset q$	$p \supset r$	$(p \supset q)\ \&\ (p \supset r)$
T	T	T	T	T	T
F	T	T	T	T	T
T	F	T	F	T	F
F	F	T	T	T	T
T	T	F	T	F	F
F	T	F	T	T	T
T	F	F	F	F	F
F	F	F	T	T	T

3.

p	q	$\sim p$	$p\ \&\ \sim p$	$(p\ \&\ \sim p) \supset q$
T	T	F	F	T
F	T	T	F	T
T	F	F	F	T
F	F	T	F	T

4.

q	r	$\sim q$	$\sim q \lor r$
T	T	F	T
F	T	T	T
T	F	F	F
F	F	T	T

5.

p	q	r	$p \supset q$	$q \supset r$	$(p \supset q)\ \&\ (q \supset r)$	$p \supset r$	$[(p \supset q)\ \&\ (q \supset r)] \supset (p \supset r)$
T	T	T	T	T	T	T	T
F	T	T	T	T	T	T	T
T	F	T	F	T	F	T	T
F	F	T	T	T	T	T	T
T	T	F	T	F	F	F	T
F	T	F	T	F	F	T	T
T	F	F	F	T	F	F	T
F	F	F	T	T	T	T	T

6.

p	q	r	$q \supset r$	$p \supset (q \supset r)$	p & q	$[p \supset (q \supset r)]$ & $(p$ & $q)$
T	T	T	T	T	T	T
F	T	T	T	T	F	F
T	F	T	T	T	F	F
F	F	T	T	T	F	F
T	T	F	F	F	T	F
F	T	F	F	T	F	F
T	F	F	T	T	F	F
F	F	F	T	T	F	F

$\{[p \supset (q \supset r)]$ & $(p$ & $q)\}$ V r
T
T
T
T
F
F
F
F

Section 7-3

I. 1. It isn't the case that either John or Mary failed logic. De Morgan's law.

   2. Either Jane or Bill passed logic. Commutation.

   3. If Stuart graduates and his parents keep their promise, then he'll get a new car. Exportation.

   4. John passed and so did Bill and Jane. Association.

   5. If Kim cannot pass logic, then Stuart cannot either. Contraposition.

   6. Either Pete will graduate and get a new car or he will graduate and save his money for graduate school. Distribution.

   7. He can get into medical school. Double negation.

II. 1. $\sim(A \supset B) \supset \sim C$ or $C \supset (\sim B \supset \sim A)$

   2. $\sim C$ V $(A \supset B)$ or $C \supset (\sim A$ V $B)$

   3. $\sim[C$ & $\sim(A \supset B)]$

   4. $C \supset [C$ & $(A \supset B)]$ or $C \supset [A \supset (A$ & $B)]$

   5. $(C$ & $A) \supset B$

   6. $\sim C$ V $\sim D$

   7. $\sim(D$ & $C)$

   8. $\sim(E$ & $F)$ V $\sim G$

   9. $\sim[G$ & $(E$ & $F)]$

  10. $\sim[(F$ & $E)$ & $G]$

  11. $\sim[E$ & $(F$ & $G)]$

  12. $(I$ V $J)$ & H

  13. H & $(J$ V $I)$

14. $(H \& I) \lor (H \& J)$

15. $K \equiv L$

16. $(\sim K \lor L) \& (L \supset K)$

17. $(K \supset L) \& (\sim N \supset \sim M)$

18. $(K \supset L) \& (\sim\sim M \supset N)$

19. $M \supset N$

20. $(O \equiv \sim P) \& (Q \supset R)$

21. $Q \& (R \lor T)$

22. $\sim(S \equiv T) \supset \sim(Q \equiv R)$

23. $(Q \equiv R) \supset [(Q \equiv R) \& S]$

Section 7-4

I. Reference statement: $L \supset B$

1. $\sim L \supset \sim B$

2. $\sim L \supset \sim B$

3. $B \lor \sim L$ Equivalent

4. $L \lor \sim B$

5. $\sim B \supset \sim L$ Equivalent

6. $L \& \sim B$

7. $L \supset B$ Equivalent

8. $L \supset B$ Equivalent

9. $B \supset L$

10. $L \supset B$ Equivalent

11. $L \supset B$ Equivalent

12. $B \supset \sim L$

13. $\sim L \supset \sim B$

II. 1. Statements a and d are equivalent to the given statement.

2. Statements b and c are equivalent to the given statement.

3. Statement a is equivalent to the given statement.

III. All but 7 and 8 can be translated as "$p \supset q$."

IV. 1. A given number is a multiple of 4 $\supset$ that same number is a multiple of 2

2. Steve plays the piano $\supset$ Warren sings

3. It rains $\supset$ the game is cancelled

4. The sum of two given integers is seven $\supset$ those two integers cannot but be even numbers

5. Susie walks $\supset$ Susie is late

6. He is late $\supset$ he slept late

7. He studies and the exam is easy ⊃ he passes

8. Earl does not study ⊃ Earl will have to stay home

9. Fred passes ⊃ Fred studied hard

10. Texas beats Oklahoma ⊃ Texas is a better team than Oklahoma

11. One doesn't study ⊃ one doesn't pass

12. One has not completed elementary logic ⊃ one cannot enroll in symbolic logic

CHAPTER 8

Section 8-1

I.   1. None   2. M.P.   3. None   4. Adj.
     5. Chain   6. Disj. Add.   7. None
     8. Conj. Simp.   9. None   10. None   11. None
    12. Disj. Arg.   13. None   14. C.D.
    15. None   16. None   17. None
    18. Disj. Add.   19. None   20. M.P.
    21. Conj. Simp. 22. Adj.   23. M.T.   24. Adj.
    25. C.D.

II. 1. Conj. Simp.   2. None   3. Disj. Add.
     4. Adj.   5. None   6. M.T.   7. Disj. Arg.
     8. Chain   9. Disj. Add.   10. Chain
    11. None   12. None
    13. None   14. Adj.   15. C.D.
    16. M.P.   17. C.D.
    18. Adj.   19. M.T.   20. Disj. Arg.
    21. Disj. Arg.   22. None   23. C.D.
    24. Disj. Arg.   25. Chain   26. None
    27. Chain   28. None

III. A. 3. Tomorrow is Sunday. M.P.
     B. 3. He didn't study hard. M.T.
     C. 3. If today is Saturday then I had better hurry.
     D. 3. It's Wednesday. Disj. Arg.
     E. 3. This is not a logic class. M.T.
     F. 3. Either I make good grades or I have lots of fun. C.D.
     G. 3. Either the hostess will feel better or I will. C.D.
     H. 3. This is a logic class. Disj. Arg.
     I. 3. The Cowboys did not win last year's Super Bowl. M.T.
     J. 3. I'll get an F in this course. C.D.
     K. 3. It is Sunday and it's beautiful. Adj.
     L. 3. I will get a promotion. M.P.

IV. 1.

p	q	$p \supset q$	$\sim p$	$\sim q$
T	T	T	F	F
F	T	T	T	F
T	F	F	F	T
F	F	T	T	T

Invalid, as shown by the second row.

2.

p	q	r	$p \supset q$	$q \supset r$	$p \supset r$
T	T	T	T	T	T
F	T	T	T	T	T
T	F	T	F	T	T
F	F	T	T	T	T
T	T	F	T	F	F
F	T	F	T	F	T
T	F	F	F	T	F
F	F	F	T	T	T

Valid.

3.

p	q	r	$p \supset q$	$p \supset r$	$(p \supset q) \,\&\, (p \supset r)$	p	$q \,\&\, r$
T	T	T	T	T	T	T	T
F	T	T	T	T	T	F	T
T	F	T	F	T	F	T	F
F	F	T	T	T	T	F	F
T	T	F	T	F	F	T	F
F	T	F	T	T	T	F	F
T	F	F	F	F	F	T	F
F	F	F	T	T	T	F	F

Valid

4.

p	q	$\sim p$
T	T	F
F	T	T
T	F	F
F	F	T

Valid

5.

p	q	$p \,\&\, q$
T	T	T
F	T	F
(T)	F	(F)
F	F	F

Invalid

6.

$p \supset q$
$r \supset p$
$\therefore \sim q \lor r$

p	q	r	$\sim q$	$p \supset q$	$r \supset p$	$\sim q \lor r$
T	T	T	F	T	T	T
F	T	T	F	T	F	T
T	F	T	T	F	T	T
F	F	T	T	T	F	T
T	T	F	F	(T)	T	(F)
F	T	F	F	(T)	T	(F)
T	F	F	T	F	T	T
F	F	F	T	T	T	T

Invalid

7.

$p \supset (q \supset r)$
$p \,\&\, q$
$\therefore r$

p	q	r	$q \supset r$	$p \supset (q \supset r)$	$p \,\&\, q$	r
T	T	T	T	T	T	T
F	T	T	T	T	F	T
T	F	T	T	T	F	T
F	F	T	T	T	F	T
T	T	F	F	F	T	F
F	T	F	F	T	F	F
T	F	F	T	T	F	F
F	F	F	T	T	F	F

A. 3. ~S Conj. Simp. from 2
   4. ~T M.P. from 2, 3

B. 3. X & Y Adj. 1, 2
   4. $(X$ & $Y)$ V $(Z$ & $W)$ Disj. Add.

C. 4. ~A M.T. 1, 3
   5. ~C M.T. 2, 4

D. 4. $C ⊃ B$ Chain 2, 1
   5. ~C M.T. 4, 3

E. 4. ~A M.T. 1, 3
   5. D M.P. 2, 4

F. 3. T M.P. 2, 1
   4. T V S Disj. Add.

G. 4. ~B V ~X M.P. 3, 1
   5. C V Y C.D. 2, 4

H. 4. ~C M.P. 3,1
   5. D Disj. Arg. 2, 4

I. 4. $X ⊃ Z$ Chain 1, 2
   5. Z M.P. 4, 3

J. 4. Y M.P. 1, 3
   5. Z M.P. 2, 4

K. 4. ~Y M.P. 1, 3
   5. ~W M.T. 2, 4

L. 4. ~X M.T. 1, 3
   5. Z Disj. Arg. 2, 4

M. 4. ~V Disj. Arg. 1, 3
   5. ~W M.T. 2, 4

N. 3. ~$(X$ & $Y)$ Conj. Simp. 1
   4. ~$(J$ V ~$K)$ M.T. 2, 3

O. 4. ~$M ⊃$ ~O Disj. Arg. 3, 1
   5. ~$L ⊃$ ~O Chain 2, 4

P. 4. ~R M.T. 2, 1
   5. $(S$ V $U)$ & ~R Adj. 3, 4

Q. 3. S V T M.P. 2, 1
   4. L Conj. Simp. 1
   5. L & $(S$ V $T)$ Adj.

R. 3. $J ⊃$ ~K Conj. Simp. 1
   4. $J ⊃ S$ Chain 3, 2

S. 3. ~$(X$ & $Y) ⊃ (J$ & $K)$ Chain 1, 2
   4. $[$~$(X$ & $Y) ⊃ (J$ & $K)]$ V $[(L ⊃$ ~$M)$ & $A]$ Disj. Add. 3

T. 3. A V B Disj. Add. 1
   4. B Disj. Arg. 3, 4

U. 3. ~N M.P. 2, 1
   4. R Disj. Arg. 1, 3

V. 4. ~$(O$ V $P)$ M.P. 1, 3
   5. Q & R Disj. Arg. 3, 2

W. 3. ~W V K Conj. Simp. 1
   4. K Disj. Arg. 3, 2

X. 3. ~$(X$ & $Y) ⊃ (J$ & $K)$ Chain 2, 1
   4. $[$~$(X$ & $Y) ⊃ (J$ & $K)]$ V $[(X$ V $L) ⊃ M]$ Disj. Add. 3

Y. 4. ~B V $(R$ & $S)$ Disj. Arg. 2, 3
   5. C V T C.D. 1, 4

Z. 4. $X ⊃ A$ Chain 1, 3
   5. $(B$ V $Q)$ & $(X ⊃ A)$ Adj. 2, 4

AA. 4. A & B Disj. Arg. 1, 3
    5. $($~E V ~$F)$ & $(A$ & $B)$ Adj. 2, 4

BB. 4. ~$(A ⊃ R)$ M.T. 1, 3
    5. K & L Disj. Arg. 2, 4

CC. 3. $K ⊃ L$ Disj. Arg. 2,1
    4. $(K ⊃ L)$ & ~J Adj. 3, 1

DD. 4. H & F M.P. 1, 3
    5. G & $(H$ & $F)$ Adj. 3, 4
    6. $[E ⊃ (J$ & $I)]$ & $[G$ & $(H$ & $F)]$ Adj. 2, 5

EE. 2. ~S & ~T Conj. Simp. 1
    3. ~S Conj. Simp. 2
    4. ~S & $($~S & ~$T)$ Adj. 3, 2

FF. 4. ~$(J$ & $K)$ Conj. Simp. 1
    5. ~$(A$ & $B)$ M.T. 3, 4
    6. ~C Disj. Arg. 2, 5

GG. 4. $X ⊃ (X$ & $Y)$ Conj. Simp. 1
    5. $(X$ & $Y)$ V D C.D. 4, 2, 3

HH. 5. L Conj. Simp. 4   II. 5. $\sim I$ M.T. 1, 4
    6. $L \vee (M \& N)$ Disj. Add. 5   6. $\sim\sim K \& \sim\sim J$ Disj. Arg. 2, 5
    7. $(R \& S) \supset T$ M.P. 2, 6   7. $\sim\sim K$ Conj. Simp. 6
    8. S M.P. 1, 3   8. $\sim L$ M.T. 3, 7
    9. $R \& S$ Adj. 3, 8   9. $\sim L \vee \sim J$ Disj. Add. 8
   10. T M.P. 7, 9

Section 8-5

1.

p	q	r		$p \& q$	$p \vee r$	r
T	T	F		T	T	F

2.

p	q	r		$p \supset (q \supset r)$	p	r
T	F	F		T	T	F

3.

p	q	r		$p \supset q$	$p \vee r$	q
F	F	T		T	T	F

4.

p	q	r		$p \supset q$	$q \supset r$	$p \& r$
F	F	F		T	T	F

5.

p	q	r		$p : q$	$p \vee r$	$q \supset \sim r$
T	T	T		T	T	F

6.

p	q	r	s		$(p \supset r) \& (s \supset q)$	$r \vee q$	$p \vee s$
F	T	T	F		T	T	F

7.

p	q	r		$p \supset q$	$p \vee r$	$q \vee \sim r$
F	F	T		T	T	F

8.

p	q	r		$(p \supset q) \vee (q \supset r)$	$p \vee q$	$q \& r$
T	T	F		T	T	F

CHAPTER 9

Section 9-1

1. R_J 2. $\sim J_S$ 3. $R_J \supset R_S$ 4. $(R_D \vee J_S) \supset J_S$

5. $\sim D_T$ 6. D_S 7. $D_S \& S_S$

Section 9-3

1. $(\exists x)(Sx \& Cx)$

2. $(\exists x)(Sx \& Qx \& \sim Cx)$

3. $\sim(\exists x)(Px \& Fx); \ (x)(Px \supset \sim Fx)$

4. $(\exists x)(Mx \& Lx)$

5. $(x)(Wx \supset Mx)$

6. $(\exists x)(Bx \& \sim Fx); \ \sim(x)(Bx \supset Fx)$

7. $(x)(Tx \supset Ex)$

8. $(x)[Tx \supset (Ex \& Kx \& Wx)]$

9. $(x)(Tx \supset \sim Ix); \ \sim(\exists x)(Tx \& Ix)$

10. $(x)(Fx \supset Mx)$

11. $(\exists x)(Sx \& \sim Ox)$

12. $(\exists x)(Lx \& Ux)$

13. $(x)(Tx \supset {\sim}Rx)$

14. $(x)[Mx \supset (Qx \ \& \ Bx)]$

15. $(x)[(Bx \ \& \ Tx) \supset Cx]$

16. $(x)(Ax \supset Dx)$

17. $(x)[Px \supset (Ex \ \& \ Sx)] \supset (\exists y)(Fy \ \& \ Ry)$

Section 9-4

I. 1. a. ${\sim}(x)(Px \supset {\sim}Sx)$
   b. $(\exists x)(Px \ \& \ Sx)$
   We can derive b from a as follows, using only equivalence rules.
   Hence the last line is equivalent to the first.
   (1) ${\sim}(x)(Px \supset {\sim}Sx)$
   (2) $(\exists x){\sim}(Px \supset {\sim}Sx)$ Q.N. Rule 1
   (3) $(\exists x){\sim}({\sim}Px \vee {\sim}Sx)$ Conditional Exchange
   (4) $(\exists x){\sim}{\sim}(Px \ \& \ Sx)$ De Morgan's Law
   (5) $(\exists x)(Px \ \& \ Sx)$ Double Negation

   2. a. ${\sim}(x)(Sx \supset Dx)$
   b. $(\exists x)(Sx \ \& \ {\sim}Dx)$
   We can derive b from a, using equivalence rules.
   (1) ${\sim}(x)(Sx \supset Dx)$
   (2) $(\exists x){\sim}(Sx \supset Dx)$ Q.N. Rule 1
   (3) $(\exists x){\sim}({\sim}Sx \vee Dx)$ Conditional Exchange
   (4) $(\exists x)({\sim}{\sim}Sx \ \& \ {\sim}Dx)$ De Morgan's Law
   (5) $(\exists x)(Sx \ \& \ {\sim}Dx)$ Double Negation

II. 1. (1) ${\sim}(\exists x)[(Ax \vee Bx) \vee Cx]$ Denial of a
   (2) $(x){\sim}[(Ax \vee Bx) \vee Cx]$ Q.N. Rule 2
   (3) $(x){\sim}[Ax \vee (Bx \vee Cx)]$ Association
   (4) $(x){\sim}[{\sim}{\sim}Ax \vee (Bx \vee Cx)]$ Double Negation
   (5) $(x){\sim}[{\sim}Ax \supset (Bx \vee Cx)]$ Conditional Exchange

   2. (1) ${\sim}(x)(Gx \supset {\sim}Hx)$ Denial of a
   (2) $(Fx){\sim}(Gx \supset {\sim}Hx)$ Q.N. Rule 1
   (3) $(Fx){\sim}({\sim}Gx \vee {\sim}Hx)$ Conditional Exchange
   (4) $(Fx){\sim}{\sim}(Gx \ \& \ Hx)$ De Morgan's Law
   (5) $(Fx)(Gx \ \& \ Hx)$ Double Negation

   3. (1) ${\sim}{\sim}(x){\sim}Fx$ Denial of a
   (2) $(x){\sim}Fx$ Double Negation
   (3) ${\sim}(\exists x)Fx$ Q.N. Rule 2
   (4) ${\sim}(\exists x){\sim}{\sim}Fx$ Double Negation

   4. (1) ${\sim}(x)[(Ax \ \& \ Bx) \supset Cx]$ Denial of a
   (2) $(\exists x){\sim}[(Ax \ \& \ Bx) \supset Cx]$ Q.N. Rule 1
   (3) $(\exists x){\sim}[Ax \supset (Bx \supset Cx)]$ Exportation

   5. (1) ${\sim}(\exists x){\sim}(Fx \ \& \ {\sim}Gx)$ Denial of a
   (2) $(x){\sim}{\sim}(Fx \ \& \ {\sim}Gx)$ Q.N. Rule 2
   (3) $(x){\sim}({\sim}Fx \vee {\sim}{\sim}Gx)$ De Morgan's Law
   (4) $(x){\sim}(Fx \supset {\sim}{\sim}Gx)$ Conditional Exchange
   (5) $(x){\sim}(Fx \supset Gx)$ Double Negation

Section 9-5

1.

Fa	Fb	Ga	Gb	${\sim}Ga$	${\sim}Gb$	$Fa \ \& \ {\sim}Ga$	$Fb \ \& \ {\sim}Gb$	$(Fa \ \& \ {\sim}Ga) \vee (Fb \ \& \ {\sim}Gb)$
T	T	T	T	F	F	F	F	F
T	T	F	T	T	F	T	F	T

262

2.

Ha	Hb	Ha & Hb
T	T	T
T	F	F

3.

Fa	Fb	Ga	Gb	Fa $\lor$ Ga	Fb $\lor$ Gb	(Fa $\lor$ Ga) $\lor$ (Fb $\lor$ Gb)
T	T	T	T	T	T	T
F	F	F	F	F	F	F

4.

Ha	Hb	Ia	Ib	Ha $\supset$ Ia	Hb $\supset$ Ib	(Ha $\supset$ Ia) & (Hb $\supset$ Ib)
T	T	F	T	F	T	F
T	T	T	T	T	T	T

5.

Ha	Hb	Ia	Ib	Ha $\equiv$ Ia	Hb $\equiv$ Ib	(Ha $\equiv$ Ia) $\lor$ (Hb $\equiv$ Ib)
T	T	T	T	T	T	T
T	T	F	F	F	F	F

Section 9-6

1. (1) $(x)Hx \supset Ix$
   (2) Ha $/\therefore Ia$
   (3) $Ha \supset Ia$ I, U.I.
   (4) Ia 3, 2, *Modus Ponens*

2. (1) $(y)(Jy \quad Ky)$
   (2) Jb $/\therefore(Fy)Ky$
   (3) $Jb \supset Kb$ I, U.I.
   (4) Kb 3, 2, *Modus Ponens*
   (5) $(Fy)Ky$ E.G.

3. (1) $(z)(Az \supset Bz)$
   (2) $(z)(Bz \supset Cz)$ $/\therefore(z)Az \supset Cz$
   (3) $Ag \supset Bg$ 1, U.I.
   (4) $Bg \supset Cg$ 2, U.I.
   (5) $Ag \supset Cg$ 3, 4, Chain Argument
   (6) $(z)(Az \supset Cz)$ 5, U.G.

4. (1) $(x)(Ax \supset {\sim}Bx)$
   (2) Bd $/\therefore{\sim}Ad$
   (3) $Ad \supset {\sim}Bd$ I, U.I.
   (4) ${\sim}{\sim}Bd$ 3, Double Negation
   (5) ${\sim}Ad$ 3, 4, *Modus Tollens*

5. (1) $(y)(Fy \supset Gy)$
   (2) $(\exists y)(Hy \& Fy)$ $/\therefore(\exists y)(Hy \& Gy)$
   (3) $Ha \& Fa$ 2, E.I.
   (4) $Fa \supset Ga$ 1, U.I.
   (5) Fa 3, Simplification
   (6) Ga 4, 5, *Modus Ponens*
   (7) Ha 3, Simplification
   (8) $Ha \& Ga$ 7, 6, Conjunction
   (9) $(\exists y)(Hy \& Gy)$ 8, E.G.

6. (1) $(\exists z)(Lz \& {\sim}Mz)$
   (2) $(z)(Lz \supset Oz)$ $/\therefore(Fz)(Oz \& {\sim}Mz)$
   (3) $Lb \& {\sim}Mb$ 2, E.I.

(4)	$Lb \supset Ob$			2, U.I.
(5)	Lb			3, Simplification
(6)	Ob			4, 5, *Modus Ponens*
(7)	$\sim Mb$			3, Simplification
(8)	Ob & $\sim Mb$			6, 7, Conjunction
(9)	$(\exists z)(Oz$ & $\sim Mz)$			8, E.G.

Section 9-7

1. If anything is a cat, then it is a mammal.
   Socrates is a mammal.
   Therefore, Socrates is a cat.

Cs	Ms	$Cs \supset Ms$	Ms	Cs
F	T	T	T	F

2.

Ad	Bd	Cd	$\sim Cd$	$Ad \supset Bd$	$Ad \lor Cd$	$Bd \supset \sim Cd$
T	T	T	F	T	T	F

3.

Da	Ea	Fa	Da & Ea	$Da \lor Fa$	Fa
T	T	F	T	T	F

4.

Ra	Sa	Ta	$Sa \supset Ta$	$Ra \supset (Sa \supset Ra)$	Ra	Ta
T	F	F	T	T	T	F

5.

Va	Wa	Ya	$Va \supset Wa$	$Wa \supset Ya$	$Ya \supset Va$
F	T	T	T	T	F

6.

Da	Ea	Fa	$Da \supset Ea$	$Ea \supset Fa$	Da & Fa
F	T	T	T	T	F

7.

Ag	Bg	Cg	Dg	$Ag \supset Bg$	$Cg \supset Dg$	$(Ag \supset Bg)$ & $(Cg \supset Dg)$	$Bg \lor Dg$	$Ag \lor Cg$
F	T	F	T	T	T	T	T	F

8.

Ba	Qa	Ra	$\sim Ba$	$\sim Ra$	$Ba \supset Qa$	$\sim Ba \lor \sim Ra$	$Qa \lor Ra$
F	F	F	T	T	T	T	F

CHAPTER 10

Section 10-1

I.

1.	RF	6.	RF or SP	11.	RF	16.	MP
2.	MP	7.	RF or SP	12.	RF	17.	RF
3.	RF	8.	RF	13.	SP	18.	RC or SP
4.	SP	9.	RC	14.	SP	19.	SP
5.	SP or RF	10.	RF	15.	MP	20.	SP

There is room for reasonable disagreement about some of these responses.

One's response sometimes depends on the imagined context of the probability statement as well as on what is stated.

II. 1. T   3. F   5. T   7. F   9. T
    2. F   4. T   6. T   8. T   10. T

III. In order to use the classical concept of probability, we must assume that all possibilities are known and that every possibility is equiprobable. There are conclusive reasons for rejecting the applicability of the principle of indifference in this case. In order for the probability of the formation of a protein molecule to be ascertained, the relative abundance of the constituents of protein a billion years ago must be known. The climatic conditions must also be known. Now if the climatic conditions were favorable to the formation of a protein molecule, and the constituents of protein were relatively abundant, then it is probable that a protein molecule formed as a result of the random (not consciously directed) mixing of atoms. If the conditions were quite otherwise, then that event is improbable. The weather conditions and relative abundance of the atomic constituents of protein cannot be ascertained *a priori*. But it would be necessary to ascertain those matters *a priori* in order for the principle of indifference to apply. Thus, it is impossible to use the "classical" concept of probability in such a case. Therefore, Lecomte du Nuoy believed he knew something that he could not have known on the basis of the information he had.

The formation of a protein molecule from its atomic constituents is a process involving a number of steps. Thus, the probability of the process occurring all at once is much lower, other things being equal, than the probability of its occurrence in stages. Hence, Lecomte de Nuoy's very description of the event is biased in favor of his result.

Section 10-2

I. A. 1. S. Although the percentage is relatively small, this information, when considered by itself, is evidence that Smedley is a bad professor.

2. W. Even if we consider this evidence alongside item 1, the evidence weakens Bullgravy's conclusion, since the vast majority of Smedley's students rate him as good or better. This illustrates the fact that initial evidence can point to one conclusion, although further investigation corroborates its opposite.

3. W.

4. S. If we considered items 3 and 4 together, the overall evidence militates against Bullgravy's conclusion. Ten percent is statistically significant, whereas two students represent less than one percent.

5. W.

6. N. This has no bearing on Smedley's ability to teach.

7. S or N. This information is indeterminate. Should a professor limit lectures to words that students already know? Should students ask about words they don't understand (or look them up)?

8. S or N. Occasionally being difficult to understand may show that Smedley is an unsatisfactory teacher. But it may be a

function of the difficulty of the material being taught, of the lack of preparation on the students' part, or of some combination.

9. W.

10. There are at least two ways to interpret this evidence. One way is to view Smedley as a professor with appropriately higher standards and to explain the complaints of some students as dissatisfaction with lower grades. (There is a correlation between being an easy grader and higher evaluations, and between being a tough grader and lower evaluations.) A second way is to view Smedley as such a bad professor that he cannot teach well enough to ensure that the students make the same grades they do in other classes. This second interpretation, however, does not tally with the evidence in item 9.

11. W.

B. W. Despite his being hard to understand at times, the vast majority of Smedley's students said his lectures were very helpful.

C. 1. W.   3. S.   5. S.   7. S.
   2. S.   4. W.   6. W.   8. W.

D. 1. S.

2. N. The inferior unit would naturally sell for less. But that does not show that the stereo purchased was a great deal.

3. W. The manufacturer's unwillingness to guarantee the stereo for as long is evidence that there have been claims on the three-year guarantee (and thus that the stereo is not all that reliable).

4. N. Although this may be a regrettable consequence from Julie's point of view, it has no bearing on the conclusion she drew.

5. W.

6. S.

7. S. This evidence may be indeterminate; it depends on the interpretation of the word good.

II. 1. This is the sort of hasty generalization you may hear in the hallway. Even if we assume that Sarah and Margaret snubbed the speaker, it should be noted that the sample cited is so small that it is likely to be unrepresentative.

2. If welfare programs were unnecessary, no recipient of a welfare check would need the funds. All the checks would be obtained fraudulently. But the fact that one recipient of a welfare check is a fraud does not prove that everyone who receives welfare is a fraud. The evidence cited is merely anecdotal and cannot justify the broad, sweeping generalization inferred from it. This is an instance of arguing from an extreme case. Compare the following argument: "I know of a defense contractor that filed a fraudulent claim. No service was rendered, and no product was delivered. This just goes to show that defense programs are unnecessary and riddled with corruption."

3. If the Palace of Versailles were typical living quarters in seventeenth- and eighteenth-century France, then seventeenth- and eighteenth-century people in France would have lived lives of luxurious splendor. But royalty surely had more luxurious living quarters than most people.

4. Shlomo's sample is too small for him to make any inference about college students generally. The claim "not one formulated a decent argument," is compatible with only a couple of students speaking. This means that it is possible that there were other students in the class who thought of a good argument but remained silent, for whatever reason. In that event Shlomo's claim would not even be true of all the students in his class, let alone all college students.

5. The inconsistency of the two accounts means that they cannot both be true. But that has no bearing on other statements in the Bible that are logically independent of the two accounts.

Section 10-3

1. This argument is in logically proper form just as it stands. The first conclusion, "There is a designer of nature," is a premise from which the second conclusion is derived. Assuming a standard concept of God, the second conclusion is much more sweeping than the first. For example, the evidence does not prove that there is exactly one designer of nature. David Hume makes this and other related points well in Section XI of _An Inquiry Concerning Human Understanding_. Hume also examines and criticizes the comparison of things in nature to artifacts in another work, _Dialogues Concerning Natural Religion_. Hume thereby questions the argument for the first conclusion. Evolutionary accounts of biological phenomena in terms of such factors as natural selection explain many instances of order without invoking a designer. These scientific explanations constitute a challenge to the presupposition that order requires a designer.

2. If the third sentence (the question) is deleted and the last two sentences are combined ("I know that similar behavior in similar bodies is accompanied by thought"), then the argument is in logically proper form. An alternative would be to delete the next-to-last sentence and put the conclusion as "I know that there are other minds." The problem is that the inference is based on only one case: the reasoner himself. "I cannot observe any mind but my own." Thus, this argument, which is called the analogical argument for other minds, constitutes a violation of criterion 3.

3. A premise and the conclusion of this _reductio ad absurdum_ argument are suppressed. A tacit premise is "The detective does have scientific evidence for the claim that the man died from a gunshot wound, despite not seeing the incident." The suppressed conclusion is "The anti-evolutionists' claim, that there is no scientific evidence for the theory of evolution because scientists have not seen the past," is false.
   There are some dissimilarities between a scientist's evidence for long-term evolutionary changes and the detective's evidence for the conclusion about the cause of death. Nevertheless, these differences have no bearing on the conclusion drawn. If the anti-evolutionists' claim is that only seeing something is scientific evidence regarding it, then the analogy is a refutation.

4. 1. This new car is the same model as the one I bought five years ago.
   2. I had the car I bought five years ago repaired only rarely.
   3. Therefore, I probably won't have to have this new car repaired very often.
   Although the models are the same, are the two cars similar in other ways that are relevant to frequency of repairs? The argument leaves open the possibility that the answer is "no." Argument 5, which follows argument 4, points out how this argument does not compare the two cars sufficiently.

5. The suppressed conclusion of this argument is either "Your belief that you won't have to have your new car repaired very often is probably false" or "The evidence you cited does not justify the belief that you won't have to have your new car repaired very often." The evidence in this argument supports the stronger (first) conclusion.

Section 10-4

1. .72	5. .8	9. 1/13	
2. .28	6. 0	10. 2/13	
3. .14	7. .42	11. fallacy of unequal chances	
4. .58	8. 5/13	12. gambler's fallacy	

CHAPTER 11

Section 11-1

1. There are two stages of the Redi experiment. Both stages are analyzed below. (a) = hypothesis being tested; (b) = test implications; (c) = corroborate or disconfirm.
   a. Any dead, decaying body by itself causes worms.
   b. If the snakes are put in an open box, worms will appear.
   c. The evidence corroborates the hypothesis.

   a. Same hypothesis.
   b. If the snakes are put in the open box with sealed holes, worms will appear.
   c. Although the evidence corroborates the hypothesis it also corroborates a hypothesis incompatible with it, namely "The decaying snakes attracted flies, who deposited eggs in them." The evidence also corroborates a variation on the original hypothesis: "Decaying bodies by themselves cause worms that develop into flies."

2. a. The worms in the decaying bodies are caused by the droppings of flies rather than by the sheer decay of the bodies.
   b. If the open and closed boxes with decaying meat are observed, worms (that eventually develop into flies) will appear in the meat of the open box but not in that of the closed box.
   c. The evidence corroborates the hypothesis.

3. a. Hereditary material is comparable to a fluid that is blended.
   b. If the tall garden pea plants are crossed with the short ones, the result will be medium-sized garden pea plants.
   c. The evidence disconfirms the hypothesis.

4. a. There are at least two alternative hypotheses under consideration here:
   "Heredity is determined by segregated (separate) factors" and
   "The factor for shortness in the plants did not disappear entirely."

b. If the tall plants that are the offspring of tall and short plants are allowed to self-pollinate, some of the offspring will be short.

c. The evidence corroborates either of the two hypotheses. Had all the offspring been tall, that would have disconfirmed both hypotheses.

5. a. Animals that co-operate with one another are probably related.

   b. The co-operative male lions within the same coalition are probably related.

   c. The evidence disconfirms the hypothesis.

6. a. Ginger relieves seasickness.

   b. The volunteers who were given a placebo or Dramamine will not fare so well as the volunteers given ginger in the "revolving chair experiment."

   c. The evidence corroborates the hypothesis. It also corroborates the hypothesis that ginger is more effective than Dramamine in relieving motion sickness.

7. a. There are two hypotheses being tested here. One (Heat is a material substance) is the calorie theory of heat. The other (Heat cannot be created or destroyed) is a logical consequence of the calorie theory of heat and the principle of the conservation of matter.

   b. If the boring of a brass gun produces heat, then there will be a corresponding reduction in the amount of material substance (weight of brass).

   c. The evidence disconfirms the first hypothesis and, by implication, the second, provided that the principle of the conservation of matter is assumed. Otherwise, disconfirming the second hypothesis implies that either the calorie theory or the principle of the conservation of matter, or both, is false.

8. a. Atmospheric pressure explains the fact that a suction pump will lift water no higher than 34 feet above the surface of the well.

   b. If the tube of mercury is inverted, submerged, and uncapped in an open vessel of mercury, the mercury will rise to 34/14 feet.

   c. The evidence corroborates the hypothesis.

9. a. Atmospheric pressure is responsible for the length of the mercury column (and other related phenomena, such as in Exercise 8).

   b. If the mercury barometer is taken to the top of the mountain, then the length of the column will be (proportionately) lower than at the foot of the mountain.

   c. The evidence corroborates the hypothesis.

10. a. At constant temperature, the volume of a fixed weight of gas is inversely proportional to the pressure exerted upon it.

    b. If the volume of the gas is cut in half twice, and then to two-thirds of the preceding volume, the pressures at which these results should occur (taking the top figure as our basis) are 30.56, 61.12, and 91.68.

    c. The evidence corroborates Boyle's law. (All the actual measurements are within 1.0 of the results predicted by Boyle's law.)

11. a. Boyle's law (see Exercise 10).

    b. If the volume of the gas is cut in half twice, and then to two-thirds of the preceding volume, the pressures at which these results should occur (taking the top figure as our basis) are 17.98, 35.96, and 53.94.

    c. Although the pressure for volume 1.0 (17.98) corroborates Boyle's law, the other two observations disconfirm Boyle's law.

12. a. The ratio of the angle of incidence (A of I) to the angle of refraction (A of R) is constant.
 b. If the angle of incidence is increased by 10 each time, then the angle of refraction (taking the first figure as our basis) should be 14, 21, 28, 35, 42, 49, and 56.
 c. Although the measurements to 30 yield results that corroborate Ptolemy's hypothesis, measurements of the A of R, where the A of I is 40 or higher, yield disconfirming evidence. The overall result is that the evidence militates against Ptolemy's hypothesis.

Section 11-2

I. 1. The first two questions are answered in the preceding section. Redi sought repeated corroboration for the hypothesis.

 2. The closed box is a control to determine whether the worms appear even if flies do not lay their eggs in the meat. Three converging statements that corroborate Redi's hypothesis that the droppings of flies caused the worms are as follows:
 a. The worms, when put into glass containers, developed into flies.
 b. Flies hovered over the open box before the worms appeared.
 c. No worms appeared in the meat in the closed box (flies could not deposit their eggs in it).
 The defender of "spontaneous generation" might defend his belief by revising it to "Dead, decaying bodies by themselves cause worms, provided that air circulates around the body." This *ad hoc* revision would not be falsified by Redi's evidence. Redi could have tested this new hypothesis by allowing air to circulate in the box while preventing flies from dropping eggs into the meat.

 3. Because the plants are tall, there must be a hereditary factor for tallness that is expressed in the plant. But if 25% of the offspring of these self-pollinated plants are short, then there must be a factor for shortness in the plants that is not expressed in the parent plants but is expressed in the offspring. The same parents' offspring are short and tall, so there must be two factors, one of which is expressed. Whenever the factor for tallness appears, the plants are tall (the result of the cross of tall and short plants). The factor for tallness is dominant, whereas shortness is recessive, as in this diagram:

First Generation   Offspring of Self-Pollinated Plants

     t   t   T   t

T	Tt	Tt		T	TT	Tt
---	----	----		---	----	----
T	Tt	Tt		t	Tt	tt

 = all tall offspring (First Generation)

 = offspring 3/4 tall, 1/4 short (Offspring of Self-Pollinated Plants)

 T = tall   t = short

 4. If the volunteers had not been particularly susceptible, and had all fared comparably in the test, it would not have been correct to infer that ginger was ineffective, since a placebo did just as well. The objection would be that, because the volunteers were not particularly susceptible, the test would not ordinarily be expected to produce motion sickness. Thus, the psychologists chose volunteers who were highly susceptible, people from whom they would expect motion sickness from ineffective treatments. The placebo was

a control to determine whether the results would be different in the absence of treatment.

5. An advocate of the calorie theory of heat could say that heat is a weightless material substance, which would be consistent with the findings. But it would be an objectionable *ad hoc* hypothesis.

6. There is not sufficient variety of evidence to justify the claim that Boyle's law is true without qualification. Whereas Boyle's law is about all gases at all temperatures, the evidence is about one gas at a single temperature. Different gases and different temperatures need to be tested.

7. The problem here is the same as in Exercise 6, except that here Boyle's law is rejected hastily. Although the results are negative, it does not follow that Boyle's law is useless for predicting the behavior of gases. Again, different gases and different temperatures need to be tested. If many different gases did not behave according to Boyle's law, then that would justify the sweeping rejection of it. (As a matter of fact, there are few exceptions to Boyle's law.)

8. At angles of incidence of 10 to 30, the ratio of the A of I to the angle of refraction is constant.

II. 1. Those who strongly advocate the belief that the earth is only 6,000 years old are violating the criterion of compatibility with well-established results.

2. The claim that God created the light "en route" to us (no more than 6,000 light years away) is an *ad hoc* hypothesis that is introduced only to protect the claim against adverse evidence. A testable but false statement has been transformed into an untestable one.

3. Schmucker's *ad hoc* hypothesis, that nature's abhorrence of a vacuum decreases with increasing altitude, is designed to protect the "horror-of-a-vacuum" hypothesis against the adverse evidence. Again, the *ad hoc* hypothesis renders a testable but false hypothesis untestable.

4. As illustrated above, an *ad hoc* hypothesis can render a claim untestable and thus incapable of being disconfirmed in any way. Fortunately, scientists are not (as a group) interested in protecting hypotheses at any cost.

5. A scientist is reputed to have responded to this argument, "And all the heroin addicts in the study began with mother's milk." The point is that the evidence gathered does not test the hypothesis. If only heroin addicts are surveyed, then the surveyors have ruled out the possibility of finding people who smoke marijuana but do not become addicted to heroin. Because their evidence does not test the hypothesis, the evidence does not corroborate it.

Section 11-3

I. 1. Yes. No.

2. No. There are adults who are not bachelors. Yes.

3. No, because a person's vision could be so nearly perfect that his vision did not need correction with prescription glasses, or his

vision could not be capable of being made better with glasses (e.g., a person afflicted with cataracts). Yes, if someone needs glasses, then his vision is not perfect.

4. If having an XX chromosome were a necessary condition for being a human female, then genetically abnormal individuals who look like females would not be human females. This is not to mention people who were born male (with XY) but who have undergone a sex-change operation. Having XX is only sufficient for being a human female, although a genetic abnormality consists of XXY.

5. No. Yes.

6. No. Yes, unless all the cat's fur fell out.

7. No. No. The election of a U.S. president depends on a majority of electoral, rather than popular, votes.

8. No. No.

9. No. Yes.

10. No. No.

II. 1. Reagan is insinuating that his assumption of the presidency caused inflation to plummet. But nothing more than the coincidence of two events has been noted. It takes _more_ to show that there is a cause-and-effect relationship between the two events. For example, it would be necessary to show that inflation would not have dropped if Carter had been elected.

2. This may be a case of confusing cause and effect. Did the lice avoid unhealthy members of the tribe because the lice would also become sick? Did the lice leave healthy persons once the lice had made them ill? The evidence cited doesn't address these questions. But the answer to the second question must be "no" if the statement is true. And if the answer to the first question were "yes," then the lice would not be promoting good health but merely accompanying people who were in good health.

3. This is an instance of the _post hoc_ fallacy. There is no evidence for the conclusion that stock prices would not have declined had Johnson not instituted a surtax. Economic factors might have caused a decline in stock market prices anyway.

5. This is probably best classified as an instance of the fallacy of accidental correlation, because the argument refers to the regular correlation of students who contracted venereal disease and having taken sex education classes. It is odd to read that sex education classes are being blamed for the incidence of venereal disease; such classes teach how it can be contracted and how prevented. Consider the following analogy: "A recent study shows that, among the youth of our city, 80% of those who contracted venereal disease last year had taken algebra classes in high school." We would not blame the algebra classes on that basis. Thus, the argument does not provide a good reason for blaming sex education classes for the incidence of venereal disease among high school students.

6. In this argument it is presupposed, without any evidence, that there is a cause-and-effect relationship between worrying and one's hair turning white. Even if that is assumed, (1) other possible explanations of the change of Furtwangler's hair color have not

been ruled out, and (2) Furtwangler's worry about something else could have caused the change. Perhaps (1) he simply reached the age at which his hair would become white, regardless of other details of his life. Another possibility is that (2) worry about his son's marriage, which was evidently in trouble about the time his daughter married, caused the change in hair color.

7. We are supposed to infer that food additives cause learning disabilities and behavioral disturbances. This argument does not rule out the very real possibility that many more people consume food additives, even in large quantities, than exhibit behavioral disturbances or have learning disabilities. Unless adjusted for inflation, an increase in the dollar value of food additives would not necessarily accompany an increase in the consumption of them. (It is not entirely clear, but "dollar value" seems to mean "the number of dollars spent.")

8. The argument does not tell us whether the juveniles who commit crimes are the same juveniles who purchase pornographic literature. Moreover, we need to know what percentage of adults who purchase pornographic literature commit crimes. If the percentage is low, then we need an explanation of how pornography could cause juveniles, but not adults, to commit crimes.

9. The study does not report how well the fat executives performed on the job. It would have to be shown that they were, as a group, just as deserving of the higher-paying jobs as their thinner competitors.

10. Rafferty has taken for granted that the professors knew and approved of their students' political activities. There are many other possible explanatory factors, none of which Rafferty considers, such as the student taking fewer courses, taking easier courses, or studying more that semester.

CHAPTER 12

Sections 12-1 and 12-2

1. The fact that some murderers have been certified sane by psychiatrists is evidence against the claim that no sane person would commit murder. Faced with this adverse evidence, the author adds a new criterion for sanity by using the word <u>really</u> in that way. A new criterion for sanity—not having murdered anyone—is introduced thereby. But that claim merely restates that author's "conclusion," rather than making a case for the psychiatrists being wrong. If not having murdered anyone were a criterion for being sane, a defense attorney could establish his client's innocence merely by establishing the client's sanity.

2. This is the same sort of logical error as in Exercise 1. In both cases a question-begging expression—"really"—is used in order to dismiss evidence that refutes the claim. Note how using a question-begging expression is like protecting a hypothesis with an objectionable *ad hoc* hypothesis (Chapter 11). A question-begging expression also often serves to transform a contingent (but false) statement into a necessary but trivial) statement (Chapter 2).

3. Sturdley's question is loaded. Presumably his friend does not believe that voting for the Republicans amounts to believing that the poor

should become poorer. Sturdley's question also presupposes that the described consequence will not occur if the Democrats are elected--or at least that people will, on the whole, be better off. But these are the kinds of claims that a person has to establish in political debate.

4. Although the elements of circular reasoning are separated by a couple of sentences, this passage boils down to "The Bullhorns are the outstanding team in the conference because the Bullhorns are the outstanding team in the conference." However, we require an independent reason for believing that claim. The intermediate steps appear at first to satisfy that demand, but the eventual reference to the very statement with which the passage begins means that no progress has been made.

5. (i) No student would lie to his favorite professor. (ii) Therefore, the student is telling the truth in saying I am his favorite professor. If the student's veracity is in question, as this attempt to establish it suggests, then Bullgravy cannot defend the claim that the student told the truth by assuming that what he said was true. Even if (i) is true, (ii) is a logical consequence only if (iii) is true and (iv) the student said (iii). But (iii) is precisely what Bullgravy is called upon to prove.

6. If everyone is caused, then even God would have a cause. But if God has a cause, then God is not the first cause (since the cause of God would be before God). The cause of God would not be the first cause, either. For if everything is caused, then the cause of God has a cause. This step can be reiterated indefinitely. Therefore, if everything is caused, then there is no first cause. And if there is no first cause, then God is not the first cause. Thus, the passage has inconsistent premises.

7. The statement "Everyone is obligated to be tolerant of the beliefs of others" is a universal moral statement that I. M. Pious claims to be true. Yet he begins by saying "There aren't any universal moral truths." I. M. Pious, therefore, has contradicted himself. The tone of his conclusion is itself dogmatic and intolerant. So there is a practical inconsistency between his belief about tolerance and the conclusion drawn.

8. J. F. Allswell's use of the word true in the phrase "true Christians" is a question-begging expression that is designed to rule out I. T. Endswell's refuting evidence about differences between Christians on the subject of hell. Allswell's use of true is like the use of really in Exercises 1 and 2. Allswell's claim about "true" Christians and God's word amounts to setting up a new criterion for being a Christian --namely, believing that sinners will fry in hell. Allswell's reply constitutes a decision about how to use the word Christian rather than a report of the beliefs of (all) Christians.

9. If it were fair (not discriminatory) to restrict women to the soprano section of the choir, this would be because they were incapable of singing anything but soprano. Thus Pope Paul VI is presupposing that women are incapable of being priests. However, that is precisely what is at issue. People who believe that the Pope's decree is discriminatory must base their accusation on the premise that women are capable of being priests. Pope Paul VI, therefore, could not defend the decree against the accusation of being discriminatory by assuming that it is non-discriminatory.

10. The sentences "The state has no right to put human beings to death, no matter how awful their crime" and "Capital punishment should be abol-

ished" express the same statement in different words. Because Sturdley
has only reworded his belief, he has not given us a reason for believing
it.

Section 12-3

I. 1. The Winston ad asks us to choose between good grammar and good
taste, as though making a flavorful cigarette ruled out the possibility of commercials that are free from grammatical errors.

2. It is possible to construe this as a slippery slope or false dilemma. Schmucker insinuates that the only alternative to dangerous and
unconstitutional police authority is a police force that is disarmed
and handcuffed. If the powers alleged to be dangerous and unconstitutional were restricted, presumably that would be different from
a disarmed and handcuffed police force. Alternatively, Schmucker's
reply could be construed as claiming that, if the police's authority
is eroded to any extent, we are headed down a path that will inevi-
tably end in a handcuffed police force. The reply to Schmucker is
that the justification for restricitng police power to what is constitutional would not justify handcuffing and disarming the police.

3. Sturdley suggested that a good reason for the 55-m.p.h. limit is
that it reduces the number of accidents. He did not say that any
measure that eliminates accidents altogether is justified. Smedley's reply amounts to a confusion between those distinct statements.
There are more options than a greater-than-55 or a 5-m.p.h. speed
limit.

4. This argument trades on a confusion between a belief being unproved
and a false belief. Suppose that the first statements in Exercises
4 and 5 are true. If so, then if Exercise 4 makes a compelling
case for atheism, Exercise 5 makes a compelling case for the belief
that God exists. Thus these arguments do not make a compelling
case for either belief.

5. This argument, like that in Exercise 4, is an instance of the fallacy of negative proof. It has been neither proved nor disproved
that every prime number is the sum of two primes. That does not
entitle us to infer either that the statement is true or that it is
false.

6. The speaker hopes that God exists and that life has a purpose but
offers no evidence for these beliefs or the presupposition that
God's existence is a prerequisite for a purpose of life. The passage is a case of wishful thinking.

7. Unless the conclusion is supposed to apply only to members of this
culture, the argument inconsistently enjoins members of other cultures not to judge our beliefs. Moreover, it does not follow, from
the assumption that moral beliefs in other cultures are different,
that they should be different. But the injunction against judging
beliefs in other cultures amounts to saying that those beliefs
should remain different.

8. The newspaper staff is trying to defend its decision to drop
"Doonesbury" against the objections of some readers. Evidently the
results of the survey are supposed to justify the conclusion that
the newspaper staff had the general support of its readers in dropping "Doonesbury." But the ballot constitutes a loaded question

that is designed to yield expected results. By asking the readers to choose between "Doonesbury" and "The Far Side," the newspaper staff rules out the possibility of responding that the readers want both. Thus, even if the poll yielded a preference for replacing "Doonesbury" with "The Far Side," the explanation could be that many readers failed to divide the loaded question.

II. 1. This is an *ad hominem* (circumstantial) argument. Although we have been given a good reason for being alert and skeptical of what the Joint Chiefs of Staff have to say, what they say can stand or fall on its own merits. Yet the author wants to disregard what the Joint Chiefs of Staff have to say altogether.

2. Getting all A's is a result of studying hard. But if a professor gave a student all A's in order to get him to study hard, getting all A's would not be a result of studying hard. Often people mistake an accidental correlation for a cause-and-effect relationship. This passage seems to be the reverse.

3. Wearing expensive clothing is likely to be a result of success, rather than its cause. After becoming successful, the wives can afford to buy such clothing. At any rate, the observation that the wives of successful men wear expensive clothing is perfectly consistent with what I've said.

4. The premises support the conclusion that socialism is inevitable, but not that it is desirable. This is an instance of the fallacy of moralism.

5. The news bulletin is a distortion of what Muskie said. Muskie would not be opposed to putting a Negro on the Democratic ticket if doing so did not mean the re-election of Nixon. But the news bulletin creates the impression that Muskie was opposed to nominating a Negro under any circumstances.

6. This is an appeal to tradition. The popularity of the Golden Rule does not demonstrate that it is "undeniably sound." The reasons for the rule's popularity probably would constitute grounds for the rule's soundness.

7. Dr. White recommended exercise in moderation to his convalescent heart patients. He did not recommend exercise with barbells. (Exercise with barbells is more than moderate for convalescent heart patients.) Almost all of the readers of the Sears ad are probably not convalescent heart patients. So Dr. White is not addressing them. Even if physicians recommend moderate exercise for everyone who is capable of it, that is not a recommendation of exercising with barbells, much less Sears barbells. The recommended exercise could consist entirely of calisthenics, walking, or both.

8. The price of the TV is included in the selling price of the car. Thus the TV is not "absolutely free." Yet some will infer that they will receive something for nothing if they buy a car.

9. Witt points out that the leg-hold trap is efficient. But that is no reason for thinking that the trap is not cruel. If amputation of a person's legs were the punishment for jaywalking, that would be an efficient way of reducing the incidence of jaywalking. Witt, in his second statement, insinuates that, if the leg-hold trap were cruel, there would have been organized and successful opposition long before now. This appeal to conventional wisdom overlooks the

fact that cruel practices can survive for some time. The Chinese practice of binding women's feet (which resulted in deformed feet) survived for centuries because small feet were considered beautiful. Consider too the institutions of slavery and segregation.

10. Would Smedley have made the sale even if he had not gargled or had used another brand? Because we do not know the answers, we do not know that Micro antiseptic had anything to do with Smedley's big sale.

11. This is an example of the *post hoc* fallacy. Did Sweden come to have one of the highest suicide rates before or after acquiring many of the trappings of a socialist country? The passage does not inform us, but the answer cannot be "before" if socialism is a cause of high suicide rates. If many of the countries with comparably high or higher suicide rates are not socialistic, then there is reason to doubt the alleged causal connection between socialism and high suicide rates. If there are socialist countries with average or low suicide rates, then the conclusion is false. Yet there is no information about the suicide rates in other socialist countries.

12. This partly is a matter of misapplying a rule. If Jack Anderson's reports were "unsubstantiated," then Anderson did not find the facts. Thus, the report would not be an instance of a journalist's right to report the facts as she or he finds them. Many rules, such as "Newspapermen have a right to express their opinions without fear of reprisal," are understood as being true, other things being equal. "Other things being equal" means "unless there are over-riding moral considerations." In this case, there is such a consideration: Anderson's report would be very damaging to Eagleton's reputation. Since such harm could befall Eagleton, Anderson's report would have to be well substantiated in order for him to express it without fear of (legal) reprisal.

13. Vincent Van Gogh is the only person of the four mentioned whose work would be studied in an art appreciation course. Poe, Stein, and Woolf are all literary figures whose work would be studied in literature courses. The author speaks of college students as though they were impressionable elementary school children. Therefore, even if the evidence cited in the premises were relevant to the conclusion, many of the premises would still be false. What is more, the premises are not even relevant to whether the course should be a part of the curriculum. A person can lead a less-than-admirable life and yet produce admirable works worth studying. It is those works that are ordinarily the focus of courses, rather than the lives of the people who produced them. The author does not want his children to emulate such individuals. If an elementary school teacher recommended that impressionable children cut off their ears or take addictive drugs, that would be grounds for firing the teacher rather than eliminating a course on the works of great artists. (I momentarily disregard the fact that the letter is about a university curriculum.) Moreover, mentioning facts about someone's life is not a recommendation that one's audience imitate that person's lifestyle or behavior.

Section 12-4

1. The issue was whether Carl Albert should resign. Rather than address the newspaper's arguments for Albert's resignation, the respondent

tries to dismiss them by pointing to the newspaper's support of Nixon. The newspaper's arguments, however, pertain to Albert, not Nixon, and must stand or fall on their own merits.

2. Nixon has poisoned the well. If the Democratic candidates refused to make their finances public, Nixon would respond that they had something to hide. If they did issue a public financial statement, Nixon could claim that the statement was incomplete and that the Democratic candidates were hiding something.

3. This is a clear case of *tu quoque*, since it is an attempt to convince some people to accept the killing of civilians at My Lai because the Viet Cong did much the same thing. There <u>would</u> be a double standard if someone accepted one but not the other, but both can be consistently condemned.

4. The punishment would be unfair if S.M.U. and the other schools had been proved to be in violation of the rules, but only S.M.U. had been punished. The accusations of the other schools, however, consist of either unsubstantiated charges or proven cases of violations for which the universities were punished. It would be unfair to punish a school on unsubstantiated charges. It would also be unfair to punish a school twice for the same proven violation. Thus, the argument is fallacious.

5. This is an instance of "appeal to tradition," since it is an attempt to show that it is okay to drive 70 m.p.h. because it is popular ("almost everybody does it"). But the popularity of a practice does not make it permissible, and the unpopularity of a practice does not make it wrong.

6. This is a case of *tu quoque*, since it is an attempt to undercut tacit criticism of a person for shoplifting. Paradoxically, the arguer is contributing to the very problem about which he complains: high prices.

7. Reagan's response is *ad hominem*. Rather than consider the reasons McGovern gave for criticizing the tax loopholes, Reagan tries to bypass the need to consider McGovern's case by attacking McGovern for using the loopholes. Though it is rhetorically effective, Reagan's reply is not good. He needs to prove that, if McGovern takes advantage of a tax loophole, it is a justifiable loophole that no one should criticize.

8. Nixon's connection with the Watergate burglary is independent of his policy on China. Disapproval of Nixon's role in Watergate simply has no bearing on whether his policy on China is good or bad. Although Nixon's long-standing anti-communism made his visits to China unexpected, that is not to say that his policy toward China is good or bad.

9. The issue is not whether foreign governmental agencies obey the law but whether they should do so. The description "follow the letter of the law" is slanted. The suggestion is that, if foreign agencies do not scrupulously follow every law, then there should be no criticism of the C.I.A., regardless of what it does. If the "commotion" was about something more serious than failure to follow the letter of the law, then there is a double standard in the argument.

10. There are some truths that only a few people know. Let us say that they are items of specialized knowledge (such as an esoteric mathematical proof) or truths that only a few are in a position to know (such as your birthdate). Now the <u>lack</u> of popular belief in those truths casts no doubt on their truth. Just so, the <u>presence</u> of popular belief does not constitute evidence for the belief's truth. An appeal to sheer numbers is unlike an appeal to widespread belief among scientists,

for such reference is an indirect appeal to the evidence scientists have. Sharing a belief with many people may be reassuring. But we must distinguish between reassurance and evidence. Since this argument is an appeal to sheer numbers, the refutation of the argument can consist merely in pointing out that it is possible for a belief to be widespread and false.

11. This is a slippery slope in which it is said that anything that would justify giving up the foreign language requirement would justify eliminating all requirements. In order to know that, we must know what grounds have been offered or could be offered for eliminating the foreign language requirement. Then the elimination of all other requirements must be deduced from those grounds. The slippery slope in question is an easier claim to make than it is to justify.

   The second paragraph is a transparent appeal to tradition. The problem is that the author does not address the reasons for the requirement being good enough for one's father and grandfather. Those reasons for the requirement having been in place, rather than the sheer fact that it has been in place, would be the reasons that could justify retaining the foreign language requirement.

   The word _illiterate_ is used as a slanted and question-begging expression. It had been suggested that the foreign language requirement be eliminated. Anyone who supports that position believes that elimination of the requirement would not result in student illiteracy. Thus critics of the suggestion need to establish that claim, rather than argue from it as a premise. Strictly speaking, the claim is just false. Illiteracy is the inability to read and write. But the inability to read and write another language does not imply an inability to read and write any language. The author's use of this slanted term constitutes an attack on a straw man, as though the opposition were not opposed to illiteracy. There is a false dilemma embedded in the argument: Either one favors keeping the foreign language requirement or one does not oppose illiteracy.

12. Would Fizzbee's statements suddenly become credible if he were a businessman? Let's stipulate that they are exactly the same statements. This shows that the connection between Fizzbee's profession and his statements is merely psychological. We may be less inclined to listen to Fizzbee's statements about salaries for teachers, given that he teaches. But the arguments for higher salaries are not made better or worse by who advocates them. Arguments stand or fall on their own merits. So our inclination not to listen to Fizzbee is not logically founded.

13. This is the same sort of argument as in Exercise 4 (about S.M.U., other universities, and N.C.A.A. regulations). It would be unfair if all the presidents named had been proved to have misused presidential power in much the same way as Nixon, and yet only Nixon had been forced to resign. However, it would be unfair if the mere accusation of abuse of presidential power were sufficient to force a resignation. In this passage we have the mere accusation of such abuse regarding the other presidents, but that is not true in Nixon's case. Evidence that may emerge after the presidencies of each of the three mentioned does not count, since we are speaking of grounds for forcing a president to resign. If it had been shown in 1986, for example, that FDR abused presidential power in 1941, that would not prove that we knew FDR should have been forced to resign in 1941 since, by hypothesis, the evidence to back up the forced resignation was lacking. In Nixon's

case the evidence was present while he was in office. We have a mere accusation regarding Nixon's contemporaries, his accusers. If the accusation were true, then Nixon and his guilty accusers should be treated similarly.

14. This is an appeal to tradition. Monks' argument does not address reasons that could be given for outlawing cockfighting. Its popularity with those three American patriots does not constitute a reason for retaining it, unless it is presupposed that they could not be fans of anything that should be outlawed. But there is no reason to make that assumption. It might be pointed out that several famous and (otherwise) admired American patriots owned slaves. Perhaps even the people Monks mentioned owned slaves. That would not constitute a justification for slavery.

15. This is a clear-cut case of the *post hoc* fallacy. Monks is suggesting that outlawing cockfighting causes powerful nations to become meek. The only evidence offered is that England outlawed cockfighting before becoming a weaker nation. But several things happened before England became a weaker nation, many of which were not causes of England's declining power. No reason is given for singling out the outlawing of cockfighting from among the many events that occurred between England's powerful and her weakened state. There is also the suggestion that legalized cockfighting caused England's strength. But the only evidence given is that there was cockfighting during England's strong period. Again, many things occurred during that time, and many of them had nothing to do with England's strength.

16. This is an example of the genetic fallacy. It does not follow, from the assumption that belief in God arises from fear of the unknown and a need for a father figure, that the belief is false or unfounded. Although wishing that something were the case is not a reason for believing it, we should not fall into the trap of thinking that the fact that it is wished for is a reason for disbelieving it—or for thinking that it is ill-founded. Occasionally our wishes come true; and sometimes we have good reasons for believing what we want to be true. Suppose that Charles is feeling so blue that he would like (and has a psychological need for) a hug. Suppose Charles's wife, Sally, has always been responsive and accommodating under those circumstances. In that event, Charles has good reason to believe that what he wants will come true.

CHAPTER 14

Section 14-1

1. An extended argument consists of at least two interrelated arguments that ultimately are supposed to establish a major point: the main conclusion. A leading argument is thus a part—the major part—of an extended argument, since the leading argument contains the major conclusion. An extended argument also contains subsidiary arguments, which are arguments that are supposed to establish the conclusion(s) that is (are) the premises of the leading argument.

2. The premises of an argument are sometimes controversial, doubtful, or not obviously true. In such circumstances it is necessary to formulate an argument or arguments in their defense. Such arguments are subsidiary arguments. The point of formulating subsidiary arguments, then, is to defend statements that require it, statements that are combined

with one another in order to derive further conclusions. The conclusions of subsidiary arguments, that is, are premises of leading arguments.

3. If an inductive argument were misidentified as deductive, then a reliable inductive argument might be rejected as invalid. If a deductive argument were misidentified as inductive, then an invalid deductive argument might be accepted as a reliable, or even a strong, inductive argument. Since we do not want to reject acceptable arguments or accept bad arguments, it is important to distinguish deductive from inductive arguments before evaluating them.

4. A subsidiary argument is an attempt to establish a premise of a leading argument. A subsidiary argument, then, is an argument that helps to make the major point (the main conclusion).

5. If an argument in an exercise had clearly true premises and a recognizably false conclusion, then it obviously would be invalid. If the argument were obviously invalid, there would be no need to refute it by analogy. Therefore, if there is a need to refute it by analogy, the argument must not be obviously invalid. Thus, the argument in the exercise must not have obviously true premises in conjunction with a recognizably false conclusion. Therefore, the student's correct observation that the argument he is being asked to refute does not have obviously true premises and a clearly false conclusion amounts to saying that the problem has not been solved for him already! The refutation itself, however, must have clearly true premises and a recognizably false conclusion. The point of a refutation by analogy is to prove the invalidity of the argument being refuted and to make the invalidity of the argument clear to one's audience. An invalid argument, unlike a valid one, has a form such that it can have true premises and a false conclusion. Thus, the refutation must have the same form as the argument being refuted, all true premises, and a false conclusion. But in order for the point to be clear to one's audience, the audience must recognize the truth of the premises and the falsehood of the conclusion. Thus, the refuting argument must not have premises that only a limited number of people recognize as true. Moreover, the conclusion must not be one that only a limited number of people know to be false.

Section 14-2

1. SP_1: Either things that began to exist are causes of themselves or they were caused by something else.

   SP_2: If anything that began to exist were its own cause, it would have to exist before it began to exist.

   SP_3: It is impossible for something (that began to exist) to exist before it began to exist.

   P_1: Everything that began to exist is caused by something else (that existed beforehand).

   P_2: There must be a beginning of the chain of causes.

   P_3: If there must be a beginning of the chain of causes, then there is a first cause that (a) does not begin to exist, (b) is not caused, but (c) causes everything else.

   MC_1: There is a first cause, which (a), (b), and (c).

P_4: Everyone calls this first cause "God."

MC_2: God exists.

SP_4: If there were no beginning of the chain of causes, then there would be no first cause.

SP_5: If there were no first cause, then nothing thereafter would exist, and nothing would exist now.

SP_6: To take away the cause is to take away the effect.

SP_7: Something exists.

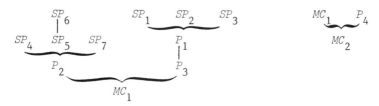

2. MC_1: Aquinas's "second way" does not even prove that there is a first cause, much less God's existence.

MC_2: The subsidiary causal argument (SCA) commits the fallacy of equivocation.

P_1: In order for the first premise of the SCA (SP_4 of Exercise 1) to be true, "There is no first cause" must mean "Everything is caused."

SP_1: In order for the second premise of the SCA (If there were no first cause, nothing thereafter would exist, and nothing would exist now") to be true, then "There is no first cause" cannot mean "Everything is caused."

SP_2: If everything is caused, then there is always something or other that began to exist that causes subsequent things to begin to exist.

SP_3: "There is always something or other that began to exist that causes subsequent things to begin to exist" is compatible with things existing now.

P_2: The second premise of the SCA (SP_5 of Exercise 1) means "If at one time nothing existed, then nothing would exist now."

SP_4: Only the interpretation in P_2 renders the second premise of the SCA true.

SP_5: The interpretation in P_2 fits Aquinas's statement "To take away the cause is to take away the effect."

SP_6: Aquinas has in mind taking away the existence of things, which would make it impossible for things to exist now.

P_3: The supposition that everything is caused does not imply that at one time nothing existed.

P_4: "There is no first cause" means two different things in the premises of the SCA.

P_5:   The SCA would be valid only if "There is no first cause" meant the same thing in both premises.

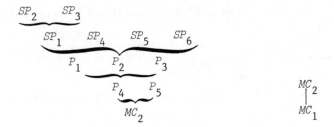

3. (A) Every statement in the religious text is true.
    (B) The religious text states that God exists.
    (C) Therefore, God exists.

P_1:   The (a) refusal to acknowledge the justice of the demand of a proof of (A) by declaring that the fact that a statement is in the book itself makes it true is absurd.

SP_1:   If the fact that a statement occurred in a book by itself made it true, then contradictory statements would both be true.

SP_2:   We are given no reason to prefer the statement in the religious text to statements in a book in which atheism is advocated.

P_2:   If someone tried (d) to prove the infallibility of the book by claiming that God inspired (or wrote) the book, then the argument would be question-begging.

SP_3:   The argument (A-C) is supposed to prove God's existence.

SP_4:   Strategy (d) presupposes God's existence.

SP_5:   If someone (b) attempted to prove all the statements in the religious text and succeeded, then God's existence would have been proved.

SP_6:   But if God's existence had been proved, then there would be no need to argue from the authority of the book.

$P*_6$:   If someone attempted (b) and succeeded, then there would be no need to argue from the authority of the book.

P_3:   The proof of God's existence would be preferable to an argument from the authority of the religious text.

SP_7:   In order to know whether the argument from the authority of the religious text is any good, a direct argument for God's existence must be considered.

SP_8:   But one does not need to consider whether the religious text is authoritative in order to assess direct arguments for God's existence. (Direct arguments can be assessed independently.)

SP_9:   The degree of success of (c)--in arguing for (A) by establishing a subset of the book's statements--is a function of the evidential or logical connection between the statements established and God's existence.

SP_{10}:   If the appropriate connection does not obtain, the defense is unsuccessful.

SP_{11}: But if the connection is there, then an independent argument for God's existence could be formulated thereby (independent of the authority of the religious text).

$P*_7$: If (c) is successful, the proof of God's existence is logically independent of the authority of the text.

P_4: If either (b) or (c) were successful, then the religious text's authority would be <u>irrelevant</u> to the proof of God's existence.

P_5: Neither (a) nor (d) is successful.

MC: No argument from the authority of a religious text proves God's existence.

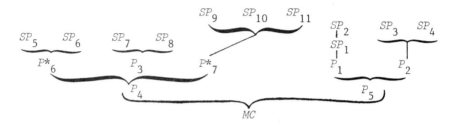

4. SP_1: If God is all-knowing, God knows about all pain, suffering, and wrongdoing.

SP_2: If God is all-powerful, God is capable of eliminating pain, suffering, and wrongdoing.

SP_3: If God is completely good and benevolent, God wants to eliminate pain, suffering, and wrongdoing.

SP_4: By definition, God is all-knowing, all-powerful, completely good and benevolent.

$P*_1$: (If God exists, then) God knows about, is capable of eliminating, and wants to eliminate pain, suffering, and wrongdoing.

P_2: If God knew about all pain, suffering, and wrongdoing, were capable of eliminating those things, and wanted to eliminate them, then there would be considerably less pain, suffering, and wrongdoing than there is.

P_3: The only way God could allow any pain, suffering, and wrongdoing is if instances of them were necessary for some greater good.

P_4: Some instances of pain, suffering, and wrongdoing promote a greater good.

P_5: Some (many) instances of pain, suffering, and wrongdoing do not promote a greater good.

MC_1: There is no individual that is all-knowing, all-powerful, completely benevolent, and good.

MC_2: God does not exist.

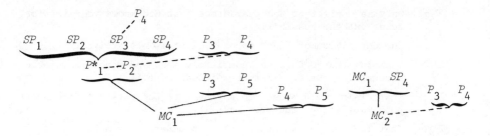

5. P_1: The word "God" means "the being that is perfect in every possible way."

P_2: The being that is perfect in every possible way must actually exist.

MC: God actually exists.

SP_1: Only something that actually exists could exist independently.

SP_2: No product of thought could exist independently.

SP_3: Existing independently is a perfection.

P_3: If the being that is perfect in every possible way were only a product of thought, it would not be perfect in at least one way.

P_4: It is impossible for the being that is perfect in every possible way not to be perfect in at least one way.

P_5: The being that is perfect in every possible way is not a mere product of thought.

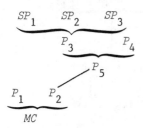

6. MC_1: The definition of "God" is not arbitrary.

MC_2: The attempt to solve the problem of evil by changing the definition of "God" amounts to abandoning beliefs that are essential to religious practices.

SP_1: Denying God's omniscience in order to solve the problem of evil amounts to explaining evil's existence in terms of God's ignorance of it.

SP_2: If God were ignorant of all evil, God would be ignorant of a lot.

SP_3: The believer has left open the possibility that God may not know that human beings exist.

SP_4: If God may not know that human beings exist, then belief in God would lose its (religious) significance.

SP_5: Only an omniscient God guarantees that God knows we exist (or rules out the possibility in SP_3).

$P*_1$: The definition of "God" as omniscient is not arbitrary.

SP_6: Claiming that God is not completely good and benevolent would account for the co-existence of God and evil.

SP_7: That claim would amount to saying that God does not care about pain, suffering, and wrongdoing.

SP_8: That (SP_7) is not an acceptable consequence for a believer.

$P*_2$: The definition of "God" as completely good and benevolent is not arbitrary.

SP_9: Claiming that God is not omnipotent would account for the co-existence of God and evil.

P_3: In order to account for all pain, suffering, and wrongdoing, God would have to be considerably less than all-powerful.

SP_{10}: The claim that God is not omnipotent is an attempt to account for evil by saying that God cannot control any of it.

SP_{11}: If human beings often can control pain, suffering, and wrongdoing, then God would be less powerful than people.

P_4: A God that is less powerful than people (or considerably less than all-powerful) is not a God worth worshipping.

$MC*_3$: Changing the definition of "God" is an inadequate attempt to solve the problem of evil.

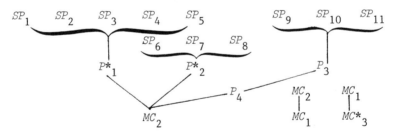

7. P_1: There has to be some evil in order for there to be good.

P_2: It is better for there to be good and some evil than neither good nor evil.

MC_1: God can allow the evil there is and still be completely good and benevolent.

P_3: The problem with this proposal is that a false dilemma is embedded in it.

SP_1: The only two possible universes in the proposal are: (a) good with all the pain, suffering, and wrongdoing there is, and (b) neither good nor evil.

SP_2: There are other possible universes, such as (c) the same amount of good with somewhat less evil, or (d) the same amount of good with much less evil.

P_4: Even if the "contrast proposal" included an argument against the possibility of an all-good universe, that does not mean that God could have created a universe with as much evil as there is.

P_5: The "contrast proposal" would at best justify only a small amount of pain, suffering, and wrongdoing.

$MC*_2$: The "contrast proposal" is an inadequate attempt to solve the problem of evil.

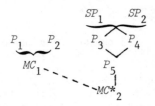

Section 14-3

Many of the moral standards are so general that an argument for several of the moral judgments can be formulated using them. But there is an ambiguity regarding "moral action." Does the term mean what is morally obligatory, what is permissible, or both? The divine command standard, for example, only seems to fit obligatory actions, for God would not seem to <u>command</u> what is <u>permissible</u>. The relativist standard mentions only what is "right or obligatory," neglecting to mention permissibility.

1. (a) I sometimes approve of making a false claim to an insurance company.
   (b) subjectivist standard
   (c) Thus, it is okay to make a false claim to an insurance company.

   (a) I disapprove of making false claims to an insurance company, and I am made happy by people telling insurance companies the truth.
   (b) subjectivist standard
   (c) It is not okay to make false claims to an insurance company.

These two arguments illustrate the fact that a subjectivist standard can be used to "justify" any moral judgment whatsoever.

2. (a) A majority of people in society S accept premarital sex, provided that the sexual partners are in love.
   (b) relativist standard
   (c) Thus, premarital sex is okay if you're in love.

   (a) A few people changed their minds about premarital sex for people in love. The slim majority has become a minority. Now a majority of people in society S disapprove of premarital sex even if the sexual partners are in love.
   (b) relativist standard
   (c) Thus, premarital sex is wrong even if the sexual partners are in love.

These arguments reveal a point about the relativist standard--namely, that even if one relativizes one's judgments to a given society, moral knowledge and moral truth depend on changeable shifts in public opinion. You would have to know what the latest popular opinion is in order to know whether some action is right, wrong, or okay.

3. (a) It is human nature that people are lustful and would (at least) like to be promiscuous. Were it not for fear of unwanted pregnancy and disease, there would be even more sexual activity. Consider primitive societies, in which such fears play minor roles: there is a great deal of sexual activity with many partners. Consider the increase in sexual activity that accompanied the availability of birth control pills.
   (b) natural law standard
   (c) Promiscuous sexual activity (and thus premarital sex) is okay, whether or not you're in love.

   Suppose we disregard the fear of pregnancy. Then the argument above could be used as an argument for the permissibility of homosexuality. The natural law standard, however, is often used in order to argue for the impermissibility of homosexuality, as when people express disapproval of homosexuality by saying, "Homosexuality is unnatural." This points to the vague generality of the natural law standard. It is not clear what constitutes "harmony with nature or with universal laws of nature."

4. (a) It can be desired, with consistency, that every rational being refrain from experimenting on animals when the research can be conducted using volunteers or plants.
   (b) Kantian standard
   (c) moral judgment 4

   (a) Most members of society S accept experimenting on animals even when the research can be conducted on volunteers or plants.
   (b) relativist standard
   (c) Moral judgment 4 is false.

   Is it possible for a relativist to speak of a moral judgment being false? Or must the relativist say that the moral judgment is false in S? What does "false in S" mean?

5. (a) I intuit or see that it is wrong to pass judgment on others.
   (b) intuitionist standard
   (c) moral judgment

   (a) In society S it is acceptable to pass judgment on others. It is even acceptable to be intolerant of the beliefs of others.
   (b) relativist standard
   (c) Moral judgments 5 and 6 are false.

   Some people believe that openmindedness requires acceptance of the relativist standard. I have just shown that the relativist standard can be used in order to "justify" intolerance and self-righteous judgment of others. Moreover, I can show how a non-relativist standard can be used to argue for moral judgment 6. (The intuitionist standard is at least intended to be non-relativistic.) So, acceptance of the relativist standard is neither a necessary nor a sufficient condition for openmindedness.

6. (a) Rational agents can be treated as ends in themselves (rather than as means to an end) only if everyone is tolerant of the beliefs of others.
   (b) Kantian standard
   (c) Moral judgment 6 is true.

7. (a) act—utilitarian standard
    (b) A person should keep his promise only if doing so will produce the best consequences.

    (a) A person cannot consistently will that everyone refrain from keeping his promise whenever keeping it would not produce the best consequences.
    (b) Kantian standard
    (c) Moral judgment 7 is false.

8. (a) God forbids working on Sunday.
    (b) divine command standard
    (c) It is wrong to work on Sunday.

    (a) If some people work on Sunday, that will produce the greatest happiness or well-being for the greatest number of people.
    (b) act—utilitarian standard
    (c) It is morally permissible to work on Sunday.

9. A utilitarian or relativist standard could be cited to argue for the truth or falsity of either moral judgment 8 or its contradictory, depending on what would produce the greatest happiness for the greatest number, or depending on what the members of the society in question found permissible, impermissible, or obligatory. (The arguments above depend on the truth of the premises, naturally, and some of the premises are dubious or false.)

10. Suppose God commanded Smith to murder her pet, much as God is alleged to have commanded Abraham to kill Isaac. The divine command standard would imply that moral judgment 10 is false. If taking care of her pet made Smith feel good, then a subjectivist standard would imply that moral judgment 10 is true.